WORLD CUP 2010

SUPERSTARS

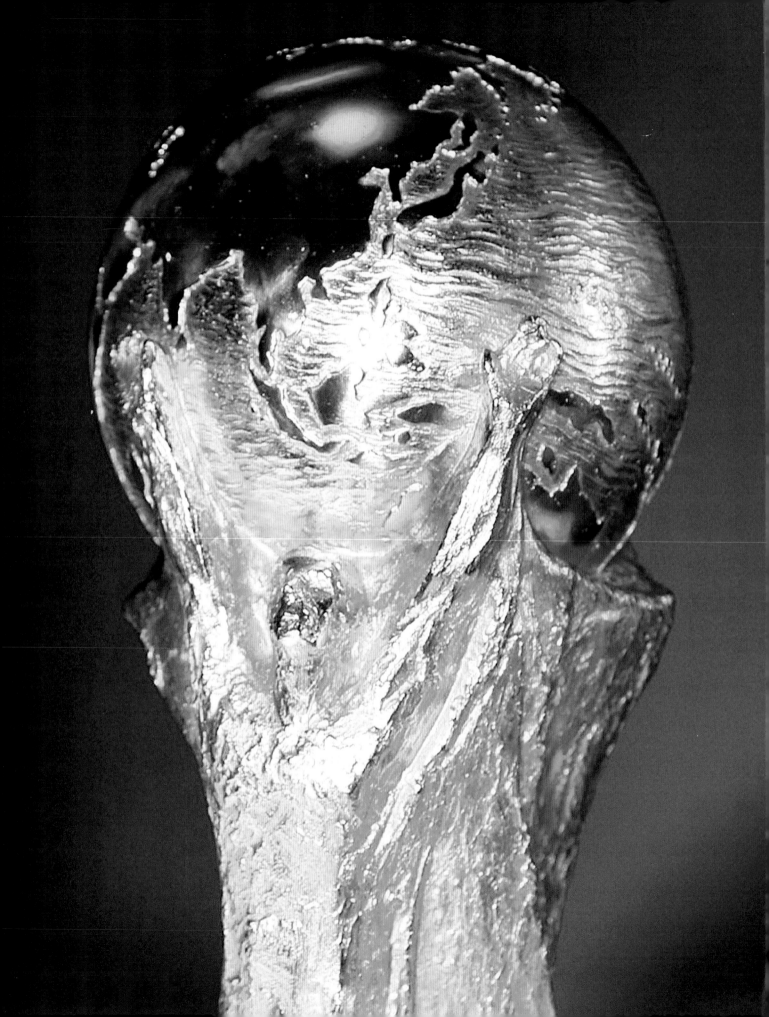

WORLD CUP 2010 🌐

SUPERSTARS

The ultimate guide to the stars of the 2010 World Cup

PAUL FISHER

PaRragon

Bath · New York · Singapore · Hong Kong · Cologne · Delhi · Melbourne

First published by Parragon in 2010
Parragon
Queen Street House
4 Queen Street
Bath BA1 1HE, UK

Copyright © Parragon Books Ltd 2010

Created and produced by Jollands Editions
Design JC Lanaway
Author Paul Fisher
Additional text Julian Flanders/Adrian Besley

All statistics are correct up to 31 January 2010.

World rankings of teams are official FIFA figures
for November 2009.

ISBN 978-1-4075-8490-4

Printed in Spain

CONTENTS

INTRODUCTION

Superlatives crowd round the 2010 World Cup. The most sought after trophy of the most popular sport on the planet will, for the first time, be contested in an African country. From 11 June to 11 July, South Africa will host football's greatest spectacle and the beautiful game, a unifier of all peoples, will be witnessed by a global TV audience larger than the total population of Great Britain.

At last the wait is almost over and all eyes are on South Africa as the 32 finalists assemble to take part in what for many is the world's most exciting sporting tournament. It all began two or three years ago when over a hundred nations from six zones (Africa, Asia, Europe, North, Central America and Caribbean, Oceania and South America) were whittled down in qualifying matches that built to a climax in the November 2009 play-offs where a number of fancied teams faced inevitable disappointment. Notable European absentees include Russia, Croatia, Scotland and the Republic of Ireland.

ABOVE *The official mascot for the 2010 FIFA World Cup is Zakumi, a leopard with green hair. His name comes from 'ZA', the international abbreviation for South Africa, and 'kumi', a word that means 'ten' in various African languages. The mascot's colours reflect those of the host nation's playing strip.*

BELOW *As the advertising billboard suggests, an entire continent can't wait for the World Cup to begin. Millions will be rooting for at least one African nation to make it through to at least the quarter-finals.*

We can't wai
Let's go 2010.

MTN
OFFICIAL SPONSOR

SOUTH
AFRICA 2010

THE FINAL DRAW

The draw for the finals was staged in Cape Town on 4 December 2009 at the Cape Town International Convention Centre in a ceremony presented by the South African actress Charlize Theron. The seeding was based on the October 2009 FIFA ranking and seven squads joined hosts South Africa as seeded teams in Pot 1. Pot 2 was composed of teams from Asia, Oceania, and North and Central America and the Caribbean. Pot 3 included teams from Africa and South America. Pot 4 had the remaining European teams. Geographical criteria meant that no two teams from the same confederation were drawn in the same group (except European teams, where a maximum of two could be in a group).

There are groups comprising three exceptionally strong teams and one underdog, and there are groups where all four teams are evenly matched. But predicting anything is hard on this occasion, because nearly all the teams are going to encounter unfamiliar conditions such as playing at altitude and the South African winter. Johannesburg will play a key role in the World Cup, hosting the opening ceremony when a star-spangled cast of international celebrities from the worlds of show business, the music industry and politics will gather.

INTERCONTINENTAL DUEL

It could be a World Cup full of surprises, with at least eight of the teams good enough to win it plus a couple of unseeded teams like France and Portugal. At root the World Cup is an intercontinental duel between Western Europe and South America. The current score is nine cup wins per continental bloc and the strongest likelihood is that Brazil, Argentina, Germany, Italy, England and France (one World Cup each), Spain and the Netherlands (no wins) will make it through to the quarter-finals. Any of these countries that haven't reached the fifth game of the tournament will be seen to have failed while any other team breaking into that elite eight will legitimately claim a triumph. South Africa could exploit home advantage though Côte d'Ivoire look a better African bet. The North Koreans sprung a surprise in 1966 and Australia could do it. Ditto the United States. Come the semi-finals, however, and the elite are likely to meet the elite and everything points to a reassertion of the status quo. While millions of hearts might say otherwise, the head tells us that the African and Asian World Cup duck will not be broken.

In early June, when teams have settled into unfamiliar training compounds, grizzled coaches will make their final selections and gather their young charges around them to tell of simple arithmetic. 'You are seven games away from lifting the World Cup,' they'll say

ABOVE *FIFA president Sepp Blatter unveiling the official World Cup poster.*

> ❝ **Portraying a country in the shape of a man heading a ball is a new idea with potent symbolism .... highlighting the pride and passion of the African continent and her people. It represents the African dream come true.** ❞
>
> FIFA PRESIDENT
> SEPP BLATTER

STARS OF WORLD CUP HISTORY

History is being made with the World Cup going to Africa for the first time. In the action-packed weeks of June and July 2010, South African football grounds will see high-paced games in a tournament that takes place during the host country's winter. The venues are spectacular, with the conditions inside cool and so therefore far better suited to the beautiful game than the heat and humidity that often slows summer soccer tournaments down.

Fast or slow, the World Cup always yields a hero or two and a pick of the all-time greats are featured on the next few pages. And in the main body of the book are profiles of over fifty players who are already stars, one of whom will emerge to make history as the 2010 World Cup superstar. Will it be Drogba or Rooney, Messi or Robinho, Xavi or Ronaldo – or some other player altogether?

And would we reach a majority verdict on the greatest player of this or earlier decades? Probably not. Though we all know the simple rules of the game and recognize quality when we see it, we're experts with our own points of view. What follows in these pages are facts and a few opinions to fuel disputes that will echo on for so long as the game is played.

PELÉ, Brazil

1950s and 1960s

The greatest player in the world won a World Cup medal in 1958, 1962 and 1970. His sheer speed of thought and precision of action are commemorated in grainy black-and-white footage where the quality of play still retains its freshness. It is possible that in 2010 another 17 year old will burst onto the scene to score a semi-final hat-trick. Possible, but not likely because no other player has quite matched Pelé's skill. After playing an astonishing 1,366 competitive matches and scoring 1,283 first-class goals (12 in World Cup finals), he became a footballing ambassador and, now approaching his 70th birthday, he will be there among the crowds for the 2010 World Cup in South Africa.

BOBBY MOORE, England

1960s

It is a personal and national pinnacle of achievement when a country's football captain lifts the World Cup. Their face and their style will become familiar to those unborn at the moment of triumph. Most English people who were alive in 1966 can well remember where they were the day Bobby Moore raised the small trophy that meant so much. Football fans will remember a young man of poise who organized his defence and kept cool in needle matches against Argentina, Portugal and West Germany. His was the inspiration that won the day for England 44 years ago.

WORLD CUP FINALS

YEAR	HOST	WINNER			RUNNER-UP	PLAYER OF THE TOURNAMENT
1930	Uruguay	Uruguay	4	2	Argentina	José Nasazzi (Uruguay)
1934	Italy	Italy	2	1	Czechoslovakia	Giuseppe Meazza (Italy)
1938	France	Italy	4	2	Hungary	Leônidas (Brazil)
1950	Brazil	Uruguay	2	1	Brazil	Zizinho (Brazil)
1954	Switzerland	West Germany	3	2	Hungary	Ferenc Puskás (Hungary)
1958	Sweden	Brazil	5	2	Sweden	Didi (Brazil)
1962	Chile	Brazil	3	1	Czechoslovakia	Garrincha (Brazil)
1966	England	England	4	2	West Germany	Bobby Charlton (England)
1970	Mexico	Brazil	4	1	Italy	Pelé (Brazil)
1974	West Germany	West Germany	2	1	Netherlands	Johan Cruyff (Netherlands)
1978	Argentina	Argentina	3	1	Netherlands	Mario Kempes (Argentina)
1982	Spain	Italy	3	1	West Germany	Paolo Rossi (Italy)
1986	Mexico	Argentina	3	2	West Germany	Diego Maradona (Argentina)
1990	Italy	West Germany	1	0	Argentina	Salvatore Schillaci (Italy)
1994	USA	Brazil (3–2 on pens)	0	0	Italy	Romário (Brazil)
1998	France	France	3	0	Brazil	Ronaldo (Brazil)
2002	Japan/Korea Rep.	Brazil	2	0	Germany	Oliver Kahn (Germany)
2006	Germany	Italy (5–3 on pens)	1	1	France	Zinédine Zidane (France)

STARS OF WORLD CUP HISTORY

DIEGO MARADONA, Argentina

1980s

Diego Maradona scored what FIFA voted as the goal of the century during the 1986 World Cup quarter-final between Argentina and England. Maradona is shown below beating Terry Fenwick on a run from his own half that included 11 perfect touches. He also dribbled past Glenn Hoddle, Peter Reid, Kenny Sansom, Terry Butcher and the goalkeeper Peter Shilton. Argentina beat England 2–1 and went on to claim top slot in a World Cup tournament Maradona dominated as no other player has before or since.

JOHANN CRUYFF, Netherlands

1970s

The greatest player never to have won a World Cup took football onto a new plain when he operated at the heart of the 1970s' Dutch team that pioneered *totaalvoetbal* ('total football'). This system has players switching positions in an abandonment of traditional formations that could only work with the most skilled players. Cruyff took up the most positions as he moved from centre forward, back into midfield and then out to the wing. While total football did not catch on, Cruyff left a tactical legacy; his defence-bamboozling positional flexibility is how other skilled playmakers such as Wayne Rooney, Lionel Messi and, above all, Cristiano Ronaldo are likely to be deployed in South Africa.

WORLD CUP NUMBERS

665 MILLION
The amount in rands that the South African government claims to be spending on crowd-control equipment including helicopters, water cannons, a hundred BMWs for highway patrol and body armour.

30 MILLION
The amount in dollars that goes to the World Cup winner from a prize-money pot totalling US$420 million.

200,000
The number of spectators who squeezed into the Maracana Stadium for the 1950 World Cup final between hosts Brazil and Uruguay.

94,700
The capacity of Soccer City in Johannesburg, venue for the 2010 World Cup final.

41,400
The number of police officers who will be on World Cup duty.

5,000
The number of square metres of satellite dishes linking the International Broadcast Centre in Johannesburg to the outside world.

64
The number of matches to be played.

41
The number of matches in 2006 where the team that scored first won the game.

36
The height in centimetres of the World Cup trophy, which is made of gold and malachite.

8
The number of matches in 2006 when a team came from behind to win.

Zidane

Ronaldo

ZINÉDINE ZIDANE, France
1990s

In France's 1998 World Cup final victory, Zinédine Zidane scored two rare headed goals against the reigning champions, Brazil. In his 106 international matches, Zidane scored 298 goals mostly with his feet. The goal scoring marks him as special but he is remembered most for the uniquely elegant and appropriate way he dominated big games from central midfield. In the turmoil of hotly contested international matches, Zidane was the man who seemed to have time and space on his hands.

RONALDO, Brazil
1998, 2002, 2006

Was there ever a more opportunistic goal scorer than Ronaldo? His 15 goals scored across three World Cup finals in 1998, 2002 and 2006 are a record. In the 2002 World Cup he found the net eight times including twice in the final when Brazil beat Germany. He is one of the greatest strikers in the history of world football, and his presence would petrify defences before he ever set off on one of his darting runs or mazy dribbles. No wonder they called him 'The Phenomenon'.

THE VENUES

A rapid 12 billion rand building effort has resulted in five new stadiums and five extensively improved grounds for the 64 matches of the 2010 World Cup. The matches take place throughout South Africa, with the action beginning and ending in Johannesburg. Many of the stadiums will be officially relabelled during the tournament – the FIFA-approved names are used on these pages.

BELOW The earth-coloured walls of Johannesburg's Soccer City stadium make it appear in the cityscape as an African cooking pot, an effect enhanced when the exterior is lit from below to create the impression of fire.

JOHANNESBURG *Soccer City*

Capacity: 94,700

Matches: Five group matches, one last-16 match, one quarter-final, the final

Soccer City is in Soweto, where the majority of Johannesburg's black population lives. This landmark ground is the home of South African football and gained a deeper political significance when it hosted a mass rally on Nelson Mandela's release from prison in 1990. Ground improvements for the World Cup include a roof, an extended upper tier plus enhanced changing rooms and floodlights.

JOHANNESBURG *Ellis Park Stadium*

Capacity: 61,000

Matches: Five group matches, one last-16 match, one quarter-final

Built as a rugby union stadium, Ellis Park has been upgraded with new upper tiers behind each of the goals. It is the home ground of Orlando Pirates FC. A Nelson Mandela African XI played a World All Stars XI in a farewell match when South Africa's first black president retired from office.

CAPE TOWN *Green Point Stadium*

Capacity: 69,070

Matches: Five group matches, one last-16 match, one quarter-final, one semi-final

This new stadium, which replaces an earlier stadium, has a dramatically low and sweeping silhouette that dominates a coastal strip in Cape Town's city centre between the Atlantic Ocean and Table Mountain. The new showpiece facility has a retractable dome-shaped roof.

DURBAN *Senzangakhona Stadium*

Capacity: 70,000

Matches: Five group matches, one last-16 match, one semi-final

A pair of archways high above the roof makes this three-tiered stadium an eye-catching venue. Named after a Zulu king, it is on the site of the old King's Park Stadium where South Africa's first post-apartheid soccer international was played and where it played England in 2002.

MANGAUNG/BLOEMFONTEIN *Free State Stadium*

Capacity: 48,070

Matches: Six group matches, one last-16 match

The Free State Stadium doubles as a rugby union venue when it isn't used as a home ground of Bloemfontein Celtics Premier Soccer League team. It has had its capacity increased with the addition of a second tier to the main western grandstand and has installed new floodlights, electronic scoreboards and turnstiles.

NELSPRUIT *Mbombela Stadium*

Capacity: 46,000

Matches: Four group matches

A translucent roof raised on cantilevers designed to look like a row of giraffes' necks is the dominant feature of this new stadium outside Nelspruit. The architectural innovation allows spectators a view of nearby game reserves in a rural stadium next to the Kruger National Park, providing a memorable venue for first- and second-round matches.

POLOKWANE *Peter Mokaba Stadium*

Capacity: 46,000

Matches: Four group matches

This new sports venue, named after a former leader of the ANC Youth League, has been built near to the Pietersburg Stadium, which was too small to meet FIFA requirements.

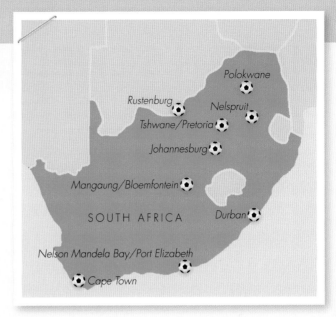

After the World Cup, the stadium will become a centre for football in Limpopo, the province with the largest number of registered football players in the country.

NELSON MANDELA BAY/PORT ELIZABETH
Nelson Mandela Bay Stadium

Capacity: 49,500

Matches: Five group matches, one last-16 match, one quarter final, losing semi-finalists

Despite not having a team in the Premier Soccer League, Port Elizabeth is football crazy and this was the first of the new South African World Cup arenas to be completed. The five-tier coastal stadium has two rings of skyboxes and looks over a lake in the middle of the city.

RUSTENBURG *Royal Bafokeng Sports Palace*

Capacity: 42,000

Matches: Five group matches, one last-16 match

Rustenburg's stadium, located 12 km/8 miles from the city centre and a half-hour drive from Sun City, is named after the local Bafokeng people. Many Premier Soccer League games are played here, and its ground was upgraded in time to host the FIFA Confederations Cup in March 2009.

TSHWANE/PRETORIA *Loftus Versfeld Stadium*

Capacity: 51,760

Matches: Five group matches, one last-16 match

The home ground of the Mamelodi Sundowns football team dates back to 1903. All four stands have been rebuilt since the late 1970s to create an imposing arena that rises steeply on all sides. Minimal upgrading was necessary to qualify the stadium as a World Cup venue.

MATCH SCHEDULE

The 32 teams have been divided into eight groups of four. In Stage 1 each team will play each other once in a league system and the top two from each group will proceed to Stage 2 (the round of 16), from when the competition will be decided on a knockout basis.

If two or more teams finish the group stage with the same number of points then the following criteria will be used to determine the final ranking: 1 Points won head-to-head. 2 Goals won head-to-head. 3 Number of goals scored head-to-head. 4 Goal difference in all group games. 5 Goals scored in all group games. 6 Drawing lots.

STAGE 1

GROUP A

| | South Africa | | France |
| | Uruguay | | Mexico |

Match	Date	Venue	
1	11 June	Johannesburg	South Africa v Mexico
2	11 June	Cape Town	Uruguay v France
17	16 June	Tshwane	South Africa v Uruguay
18	17 June	Polokwane	France v Mexico
33	22 June	Rustenburg	Mexico v Uruguay
34	22 June	Mangaung	France v South Africa

GROUP B

| | Argentina | | Greece |
| | Korea Republic | | Nigeria |

Match	Date	Venue	
3	12 June	Johannesburg	Argentina v Nigeria
4	12 June	Port Elizabeth	Korea Rep. v Greece
19	17 June	Mangaung	Greece v Nigeria
20	17 June	Johannesburg	Argentina v Korea Rep.
35	22 June	Durban	Nigeria v Korea Rep.
36	22 June	Polokwane	Greece v Argentina

GROUP C

| | England | | Slovenia |
| | Algeria | | USA |

Match	Date	Venue	
5	12 June	Rustenburg	England v USA
6	13 June	Polokwane	Algeria v Slovenia
22	18 June	Johannesburg	Slovenia v USA
23	18 June	Cape Town	England v Algeria
37	23 June	Port Elizabeth	Slovenia v England
38	23 June	Tshwane	USA v Algeria

GROUP D

| | Germany | | Ghana |
| | Serbia | | Australia |

Match	Date	Venue	
7	13 June	Durban	Germany v Australia
8	13 June	Tshwane	Serbia v Ghana
21	18 June	Port Elizabeth	Germany v Serbia
24	19 June	Rustenburg	Ghana v Australia
39	23 June	Johannesburg	Ghana v Germany
40	23 June	Nelspruit	Australia v Serbia

GROUP E

| | Netherlands | | Cameroon |
| | Japan | | Denmark |

Match	Date	Venue	
9	14 June	Johannesburg	Netherlands v Denmark
10	14 June	Mangaung	Japan v Cameroon
25	19 June	Durban	Netherlands v Japan
26	19 June	Tshwane	Cameroon v Denmark
43	24 June	Rustenburg	Denmark v Japan
44	24 June	Cape Town	Cameroon v Netherlands

GROUP F

 Italy   Slovakia

 New Zealand   Paraguay

Match	Date	Venue	
11	14 June	Cape Town	Italy v Paraguay
12	15 June	Rustenburg	New Zealand v Slovakia
27	20 June	Mangaung	Slovakia v Paraguay
28	20 June	Nelspruit	Italy v New Zealand
41	24 June	Johannesburg	Slovakia v Italy
42	24 June	Polokwane	Paraguay v New Zealand

GROUP G

 Côte d'Ivoire   Portugal

 Brazil   Korea DPR

Match	Date	Venue	
13	15 June	Port Elizabeth	Côte d'Ivoire v Portugal
14	15 June	Johannesburg	Brazil v Korea DPR
29	20 June	Johannesburg	Brazil v Côte d'Ivoire
30	21 June	Cape Town	Portugal v Korea DPR
45	25 June	Durban	Portugal v Brazil
46	25 June	Nelspruit	Korea DPR v Côte d'Ivoire

GROUP H

 Honduras   Chile

 Spain   Switzerland

Match	Date	Venue	
15	16 June	Nelspruit	Honduras v Chile
16	16 June	Durban	Spain v Switzerland
31	21 June	Port Elizabeth	Chile v Switzerland
32	21 June	Johannesburg	Spain v Honduras
47	25 June	Tshwane	Chile v Spain
48	25 June	Mangaung	Switzerland v Honduras

STAGE 2/KNOCKOUT ROUND OF 16

Match	Date	Venue	Winners Group	v	Runners-up Group
49	26 June	Port Elizabeth	A	v	B
50	26 June	Rustenburg	C	v	D
51	27 June	Mangaung	D	v	C
52	27 June	Johannesburg	B	v	A
53	28 June	Durban	E	v	F
54	28 June	Johannesburg	G	v	H
55	29 June	Tshwane	F	v	E
56	29 June	Cape Town	H	v	G

QUARTER-FINALS

Match	Date	Venue	Winners Match	v	Winners Match
57	02 July	Port Elizabeth	53	v	54
58	02 July	Johannesburg	49	v	50
59	03 July	Cape Town	51	v	52
60	03 July	Johannesburg	55	v	56

SEMI-FINALS

Match	Date	Venue	Winners Match	v	Winners Match
61	06 July	Cape Town	57	v	58
62	07 July	Durban	59	v	60

QUARTER FINALS THIRD PLACE PLAY-OFF

Match	Date	Venue	Losers Match	v	Losers Match
63	10 July	Port Elizabeth	61	v	62

FINAL

Match	Date	Venue	Winners Match	v	Winners Match
64	11 July	Johannesburg	61	v	62

KNOCKOUT ROUNDS

In the knockout rounds, if a match is level after 90 minutes, a further 30 minutes' extra time will be played. If the score is level after extra time, there will be a penalty shoot-out.

SOUTH AFRICA

GROUP A ▶

On Friday 11 June 2010, in Johannesburg's Soccer City, South Africa will kick off the World Cup in their opening match against Mexico. The home side will do what World Cup home sides do and play out of their skins to imprint some new names – Teko Modise, Thembinkosi Fanteni and Katlego Mphela – onto the global consciousness.

RIGHT *Come June 2010, the footballing world will echo to the sounds of the vuvuzela and the chant 'Bafana Bafana' in support of the host nation.*

BELOW *Rustenburg, June 2009: Katlego Mphela scores for South Africa during their third place play-off against Spain in the Confederations Cup.*

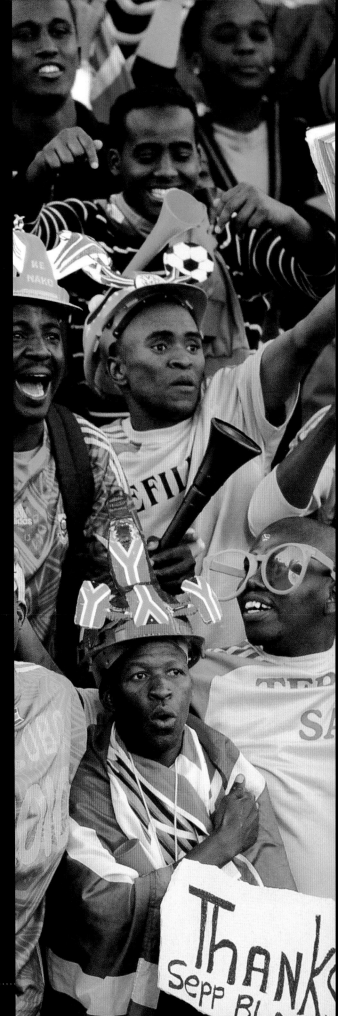

Throughout the decades of apartheid, football developed in isolation from the rest of the world. The fiercely competitive national league did, however, develop a level of proficiency and in 1992 'Bafana Bafana' ('The Boys, The Boys') marked its post-apartheid international debut with a 1–0 victory over Cameroon. Four years later, Bafana Bafana lifted the African Nations Cup and then qualified for the World Cups in France 1998 and in Korea and Japan 2002.

All this amounted to achievements enough for South Africa to be chosen as the first African country to host the World Cup. Expectations for the tournament are as continental as they are national and Abedi Pelé, the former Ghana football captain and now a spokesman for the South African Football Association, says: 'African teams are coming to this African World Cup to showcase their talent and this is our best chance of getting close to the trophy itself. In the history of the World Cup only Brazil has won it outside their own continent, in Sweden in 1958 and in Japan in 2002. But here in Africa we will definitely have one team that will go far – and when I say go far I mean as far as getting the trophy. When I say this people laugh, but I believe it. I believe Africa is going to do very well. Look at South Africa. They have learned about their weaknesses in this Confederations Cup, and they will get better over the next 12 months.'

The 2009 Confederations Cup was a rehearsal for the big 2010 event with South Africa hosting a competition featuring the champions of the world's six regional football federations, plus Italy as the current World Cup holder. South Africa reached the semi-finals and came a creditable fourth after losing 3–2 in the runners-up game against a weakened Spanish team. A brace of Katlego Mphela goals took the game to extra time and provided a climax to a campaign that revealed South Africa as a footballing lion that can bite as well as roar.

The Confederations Cup was played against spectacular backdrops and, in breaks of play, commentators concentrated on the scenery and on the long horns blown by South African supporters. The *vuvuzela* will irritate and intimidate opponents in equal measure, and the only thing more annoying than its distinctive noise will be the noise of people complaining about it. 'Bafana Bafana' is a South African chant that will circle the globe, with every football fan looking forward to high-pressure South African play and rooting for a team that could advance far on a wave of national and international enthusiasm.

HOW THEY'LL LINE UP

South Africa's reliance on Brazilian mercenaries reveals a hope that a crash course might inculcate C-grade South African pupils with A-star South American flair. However, Brazilians believe in grit as well as samba and both Santana and Parreira are pragmatists who build from defences and midfields drilled to control possession before going for flat-out attack. The difference between the two is that Parreira provides a dash of added inspiration, and that is why he got his job back in October 2009.

Khune

Masilela   Khumalo   Sibaya   Gaxa

Modise   Tshabalala   Pienaar   Mashego

Mphela   Fanteni

POSSIBLE SQUAD

Goalkeepers

Brian Baloyi (Mamelodi Sundowns), **Rowen Fernández** (Arminia Bielefeld), **Itumeleng Khune** (Kaizer Chiefs)

Defenders

Matthew Booth (Mamelodi Sundowns), **Siboniso Gaxa** (Mamelodi Sundowns), **Morgan Gould** (Supersport United), **Bongani Khumalo** (Supersport United), **Tsepo Masilela** (Maccabi Haifa), **Innocent Mdledle** (Orlando Pirates), **Aaron Mokoena (C)** (Portsmouth), **Bryce Moon** (Panathinaikos)

Midfielders

Lance Davids (Supersport United), **Kagiso Dikgacoi** (Fulham), **Benson Mhlongo** (Orlando Pirates), **Teko Modise** (Orlando Pirates), **Steven Pienaar** (Everton), **MacBeth Sibaya** (Rubin Kazan), **Siphiwe Tshabalala** (Kaizer Chiefs), **Elrio van Heerden** (Blackburn Rovers)

Forwards

Thembinkosi Fanteni (Maccabi Haifa), **Katlego Mashego** (Orlando Pirates), **Katlego Mphela** (Mamelodi Sundowns), **Bernard Parker** (FC Twente)

ROUTE TO THE FINALS

INTERNATIONAL MATCHES PLAYED IN THE RUN-UP TO THE WORLD CUP DRAW

Date	Home		Away
14.06.09*	South Africa 0	0	Iraq
17.06.09*	South Africa 2	0	New Zealand
20.06.09*	South Africa 0	2	Spain
25.06.09*	South Africa 0	1	Brazil
28.06.09*	South Africa 2	3	Spain
12.08.09	South Africa 1	3	Serbia
05.09.09	Germany 2	0	South Africa
08.09.09	Republic of Ireland 1	0	South Africa
19.09.09	South Africa 1	0	Madagascar
10.10.09	Norway 1	0	South Africa
13.10.09	Iceland 1	0	South Africa
14.11.09	South Africa 0	0	Japan
17.11.09	South Africa 0	0	Jamaica

*Confederations Cup. All other matches friendlies.

FINALS GROUP A

South Africa play		Date	Venue
	Mexico	11 June	Johannesburg (Soccer City)
	Uruguay	16 June	Tshwane/Pretoria
	France	22 June	Mangaung/Bloemfontein

VITAL STATISTICS

World ranking 86th	Keeper and defence 6/10
Midfield 7/10	Attack 5/10

Strengths and weaknesses The last three World Cups showed how home crowds boost the host team's performance. South Africa's awesome support guarantees it home advantage in trumps, though in the end it's the players who have to turn advantage into victories. Every neutral will be rooting for them.

How far will they go? An enormous amount hinges on the opener. If South Africa pinch at least a point against Mexico, confidence will soar. National and continental fervour might then buoy them to the knockout round. The excitement would echo around the planet.

COACH **Carlos Alberto Parreira**

Born 27 February 1943
Record: P22, W10, D4, L8

Parreira has led four teams to the World Cup: Kuwait, UAE, Saudi Arabia and his native Brazil, who won under him in 1994. He now has the task of bringing Brazilian flair to the breakneck South African style of play. He took on management of South Africa in 2007 at ten times the salary of the national president, then left after 18 months when his wife fell ill. The Brazilian experiment continued with Parreira's own nominee, but the ultra-defensive Joel Santana led South Africa to a rotten run of results. Come autumn 2009, it was exit Joel and hello again to Carlos who returned with the same daunting brief of finding glory for a new nation with no footballing pedigree and the perceived advantage of playing at home.

OPPOSITE *South Africa v Spain, Confederations Cup third place play-off, Royal Bafokeng Stadium, Rustenburg, South Africa, 28 June 2009: (back row, left to right) Mokoena, Booth, Khune, Sibaya, Dikgacoi, Gaxa; (front row) Modise, Pienaar, Parker, Masilela, Tshabalala.*

Steven Pienaar

Steven Pienaar is a midfield regular in a South African team that has its greatest strength in midfielders. His many fans at Everton and back home in South Africa hope his unspectacular style will yield his country some spectacular results.

His nickname is the 'Mighty Peanut' and his dynamic skills have found expression for club and country. He's a senior member of the South Africa squad, with the European experience lacking in many of his younger teammates. His reputation as a boy wonder at Ajax Cape Town, a feeder club for Ajax Amsterdam, put him on the European conveyor belt. He was part of an attack-minded Ajax team that won the Dutch League in 2002 and 2004 and reached the quarter-finals

PLAYER FACT FILE

Name: Steven Pienaar
Position: Midfielder
Caps: 46
Goals: 2
Team: Everton
Date of birth: 17 March 1982
Height: 176 cm/5 ft 9¼ in
Weight: 66 kg/145 lb
Previous clubs: Ajax, Borussia Dortmund
International debut: 23 May 2002 v Turkey
Previous World Cups: 2002

STYLE GUIDE

Steven Pienaar is a left-footed player who mixes toughness with cunning. He's a players' player who operates on either side of midfield to bring balance to any side. He'll thrive in a fight for the ball and is equally adept at breaking up opposition play or taking on the role of playmaker.

LEFT AND OPPOSITE *The poised Steven Pienaar shows his control as he marshalls South Africa's midfield.*

Katlego Mphela

Katlego Mphela plays for Mamelodi Sundowns and has gained experience abroad with the French club RC Strasbourg. With a strike rate for South Africa of one goal every other match, a nation's hopes could rest on his slim shoulders and his presence of mind in front of goal. Crowds are going to be willing him to repeat his goal-scoring feats in the Confederations Cup third-place play-off against Spain, when he hit the net twice. His 73rd-minute strike looked like being enough until a flurry of late activity. Spain scored in the 88th and 89th minutes and Mphela then produced the goal of the tournament with a free kick from thirty metres.

> ## 66 He is our best player by an absolute mile. 99

PHIL NEVILLE
EVERTON MANAGER

of the 2003 Champions League. Then he spent a frustrating year at Borussia Dortmund before moving to Everton in 2007 for the low fee of £2 million.

His quick passing game has established him as a fixture in a creative Everton midfield and when he advances forward the Toffees' fans anticipate one of his fierce shots on goal. His gathering confidence at club level has helped his country, and he played a key role in the 2009 Confederations Cup and the 2010 African Cup of Nations.

Pienaar was brought up in a Johannesburg township and has not forgotten his roots or his good fortune (he is involved with a charity that helps young people when they get out of jail). Interviewed after the final draw, he expressed the hopes of his team: 'For us to go to the second round, that is the expectation of the people. I think we can get out of the group. Mexico and Uruguay play quite similar to us, only France will be a bit of a challenge for us. The crowd will boost the players and we will be confident with them behind us. We hope they will be behind us.'

MEXICO

Mexico are in their fifth World Cup finals in a row. In Germany 2006, they were one of eight top-seeded teams and progressed to a second-round defeat against Argentina. This time, their standing is lower, largely due to inept administration that has seen a merry-go-round of coaches.

Javier Aguirre led Mexico to second place in the Copa América 2001 and on to the 2002 World Cup. Ricardo Lavolpe had the manager's job in 2006 and he was replaced by Hugo Sánchez, who was replaced by Jésus Ramirez, who was replaced by Sven-Göran Eriksson, who was replaced – in an April 2009 World Cup qualification crisis – by one Javier Aguirre.

'For me, it is an honour to return home,' Aguirre said. 'May the player who comes, come with pride, with identity, with love for the jersey. Let this be a prize, not a punishment, because this is a prize for our careers.' After the pep talking came defeat against El Salvador. Then the former Mexican player and manager turned things round with a run of five qualifier wins including one against the USA, their main local rivals. A second victory over the USA in the CONCACAF Gold Cup has convinced fans that their troubles are behind them.

It is hard identifying influential players from regimes that selected over fifty players during qualification. Those who stand out are two formidable defenders, the captain Rafael Márquez of Barcelona and the solid and aggressive left back Carlos Salcido of PSV Eindhoven. Others who could make a mark in South Africa are the midfielder Andrés Guardado and the goalkeeper Guillermo Ochoa. A forward to note is Arsenal's Carlos Vela, a 21 year old who has shown promise for club and country. At the other end of the age range is Cuauhtémoc Blanco who has a fitness and a brilliance that belies his years. He will be 37 in July 2010 but he put up a good case for his selection in the winning run that secured qualification for Javier Aguirre's winning version of El Tri.

ABOVE *National captain Rafael Márquez pictured after helping to secure his team a World Cup place in a 4–1 victory over El Salvador at the Azteca Stadium.*

ABOVE *Arsenal's Carlos Vela went straight to his manager Javier Aguirre after he had scored a last-minute goal to complete Mexico's 4–1 thrashing of El Salvador.*

POSSIBLE SQUAD

Goalkeepers

José de Jesús Corona (Cruz Azul), Guillermo Ochoa (América), Oswaldo Sánchez (Santos)

Defenders

José Antonio Castro (UANL), Efraín Juárez (UNAM), Jonny Magallón (Guadalajara), Rafael Márquez (C) (Barcelona), Héctor Moreno (AZ), Ricardo Osorio (Stuttgart), Óscar Rojas (América), Carlos Salcido (PSV Eindhoven)

Midfielders

Lucas Ayala (UANL), Israel Castro (UNAM), Pablo Barrera (UNAM), Andrés Guardado (Deportivo La Coruña), Giovani dos Santos (Tottenham Hotspur), Gerardo Torrado (Cruz Azul)

Forwards

Omar Arellano (Guadalajara), Cuauhtémoc Blanco (Chicago Fire), Enrique Esqueda (América), Guillermo Franco (West Ham United), Miguel Sabah (Morelia), Carlos Vela (Arsenal)

ROUTE TO THE FINALS

CONCACAF FINAL STAGE – FINAL TABLE

Team	P	W	D	L	F	A	Pts
USA	10	6	2	2	19	13	20
Mexico	10	6	1	3	18	12	19
Honduras	10	5	1	4	17	11	16
Costa Rica	10	5	1	4	15	15	16
El Salvador	10	2	2	6	9	15	8
Trinidad & Tobago	10	1	3	6	10	22	6

FINALS GROUP A

Mexico play		Date	Venue
	South Africa	11 June	Johannesburg (Soccer City)
	France	17 June	Polokwane
	Uruguay	22 June	Rustenburg

VITAL STATISTICS

World ranking 15th Keeper and defence 7/10
Midfield 6/10 Attack 5/10

Strengths and weaknesses Mexico have strong ingredients to form the tastiest of teams. But is there a recipe for success? Too many management cooks spoiled the Mexican broth until Aguirre returned.

How far will they go? A group that pits them against the hosts and a 2006 finalist suggests an early bath for the Mexicans.

LEFT *Mexico v El Salvador, World Cup qualifying match, Azteca Stadium, Mexico City, 10 October 2009: (back row, left to right) Osorio, Vela, Márquez, Ochoa, Israel Castro, Torrado; (front row) Franco, Juárez, Guardado, Salcido, Blanco.*

URUGUAY

Statistics can shed a joyous light on Uruguay. *La Celeste* (the Sky Blue) won – as host nation – the inaugural World Cup in 1930, won again in 1950, and qualified for a further eight World Cups. Uruguay are also the smallest nation to have lifted the World Cup.

Statistics can, however, be misleading for Uruguay's World Cup record during the 21st century doesn't thrill. They tumbled out of the first round in 2002 and failed to qualify for 2006 after losing a play-off with Australia. This time round they struggled in their South America group and nearly came unstuck in a play-off against Costa Rican tiddlers. After the 1–1 draw that secured their passage to South Africa, the team captain Diego Lugano said: 'I am happy to qualify, but not for the way we've clinched it. It is unbelievable that we have to suffer this way.'

The Uruguayan public suffers too, and many claim that the top players show more commitment to their high-paying European clubs. The man who catches the most criticism is manager Oscar Tabárez, who is in his second spell in charge having coached the team that qualified for Italy 1990. Tabárez has used the experience of attackers Sebastián Abreu and Diego Forlán while bringing on new players such as goalkeeper Fernando Muslera, defender Diego Godín, midfielder Nicolás Lodeiro and striker Luis Suárez. All are ones to watch.

Over the years Uruguay have produced a disproportionate number of world-class players relative to the country's size – Diego Forlán, Álvaro Recoba, José Nasazzi, Obdulio Varela, Rodolfo Rodríguez – but most of that list is history. The current question is whether the Tabárez blend of youth and experience can once again prove that small adds up to beautiful.

BELOW LEFT *Sebastián Abreu's goal in the home play-off against Costa Rica took Uruguay through to their ninth World Cup finals.*

BELOW RIGHT *Uruguay's coach Oscar Tabárez shows the strain of managing a side that nearly missed World Cup qualification.*

POSSIBLE SQUAD

Goalkeepers

Juan Castillo (Botafogo), **Fernando Muslera** (Lazio), **Martín Silva** (Defensor Sporting)

Defenders

Martín Cáceres (Juventus), **Sebastián Coates** (Nacional), **Juan Manuel Díaz** (Estudiantes De La Plata), **Diego Godín** (Villarreal), **Diego Lugano (C)** (Fenerbahçe), **Maxi Pereira** (Benfica), **Andrés Scotti** (Argentinos Juniors), **Bruno Silva** (Ajax)

Midfielders

Miguel Amado (Defensor Sporting), **Sebastián Eguren** (Villarreal), **Álvaro Fernández** (Vitória de Setúbal), **Walter Gargano** (Napoli), **Álvaro González** (Nacional), **Nicolás Lodeiro** (Nacional), **Álvaro Pereira** (Porto), **Diego Pérez** (AS Monaco)

Forwards

Sebastián Abreu (Aris Thessaloniki), **Sebastián Fernández** (Banfield), **Diego Forlán** (Atlético Madrid), **Luis Suárez** (Ajax)

BELOW *Uruguay v Costa Rica, World Cup play-off, Centenario Stadium, Montevideo, Uruguay, 18 November 2009: (back row, left to right) Forlán, Muslera, Eguren, Lugano, Godín; (front row) Álvero Pereira, Scotti, Perez, Lodeiro, Suárez, Maxi Pereira.*

ROUTE TO THE FINALS

SOUTH AMERICA QUALIFYING GROUP – FINAL TABLE

Team	P	W	D	L	F	A	Pts
Brazil	18	9	7	2	33	11	34
Chile	18	10	3	5	32	22	33
Paraguay	18	10	3	5	24	16	33
Argentina	18	8	4	6	23	20	28
Uruguay	18	6	6	6	28	20	24
Ecuador	18	6	5	7	22	26	23
Colombia	18	6	5	7	14	18	23
Venezuela	18	6	4	8	23	29	22
Bolivia	18	4	3	11	22	36	15
Peru	18	3	4	11	11	34	13

SOUTH AMERICA/CONCACAF PLAY-OFFS

14.11.09	Costa Rica 0	1 Uruguay
18.11.09	Uruguay 1	1 Costa Rica

FINALS GROUP A

Uruguay play		Date	Venue
	France	11 June	Cape Town
	South Africa	16 June	Tshwane/Pretoria
	Mexico	22 June	Rustenburg

VITAL STATISTICS

World ranking 19th	Keeper and defence 5/10
Midfield 5/10	Attack 6/10

Strengths and weaknesses While the best in the squad can play the rapid short-passing South American game, the team as a whole is renowned for stodgy stalemates rather than soufflés of soccer delight.

How far will they go? Only the sentimentalist would set any store by 20th-century form. Punters of a 21st-century persuasion will keep their hands in their pockets.

Diego Forlán

Those English fans who write off Diego Forlán as a Manchester United reject haven't been keeping an eye on Spain's La Liga, where he was top scorer in 2005 with Villarreal and in 2009 with Atlético Madrid. Neither have they paid attention to the South American qualifiers where he scored a hat-trick against Peru.

PLAYER FACT FILE

Name: Diego Martín Forlán Corazo
Position: Forward
Caps: 60
Goals: 22
Team: Atlético Madrid
Date of birth: 19 May 1979
Height: 179 cm/5 ft 10½ in
Weight: 75 kg/165 lb
Previous clubs: Independiente, Manchester United, Villarreal
International debut: 9 March 2002 v Saudi Arabia
Previous World Cups: 2002

STYLE GUIDE
Forlán's goal scoring through the past decade has depended on his pace, his speed on the turn and a two-footedness that makes his markers back away. He can sniff out chances in the penalty box and strike volleyed spectaculars from distance. He's good at set pieces too.

LEFT AND ABOVE RIGHT *Diego Forlán's eye for goal means he always keeps his eye on the ball. These photographs reveal a finely balanced player in action and show a man who is equally at ease kicking the ball with his left or his right foot. Forlán is shown above right leading with his right and winning an aerial challenge with Carlos Salazar of Venezuela. The World Cup qualifier in June 2009 was a 2–2 draw.*

At United he became Diego Forlorn when he took eight months and 27 games to score his first goal. He then hit a scoring vein of 17 goals in 95 appearances, acquiring a reputation for the shirt-off celebration – on one occasion he couldn't get rekitted in time for the kick-off and he played on, shirt in hand, until the referee ordered him off the pitch to get dressed.

When Wayne Rooney arrived at United, Forlán left. He found redemption in Spain, winning the European Golden Shoe in 2004–05 (jointly with Thierry Henry) at Villarreal and in 2008–09 at Atlético Madrid, neither of which clubs are La Liga's strongest. So, Forlán's image in Spain and Uruguay is of a goal-every-other-game phenomenon rather than a charming disappointment. Using gesture and language to convey that Forlán has goal scoring at the front of his mind, knowledgeable Uruguayan fans tap the space between their eyebrows and say their man has got it 'entre ceja y ceja'.

Diego Forlán was born with a sporting spoon in his mouth. His father Pablo played right back for Uruguay in the 1966 and 1974 World Cups and his grandfather Juan Carlos Corazo played for Independiente in Argentina. He was poised to choose a sporting career as a tennis player until deciding to follow in the family tradition. Uruguay hopes Forlán has enough 'entre ceja y ceja' to revive a national World Cup tradition.

❝ If it's about numbers of goals, I am the best striker in the world at the moment. ❞

DIEGO FORLÁN

FRANCE

GROUP A

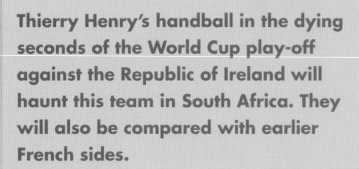

Thierry Henry's handball in the dying seconds of the World Cup play-off against the Republic of Ireland will haunt this team in South Africa. They will also be compared with earlier French sides.

The current *Les Bleus* must follow the magnificent group of players that united France in a mood of multicultural optimism and pride for the style and grace with which they won the World Cup in 1998 and then the European Championship two years later. The legacy seemed permanent and at the 2006 World Cup final it took the combination of Zinédine Zidane being sent off and a penalty shoot-out for Italy to defeat them. Further back, France were World Cup semi-finalists in 1958, 1982 and 1986. Along the way, they have been Brazil's most formidable World Cup finals opponents, having won two, drawn one and lost one in four high-level encounters.

So shall we compare the French to the Brazilians or to the Irish? Do we dwell on recent glory or on the disappointing football of more recent performances? *Les Bleus* mutated into *Les Misérables* after a sterile 2008 European Championship when negative displays of square passing across the defence didn't help upfield stars who appeared strangely anonymous and intimidated when they pulled on a French shirt. The poor form continued into World Cup qualification with a stuttering second place in an easy group and an undignified scraping through to the play-offs culminating in the famous handball that enabled the cross that got the goal that got the ticket to South Africa.

RIGHT *Let joy be slightly confined. This scene of post-match jubilation at the Stade de France shows French players and fans celebrating World Cup qualification after the concluding 1–1 play-off with the Republic of Ireland. What the picture doesn't show is another part of the pitch where Thierry Henry was sitting next to the Irish captain, Richard Dunne, offering commiseration for the handball that had given France the game.*

French newspapers demand the glories of old but understandably put a spotlight on the immediate past dwelling, in particular, on the faults of the manager Raymond Domenech. *L'Équipe* newspaper complains loudly and constantly of muddled defensive tactics and unimaginative midfield instructions from a naïve coach who is overawed by his senior players. In November 2009, the newspaper ran its ironic 'La Main de Dieu' – 'The Hand of God' – headline immediately after the disputed game to renew its campaign for a new manager. Mind you, this is the same *L'Équipe* that in May 1998 published an editorial arguing that Aimé Jacquet deserved the sack. Two months later Jacquet's team lifted the 1998 World Cup.

French teams tend to gather coherence as tournaments progress and their qualification struggle may well be an unreliable guide to how they will play in South Africa. Assuming that a contrite Thierry Henry, a resurgent Nicolas Anelka and a battling Franck Ribéry are on song – which assumes that injury hasn't kept them off the pitch altogether – then France have great potential. However, even a midfield featuring Ribéry doesn't have a dominating character with the stature of a Michel Platini or an Eric Cantona or a Zinédine Zidane. There is nobody to take up a free-attacking, playmaking role from the

> ❝ **What do I tell the players? I invite them to go out there and win. I don't need to motivate the players. I actually need to quieten them so they don't get overexcited. We need cold blood, patience and intelligence.** ❞
>
> RAYMOND DOMENECH

BELOW *In the final match of the last World Cup, the red mist fell on Zinédine Zidane and a red card had to follow. It was Zidane's final game, for he retired from top-level football after the summer of 2006.*

GREAT MATCH
2006 France 1–1 Italy
(Italy won 5–3 on penalties)

World Cup final
Olympiastadion, Berlin, Germany

The climax of the 2006 World Cup between France and Italy was more open than many had expected. The first goal came in the sixth minute when Zinédine Zidane stroked home a penalty awarded after Marco Materazzi tripped Florent Malouda. Zidane became the fourth man to have scored in two World Cup finals. Italy had equalized by half-time with Materazzi heading in an Andrea Pirlo corner from the right.

While Italy had dominated play in the first half with the man of the match Pirlo and Gennaro Gattuso controlling the pace, the game seemed to swing towards France in the second half. Thierry Henry woke up to make a couple of incisive runs and force a save from Gianluigi Buffon.

As the game moved into extra time, France regained the initiative and looked the more confident side until, with six minutes to play, disaster struck. In retaliation for unkind things being said about his mother, Zidane banged his head into a defender's chest. He was sent off. France clung on to the end for a penalty shoot-out where neither goalie made a save and which was decided when David Trézéguet hit the crossbar.

Zidane was awarded the Golden Ball as the tournament's best player.

centre of the park. The defence too has lost some sense of authority and was fragile in the air during qualifying games, especially at set pieces. That said, Bacary Sagna, Éric Abidal, William Gallas and Patrice Evra could be an awesome foursome if they gel into the kind of defensive units they operate in at club level.

But for the use of October's – as opposed to November's – world rankings by FIFA for the draw in December 2009, France's ranking as seventh in the world and its appearance in the 2006 final would have seen them seeded as a group leader. However, a potentially disastrous draw could not have been kinder for it has been their good fortune to have been drawn against a weak host nation team plus a couple of South American sides that look past their sell-by dates. This current French side will surely stand up to on-pitch comparisons with South Africa, Mexico and Uruguay.

BELOW AND RIGHT *In the dying seconds of extra time in the play-off against the Republic of Ireland, William Gallas rose to head France towards South Africa. It would have been a magnificent goal but for Thierry Henry's handling of the ball (shown clearly in the TV grab) to enable the decisive cross.*

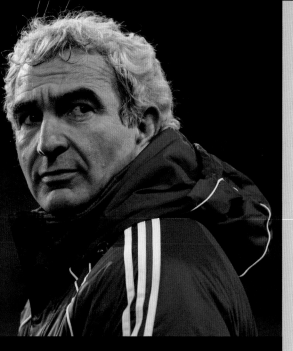

COACH **Raymond Domenech**

Born 24 January 1952
Record: P33, W17, D11, L5

Defenders of Raymond Domenech – chief amongst them being the French Football Federation – say that he is one of France's most successful managers. After all, his 33 competitive games in charge of the national team have included a World Cup final plus qualification campaigns for three successive championships.

'Good players, bad coach' claims a prosecution chorus. Pointing to dull play since Euro 2008, many people in France blame Domenech for making tactical pigs' ears from silky raw materials and then shift the ground to say he yields to player power. Then Domenech has to field complaints that it's his target man André-Pierre Gignac rather than the more popular Karim Benzema who is getting the managerial nod to go up front. There's even a story that he didn't play Robert Pirès because he distrusts Scorpios. Yet despite the unpopularity and the prickliness, Domenech has retained the services of a range of volatile talents and has largely defused conflicts on the training ground.

'My critics have the smell of blood,' he has said.' They would take great pleasure in sending me to the scaffold.' So far, Raymond Domenech has kept his head.

ROUTE TO THE FINALS

MATCHES PLAYED

Date	Home		Away
06.09.08	Austria 3	1	France
10.09.08	France 2	1	Serbia
11.10.08	Romania 2	2	France
28.03.09	Lithuania 0	1	France
01.04.09	France 1	0	Lithuania
12.08.09	Faroe Islands 0	1	France
05.09.09	France 1	1	Romania
09.09.09	Serbia 1	1	France
10.10.09	France 5	0	Faroe Islands
14.10.09	France 3	1	Austria

EUROPE QUALIFYING GROUP 7 – FINAL TABLE

Team	P	W	D	L	F	A	Pts
Serbia	10	7	1	2	22	8	22
France	10	6	3	1	18	9	21
Austria	10	4	2	4	14	15	14
Lithuania	10	4	0	6	10	11	12
Romania	10	3	3	4	12	18	12
Faroe Islands	10	1	1	8	5	20	4

EUROPE PLAY-OFFS

Date	Home		Away
14.11.09	Republic of Ireland 0	1	France
18.11.09	France 1	1	Republic of Ireland

FINALS GROUP A

France play		Date	Venue
	Uruguay	11 June	Cape Town
	Mexico	17 June	Polokwane
	South Africa	22 June	Mangaung/Bloemfontein

VITAL STATISTICS

World ranking 7th   Keeper and defence 8/10
Midfield 7/10   Attack 9/10

Strengths and weaknesses French flair and talent is unquestionable. The question mark over this team is in the detailed queries about how that talent is motivated and organized.

How far will they go? France will go to South Africa feeling their backs are against the wall. That will spur them on. By this logic, France are a quarter-final certainty.

HOW THEY'LL LINE UP

In the absence of a dominating playmaker, the tactics are decided from the front. The idea is to exploit the unpredictable passing and movement of Henry and Anelka and for them to further confuse defensive marking when they drop back into midfield or simply switch sides of the pitch. Wherever they are, Henry and Anelka can release passes crafted for either Benzema or Gignac to snap up. The engine room behind the glamour is less sure of what's going on so the attack could find itself stranded, and at the back is a defence that might be over-reliant on Hugo Lloris in goal.

POSSIBLE SQUAD

Goalkeepers

Cédric Carrasso (Bordeaux), **Hugo Lloris** (Lyon), **Steve Mandanda** (Marseille)

Defenders

Éric Abidal (Barcelona), Aly Cissokho (Lyon), Julien Escudé (Sevilla), Patrice Evra (Manchester United), Rod Fanni (Rennes), William Gallas (Arsenal), Bacary Sagna (Arsenal), Sébastien Squillaci (Sevilla)

Midfielders

Abou Diaby (Arsenal), Alou Diarra (Bordeaux), Lassana Diarra (Real Madrid), Yoann Gourcuff (Bordeaux), Sidney Govou (Lyon), Florent Malouda (Chelsea), Franck Ribéry (Bayern Munich), Moussa Sissoko (Toulouse)

Forwards

Nicolas Anelka (Chelsea), Karim Benzema (Real Madrid), André-Pierre Gignac (Toulouse), Thierry Henry (C) (Barcelona)

BELOW *France v Republic of Ireland, World Cup qualifying match, play-off second leg, Stade de France, Paris, 18 November 2009: (back row, left to right) Lloris, Alou Diarra, Gallas, Anelka, Gourcuff, Gignac, Escudé; (front row) Henry, Evra, Sagna, Lassana Diarra.*

Thierry Henry

After the handball in *that* game, Thierry Henry had five seconds to own up and redeem himself. He blew his chance, tarnishing in a moment his reputation as a man who combined gentlemanly virtues with high playing skills.

Until the last World Cup, there had been doubts about whether Henry could play well in games where the pressure is highest. That question was resolved in 2006. Playing as a lone striker, he scored three goals including the winner against Brazil, the defending champions. He was one of the dominant players in the second half of the final against Italy but did not take part in the penalty shoot-out, having been substituted in extra time with cramped leg muscles. While France lost the game, Henry emerged with a deeper reputation.

66 **Thierry will get over this. He made a mistake, like I made a mistake, even if I'm not making any comparisons. We all make mistakes.** 99

ZINÉDINE ZIDANE

A French football academy graduate, Henry began his playing career under Arsène Wenger at Monaco. Starting as a winger, he made his debut for France aged 20 and was top scorer, with three goals in each tournament, when France triumphed in the 1998 World Cup and Euro 2000. By then, following a brief spell with Juventus, he was back with Wenger, now at Arsenal, and Wenger converted him to a freer central role. Henry spent eight years with Arsenal forging a reputation as a truly great club player and honing an image so valuable to advertisers that he became one of the wealthiest sportsmen in the world. His credit only increased when he moved on to Barcelona and a Champions League medal.

In 2008, Henry was named a *Chevalier* (Knight) of the *Légion d'honneur* (France's highest honour). In the four years since the last World Cup, Henry's international reputation has shifted gear. As France fell into relative international decline, Henry developed a tendency to drift in and out of international matches and to play disjointedly, just like the team as a whole. Nonetheless, he retained enough stellar presence for Raymond Domenech to promote him to national captain. What other position would suit a *chevalier*? The time approaches when Thierry Henry must reproduce astonishing club form or be remembered more as a tarnished celebrity than a perfect gentle knight.

PLAYER FACT FILE

Name: Thierry Daniel Henry
Position: Forward
Caps: 117
Goals: 51
Team: Barcelona
Date of birth: 17 August 1977
Height: 188 cm/6 ft 2 in
Weight: 83 kg/183 lb
Previous clubs: Monaco, Juventus, Arsenal
International debut: 11 October 1997 v South Africa
Previous World Cups: 1998, 2002, 2006

STYLE GUIDE

There's an audacity to Thierry Henry's play that can occasionally move terraces full of football fans to laughter. He consistently spreads fear among defenders with his pace, his vision of surrounding play, his outrageous ball-playing skills and his sheer unpredictability. He'll variously thrust goalwards or veer left and provide assists. Or do something else entirely.

LEFT *Thierry Henry shows his poise as he moves in to shoot and score during a World Cup qualifying match against Romania.*

Nicolas Anelka

There are two not entirely unrelated aspects to Nicolas Anelka's career: first, he has never played at a World Cup finals; second, the aggregate transfer cost as he has flitted through numerous clubs adds up to nearly £90 million.

In 1997, Arsenal's new manager, Arsène Wenger, snapped up the 17 year old for £500,000. The next year France won the World Cup, Anelka was named French Young Footballer of the Year, he won the double with Arsenal and he made his international debut – in a friendly. Two years later Wenger sold his sour-faced protégé to Real

> **Nicolas kept his cool when the team was under pressure. He was probably the player who touched the ball the most.**
>
> EMMANUEL PETIT
> (FRANCE 1990–2003)
> ON ANELKA'S PERFORMANCE
> IN THE PLAY-OFFS

PLAYER FACT FILE

Name: Nicolas Sebastien Anelka
Position: Forward
Caps: 63
Goals: 14
Team: Chelsea
Date of birth: 14 March 1979
Height: 183 cm/6 ft
Weight: 77 kg/170 lb
Previous clubs: Paris St-Germain, Arsenal, Real Madrid, Paris St-Germain, Liverpool, Manchester City, Fenerbahçe, Bolton Wanderers
International debut: 22 April 1998 v Sweden
Previous World Cups: None

STYLE GUIDE

Anelka is pure footballing style. Yet the silky striker who has brought much beauty to the beautiful game was 'Le Sulk' in those difficult years when adolescent shyness pupates into youthful nonchalance. The adult Anelka has emerged into the world showing a fully fledged commitment where he has spread his wings. And smiled.

Madrid at a £20 million profit. Anelka was off on his travels, though his destinations didn't include summertime breaks in Korea and Japan in 2002 or Germany in 2006.

A perennially unsettled Anelka was deemed too much of a gamble for French tournament squads. However, things looked up on his return to English football with Bolton Wanderers. Manager Raymond Domenech brought him on in a Euro 2008 qualifier against Lithuania where Anelka scored and played a blinder. Domenech commented: 'I saw the Nicolas I like to see. When he shows these qualities, he is a candidate for a permanent place.'

Anelka finally settled at Chelsea in 2008 and fought for a permanent French place with a hitherto uncharacteristic enthusiasm and acceptance of setbacks. At Euro 2008, he was substituted in the opening match and then restricted to a sub's role in the remaining two games against the Netherlands and Italy. He battled on as a committed *bleu* and was hailed as the French saviour as he (and France) hit form towards the end of the World Cup qualifying run. He scored the only goal to win the first play-off in the Republic of Ireland.

To see Anelka's leadership and dominating forward play in both games was to witness an individualist melding into a collective without loss of flair. On form, Anelka will play a decisive role in South Africa.

ABOVE AND LEFT *Nicolas Anelka in action against the Republic of Ireland on a chilly night in Dublin on 14 November 2009. He was the star player in a 1–0 victory and is pictured taking a tumble (above) over Irish goalkeeper Shay Given and (left) firing a shot at goal.*

Patrice Evra

'He is the complete left back,' says Wilf McGuinness, a former Manchester United player and manager. 'He's almost Brazilian in style.'

Patrice Evra was almost not a French player. He was born in Senegal and arrived in Paris aged six when his diplomat father was posted to France. A cosmopolitan career has taken in Marsala in Italy, three French clubs and, from 2006, Manchester United. On his first day at Old Trafford, he asked Gary Neville where the nearest church was so he could 'thank God for letting me join the biggest club in the world'.

Through skill and hard work, his time at Man U has converted a 24 year old who didn't make it into the 2006 World Cup squad into a late-flowering first-choice international. His game matured rapidly as he adapted to English pace, though his initial struggles included a dreadful performance in a 3–1 home derby defeat to Manchester City. Evra weathered the scorn and soon became a United favourite, earning a winner's medal in the 2007, 2008 and 2009 Premier Leagues and the 2008 Champions League.

PLAYER FACT FILE

Name: Patrice Latyr Evra
Position: Defender
Caps: 26
Goals: 0
Team: Manchester United
Date of birth: 15 May 1981
Height: 173 cm/5 ft 8 in
Weight: 76 kg/168 lb
Previous clubs: Marsala, Monza, Nice, Monaco
International debut: 18 August 2004 v Bosnia and Herzegovina
Previous World Cups: None

STYLE GUIDE
Evra has an intuitive understanding of the balance between attacking and defending. He glides into forward runs down the left and knows exactly when he should stay put or scamper back into his defensive position.

LEFT *Evra puts his left foot forward to control the ball – he is shown here against the backdrop of Dutch fans during a Euro 2008 match versus the Netherlands.*

ABOVE RIGHT *Evra hard at work in the French defence, tugging at the shirt of the Serbian midfielder Gojko Kačar during a World Cup qualifier in September 2009.*

Hugo Lloris

International goalies are usually grizzled hulks by the time they become first-choice internationals. The fresh-faced Hugo Lloris is different. He'll be 24 and brimful of confidence when he starts out in South Africa in summer 2010. Lloris signed for Olympique Lyonnais in 2008, choosing a French team ahead of offers from AC Milan and Spurs. Having worked his way through the national youth teams, he secured his early right to the French goalkeeping jersey with some startlingly good performances in the qualifying matches from November 2008 onwards. His two games against the Republic of Ireland ensured that his listless teammates prevailed over a resurgent Irish team. Had the encounters not ended with such rancour, the goalkeeper would have been feted as a French saviour. While his praises were drowned out, his position between the sticks was confirmed and if France do make progress in South Africa, Lloris will have to be one of the players of the tournament.

His neat efficiency, tidiness in the tackle and straightforward distribution can make Evra seem anonymous. He usually passes beneath the referee's radar and has an excellent disciplinary record, though a fiery side was revealed in a couple of post-match spats, first with a Chelsea groundsman then with Patrick Vieira just after France had been ejected from Euro 2008. Evra, however, is normally as poised in his demeanour as he is in his play.

❝ Patrice has developed into one of the best full backs in world football and his infectious personality has helped build the team spirit that exists at Old Trafford. ❞

SIR ALEX FERGUSON

William Gallas

Gallas proclaims with every gesture that no man shall pass. He forms the ramparts of a French defensive fortress constructed around a big-hearted 'warrior'. His versatility and experience, however, are laced with volatility.

Gallas's versatility shows in the way he has operated at right back, left back and centre back for Chelsea; at right back and centre back for Arsenal; and at centre back for France. Two-footed tactical flexibility is what they teach at the Clairefontaine French football academy and Gallas has been showing off a range of defensive skills since he helped Caen out of the French second division back in 1996. Those skills were refined under the tutelage of the French World Cup winner Marcel Desailly whom Gallas partnered on his move to Chelsea in 2001. Gallas helped Chelsea to two successive Premiership titles in 2005 and 2006. By then he was partnering John Terry, and together they had a run of 16 games without conceding a goal.

Raymond Domenech has consistently selected Gallas at centre back since taking the French managerial post in 2004. First he paired Gallas with Lilian Thuram in a central partnership that took France through to the 2006 World Cup final in Germany. The current international partnership is with Éric Abidal and has held up fairly well with 10 goals against France in 12 qualifying matches. Could do better, but not bad.

The volatility is in arguments over shirt numbers, reactions to penalty decisions, demands to leave Chelsea and the gaining and the losing of the Arsenal captaincy for criticizing his teammates. Gallas has come through it all and, at 32, South Africa will be the last time he stiffens the sinews and summons up the blood to represent his country at the highest level.

RIGHT *Gallas takes flight above a couple of Republic of Ireland defenders and leaves the Irish captain Richard Dunne a frowning onlooker in the background.*

> **It's our duty to win as it's our duty to qualify for the World Cup.**

WILLIAM GALLAS

Franck Ribéry

A burden of responsibility rests on the small frame of a swift midfielder who must engage all his defiance and charm if he is to find answers to some tricky questions. Does Franck Ribéry have the style to fill the wandering playmaker gap left by Zinédine Zidane? Will hustle replace elegance? Can France replace the irreplaceable?

Ribéry is a singular man who would stand out in any crowd, not that he is the tallest of men. Before every match he raises his hands to Allah, having converted to Islam when he married a French wife of Algerian descent and adopted the Arabic name Bilal. More noticeable than the religious observance is the severe scarring on his face after a car crash when he was an infant. Most noticeable of all is the punchy stance, the trickery and the determination, the quick-fire passing and the shots, and – above all – the fact that on the pitch Ribéry looks like he is enjoying himself.

Contractual rather than personality problems had Ribéry bouncing between clubs until he established his name during two years with Marseille between 2005 and 2007. He then settled at Bayern and in his first season won the German double, was voted Bundesliga player of the year, and became only the second foreign player to be named German footballer of the year, claiming the prize ahead of Michael Ballack.

Although his international debut was less than a month before the 2006 World Cup, such was his impact that he earned selection in the team that lost so narrowly to

ABOVE *Frank Ribéry shows typical ball control under the challenge of the Lithuania defender Deividas Semberas during France's World Cup qualifying campaign.*

Italy in the finals. His first international goal was in the knockout round when he outwitted the Spanish keeper Iker Casillas to pull France level and set up a 3–1 victory. Then came the semi-final against Brazil when he asserted himself like a seasoned professional. Soon all France knew about Ribéry, who emerged from the tournament with a endorsement from Zidane.

For most people, the expectation accompanying that kind of recognition might be too heavy a weight. Ribéry is different. He has carried on adapting himself all his life; he carried on scoring in the qualifiers until an injury kept him out of the last few games. France looks forward to his return in South Africa.

66 Franck is the jewel of French football. 99

ZINÉDINE ZIDANE

ARGENTINA

GROUP B

Many football fans would consider that Argentina's progress to the World Cup finals via a play-off they barely qualified for makes them no-hopers. South American signs and portents suggest otherwise.

La Selección's four World Cup final appearances and two wins plus a record 14 Copa América titles is a set of winning statistics to convince anybody of Argentine prowess. Strong in history, the potential current squad is also strong on paper with a host of players who would make it onto any team sheet in the world. However, even with marvellous players on call, the *Albicelestes* ('light blue and whites') struggled against lesser opposition, suffering a 6–1 thrashing in Bolivia in April 2009 and shortly after a string of three defeats, before two late goals in the last two games clinched qualification.

During this time there was much contention about the appropriateness of team selection. Two of Argentina's finest players, defender Walter Samuel and midfielder Román Riquelme, hardly figured in the World Cup build-up (and would now seem to be highly unlikely to make it into the squad for South Africa). Carlos Tévez and Sergio Agüero often started from the bench while the lesser talents of Martín Demichelis and Jonás Gutiérrez were picked, if at all fit. Another regular starter, Lionel Messi – one of the players of his generation – played below par in international colours and the captain, Javier Mascherano, is not even captain of his Liverpool club side.

There has been a reliance on older players, particularly Juan Sebastián Verón. In a warm-up game immediately prior to the qualifying match that Argentina lost 3–1 to Brazil, Rolando Schiavi made his international debut. He was 36. A 35-year-old striker, Martin Palermo, figured in the penultimate qualifier against Peru. In Palermo's previous international – in 1999 – he had missed three penalties in

ABOVE *On the wet and windy night of 10 October 2009, Argentina scored a 94th-minute winner against Peru to ensure they still had a chance of World Cup qualification. Had the game been drawn, the players would have had to struggle for a place in the play-offs.*

> **Argentina's qualifying game against Peru was a travesty of football management, but one of the greatest pieces of sporting theatre imaginable.**

RICHARD WILLIAMS
THE GUARDIAN

World Cup quarter-final
Azteca Stadium, Mexico City, Mexico

Coming just four years after the Falklands War, this match took on incredible significance with the defeated Argentinians battling for a nation's pride. And so it appeared as the match got underway with Peter Beardsley and Gary Lineker being tightly marked and Maradona eclipsing the quiet Glenn Hoddle in midfield. Despite failing to get a shot at goal, England reached half-time on equal terms.

The second half was only six minutes old when Steve Hodge sliced a clearance into his own penalty area. The two captains – Maradona and Peter Shilton – contested the ball and amazingly the pint-sized genius seemed to outjump the towering keeper and the ball bounced towards the empty net. The whole stadium was fooled – only TV replays and Shilton knew Maradona had punched the ball. Four minutes later, the Argentinian hero created and scored one of the greatest World Cup goals ever, picking up the ball near the halfway line and going past three tackles before selling Shilton a dummy.

England attempted to rally, sending Chris Waddle and John Barnes on, and the latter provided a great run and cross for Lineker to nod in. Then in the dying minutes he repeated the feat. This time, just as Lineker seemed poised to equalize, a defender pushed the ball away. Argentina celebrated madly, Maradona proclaimed the 'Hand of God', and the world realized that football had found a new king.

one match against Colombia in the Copa América. But time as well as logic were defied when Palermo kept Argentina's World Cup aspirations alive with the winning goal against Peru. In the 93rd minute.

The chopper and changer in chief is, of course, Diego Maradona, and what has occurred under his management is not entirely out of character. Indeed, Argentina are moulded in their manager's image.

ABOVE *Two top number tens. Lionel Messi holds the ball under the watchful eye of Spain's Cesc Fàbregas during a friendly in Madrid in November 2009. The Argentine was named FIFA World Player of the Year in 2009 after Barcelona's haul of six successive trophies.*

LEFT *'Hand of God' and 'Tummy of God': Diego Maradona in vertical mode (above) back in 1986, when he punched the ball past Peter Shilton, and in horizontal mode (below) celebrating the goal against Peru that saved his manager's job and kept his team in the 2010 World Cup.*

They are chaotic, impetuous, inconsistent and masters at creating their own adversity. Like Maradona, the team can soak up physical and mental pressure – then, perhaps, call on the hand of God for unlikely 93rd-minute goals. Like Maradona, Argentina can dominate attention and lose. There are other similarities. Maradona delivered moments of pure footballing beauty that included sublime bits of team play as well as individual goals. Don't forget that Argentina is more often than not a formidable team of outstanding players. Nearly a quarter of a century after dominating Argentina's 1986 World Cup triumph, Maradona drew on whatever it took to hold himself and his team together in a desperate qualifying run. He could once again lead Argentina to football's pinnacle.

COACH **Diego Maradona**

Born: 30 October 1960
Record: P14, W9, D0, L5

When Maradona became Argentina's manager in 2008, a clutch of images came to mind. English media re-ran pictures of Maradona's two quarter-final goals against England in 1986. The first was 'Hand of God' stills showing his leap to punch the ball past Peter Shilton; the second, footage of what FIFA voted the greatest goal in World Cup history: Maradona is in his own half, he swivels, 11 perfect touches and his low centre of gravity has him slaloming in on goal.

Over the ensuing years the Argentinian superstar's fabled exploits on the field of play were matched by his drug-related problems off it, leading to suspension in 1991–92 and being sent home from the 1994 World Cup. By 2000 his fall from grace seemed total. Then came redemption with Maradona as TV interviewer, including a special with Fidel Castro. Cut to pictures of Maradona the manager, a greying track-suited man with a face that, as it absorbed Argentine defeats in easy qualification games, was as impassive as an Easter Island statue. The last image – and it won't be the final one – is of the exuberant belly slide celebrating the goal that kept Argentina on track for South Africa.

POSSIBLE SQUAD

Goalkeepers

Mariano Andújar (Catania), Diego Pozo (Colón), Sergio Romero (AZ)

Defenders

Martín Demichelis (Bayern Munich), Gabriel Heinze (Marseille), Emiliano Insúa (Liverpool), Nicolás Otamendi (Vélez Sársfield), Rolando Schiavi (Newell's Old Boys), Javier Zanetti (Internazionale)

Midfielders

Pablo Aimar (Benfica), Jesús Dátolo (Olympiacos, loan from Napoli), Ángel Di María (Benfica), Lucho González (Marseille), Jonás Gutiérrez (Newcastle), Federico Insúa (Boca Juniors), Javier Mascherano (C) (Liverpool), Lionel Messi (Barcelona), Enzo Pérez (Estudiantes), Juan Sebastián Verón (Estudiantes)

Forwards

Sergio Agüero (Atlético Madrid), Gonzalo Higuaín (Real Madrid), Martín Palermo (Boca Juniors), Carlos Tévez (Manchester City)

BELOW *Argentina v Peru, World Cup qualifier, Monumental Stadium, Buenos Aires, Argentina, 10 October 2009: (back row, left to right) Gutiérrez, Schiavi, Romero, Higuaín, Insúa, Heinze; (front row) Messi, Pérez, Di María, Aimar, Mascherano.*

HOW THEY'LL LINE UP

A consideration of the Argentine line-up is just another way of talking about the manager, so who knows how this team will line up in South Africa? The only certainty is that it is difficult to talk of squads and tactics for a team that has fielded over 80 players in 13 matches. Judging by the qualifying run-up, Argentina will put Gabriel Heinze and Javier Zanetti in defence with the full-back positions up for grabs. Javier Mascherano, Pablo Aimar, Juan Sebastián Verón and Carlos Tévez are the most likely midfield quartet with Mascherano as the anchor and Tévez advancing forward. And Lionel Messi will advance still further into the hole behind a striker such as Gonzalo Higuaín. Recent tactics suggest that a tendency for flat-out attacking will leave the defence exposed.

VITAL STATISTICS

World ranking 8th
Keeper and defence 7/10
Midfield 7/10   **Attack** 8/10

Strengths and weaknesses The select of *La Selección* players are among the best footballers on the planet. Maradona is among the weirdest of managers in football history … but that needn't necessarily be a weakness.

How far will they go? Argentina sneaked in ahead of France as a top seed and had a favourable draw. The opening game against Nigeria will be the strongest challenge of an easy group.

ROUTE TO THE FINALS

MATCHES PLAYED

Date	Home		Away
13.10.07	Argentina	2	0 Chile
16.10.07	Venezuela	0	2 Argentina
17.11.07	Argentina	3	0 Bolivia
20.11.07	Colombia	2	1 Argentina
15.06.08	Argentina	1	1 Ecuador
18.06.08	Brazil	0	0 Argentina
06.09.08	Argentina	1	1 Paraguay
10.09.08	Peru	1	1 Argentina
11.10.08	Argentina	2	1 Uruguay
15.10.08	Chile	1	0 Argentina
28.03.09	Argentina	4	0 Venezuela
01.04.09	Bolivia	6	1 Argentina
06.06.09	Argentina	1	0 Colombia
10.06.09	Ecuador	2	0 Argentina
05.09.09	Argentina	1	3 Brazil
09.09.09	Paraguay	1	0 Argentina
10.10.09	Argentina	2	1 Peru
14.10.09	Uruguay	0	1 Argentina

SOUTH AMERICA QUALIFYING GROUP – FINAL TABLE

Team	P	W	D	L	F	A	Pts
Brazil	18	9	7	2	33	11	34
Chile	18	10	3	5	32	22	33
Paraguay	18	10	3	5	24	16	33
Argentina	18	8	4	6	23	20	28
Uruguay	18	6	6	6	28	20	24
Ecuador	18	6	5	7	22	26	23
Colombia	18	6	5	7	14	18	23
Venezuela	18	6	4	8	23	29	22
Bolivia	18	4	3	11	22	36	15
Peru	18	3	4	11	11	34	13

FINALS GROUP B

Argentina play	Date	Venue
Nigeria	12 June	Johannesburg (Ellis Park)
Korea Republic	17 June	Johannesburg (Soccer City)
Greece	22 June	Polokwane

Javier Mascherano

Diego Maradona's first managerial move when he took over Argentina towards the end of 2008 was to appoint Javier Mascherano as team captain. 'I believe he is the Argentinian player who is closest to the idea I have about the Argentinian shirt – sweat for it, sacrifice for it, being a professional, being close to the teammate,' Maradona said. 'I will convince him. He will be my captain.'

The recognition came at the end of a swirl of off-field controversy. Immediately after the last World Cup, Mascherano had moved to West Ham from the Brazilian club Corinthians. He arrived in London with fellow Argentinian Carlos Tévez as part of a complex deal in which Media Sports Investments, the company with an interest in both players' registrations, was attempting a takeover of West Ham. A disastrous three-month playing stint at West Ham ended with a loan to Liverpool in February 2007. Financial and procedural entanglements meant it took a year for the Liverpool move to be ratified in an £18.6 million deal that finally cut Mascherano's links to Media Sports Investments. Despite the distractions, his play was unaffected.

The Liverpool manager Rafael Benítez has made Mascherano a pivot of his team calling him a 'monster of a player' and deploying him deep to release the passing talents of Steven Gerrard and Xabi Alonso. Alonso, Mascherano's midfield colleague until summer 2009, comments: 'Javier has a cool mind on the pitch. He is analysing and thinking about the game in each moment.'

El Jefecito ('the little chief') bosses games from ahead of the defence and he approaches the 2010 World Cup as a mature player in his mid-twentiess with a wealth of international experience. However, aside from two Olympic medals, he has not been an international tournament winner. Teammates twice voted him player of the tournament after losing finals in the last two Copa Américas. He was in the team that lost 4–1 to Brazil in the 2005 Confederations Cup final and in the 2006 World Cup, he played every minute of every game until a quarter-final defeat against Germany.

PLAYER FACT FILE

Name: Javier Alejandro Mascherano
Position: Midfielder
Caps: 55
Goals: 2
Team: Liverpool
Date of birth: 8 June 1984
Height: 171 cm/5 ft 7 in
Weight: 66 kg/146 lb
Previous clubs: River Plate, Corinthians, West Ham United
International debut: 16 July 2003 v Uruguay
Previous World Cups: 2006

STYLE GUIDE
Games at the top level are won and lost in midfield and Mascherano is a midfield match-winner. He is one of those unflashy footballers whose praises are shouted loudest by managers and teammates. A professional's professional, he is valued for his work rate, his commitment, his concentration, his tackling, his straightforward passing and his positional sense. He has the talents of mind and anticipation to quietly dominate midfield tussles and to negate more flamboyant talents.

ABOVE RIGHT *Javier Mascherano (left) scrapping for the ball with Uruguay defender Andres Scotti during the last World Cup qualifying match. Mascherano*

Only Messi was on the field for more minutes than Mascherano during Argentina's rocky World Cup qualifying campaign. Though Mascherano stuttered in the early games, he regained form for the last-gasp 2–1 victory over Peru and in the 1–0 win in Uruguay. In the end Mascherano did more than enough to vindicate his manager's faith and to secure his claim to the captain's armband in South Africa.

> **Mascherano is, possibly, the best central midfielder in the world. With him on the pitch a coach can sleep easily.**
>
> DIEGO MARADONA

Lionel Messi

Lionel Messi's skills on the ball are astonishing. He's one of the most exciting players of his generation and his quality is apparent from the farthest corners of the largest stadiums.

PLAYER FACT FILE

Name: Lionel Andrés Messi
Position: Midfielder
Caps: 43
Goals: 13
Team: Barcelona
Date of birth: 24 June 1987
Height: 169 cm/5 ft 6½ in
Weight: 67 kg/148 lb
Previous clubs: None
International debut: 17 August 2005
v Hungary
Previous World Cups: 2006

STYLE GUIDE

Messi has the versatility to switch between playmaking and flat-out goal-scoring roles. He runs with the ball close to his feet and his cards close to his chest. He uses his guile to shield the ball and his intentions, whisking past defenders who often find it impossible to counter the composure and balance of a man who delivers the rapier pass or the snap shot in ways they haven't quite anticipated. Then there are cool-headed corners, free kicks and penalties.

<blockquote>
❝ I have seen the player who will inherit my place in Argentine football and his name is Lionel Messi. ❞

DIEGO MARADONA
</blockquote>

It's hard to believe that the boyish-looking man with the slight frame and shuffling, stoop-shouldered stance is riding tackles, looking up, accelerating, turning into unimagined spaces and firing fierce shots. It is harder still to believe that he needed growth hormones to reach his adult height of 1.69 m/5 ft 6½ in and to achieve his stature as arguably the world's best player.

When Messi's Catalan relatives introduced him to Barcelona in 2000, the 12 year old received treatment for Fragile X syndrome. In 2004 he became the youngest player to appear in a La Liga match, and the youngest to score a league goal. That season Barcelona won La Liga, then the Champions League the following season. Messi has gone from strength to strength and is the key to Barcelona's dominance in Spain and Europe.

International progress was a fraction less assured: he came on as a substitute against Hungary in 2005 only to be sent off two minutes later for elbowing a defender. He played a minor part in Argentina's 2006 World Cup campaign, but four years on he is fully established in the national side, the only Argentinian to play in all 18 qualifying matches. Maradona gave him the number ten shirt for the World Cup qualifier against Venezuela and Messi repaid the favour by opening the scoring in a 4–0 win.

Messi's power, balance and strength – if not his physique – soon drew comparisons between him and Maradona. 'Messidona' is the clumsy nickname to catch the elegance of the ball-playing prodigy who, in a 2007 Spanish Cup semi-final against Getafe, scored a goal to compare with Maradona's 'Goal of the Century' against England in the 1986 World Cup. Both players ran over sixty metres to dribble past opponents before shooting from similar positions on the right to score and then wheel off towards the corner flag.

There will more than likely be goals from Messi in South Africa – more than likely something astonishing to witness and remember from a player with talent enough to fit the Argentine number ten shirt.

OPPOSITE AND ABOVE *Lionel Messi's extraordinary balance has him wriggling free of a Peruvian challenge (opposite) and firing off a snap shot against Venezuela (above).*

Carlos Tévez

What you see of Carlos Tévez is what you get: a fireball of skill in perpetual motion, with body language that projects absolute irrepressibility. Nobody stands in his way.

Scythed with a tackle and Tévez will be on his feet again before anyone can shout foul. Beat him down in any way and he'll get straight up. The unpretentious playing style is reflected in the way he has refused cosmetic surgery on the scar from a childhood burn that extends from his right ear to his chest.

ABOVE RIGHT *Carlos Tévez at full tilt running at the unfortunate José Manuel Velásquez of Venezuela. The number 16, Roberto Rosales, has sensibly stepped aside.*

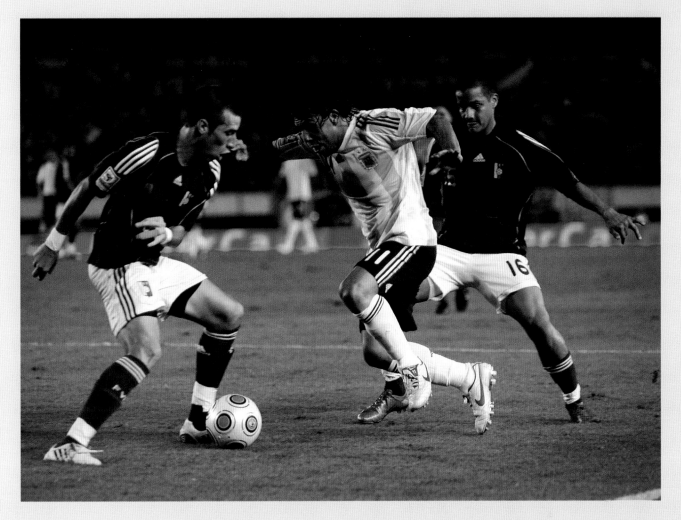

Tévez's whirlwind British career has seen him inspire West Ham to Premiership survival in 2007 and score the only goal in a last-game-of-the-season clincher against Manchester United. He is still revered in east London and was a shoo-in as West Ham's Hammer of the Year in 2007. He then moved north and helped Manchester United to two Premiership titles and the Champions League, before switching to oil-rich Manchester City in summer 2009 on a £7.8 million a year salary.

Tévez is a hero in South America too. Diego Maradona reckons him the 'Argentine prophet for the 21st century'; at Corinthians in 2005, the Brazilian Football Confederation named him the league's best player, the first non-Brazilian to win the award since 1976. Throughout all the unlikely moves – from Argentina to Brazil to east London and both sides of the Manchester football divide – his national commitment has been a singular force and he has figured as a foil to the silkier skills of Lionel Messi.

His competitive streak saw him sent off twice in a three-game stretch during qualifying for the 2010 World Cup, first against Colombia in November 2007 after he kicked the fullback and a year later for a rash tackle in Argentina's 1–1 draw with Paraguay. Thereafter, Maradona tended to use him as a substitute. Perhaps this is where he'll remain, although it would be truly strange if a talent such as Tévez was to spend too much time on the bench in South Africa.

> **" He's an international of the highest class who possesses all the attributes. "**
>
> MARK HUGHES, FORMER MANCHESTER CITY MANAGER

Javier Zanetti

Zanetti is a clean player who has done much to rehabilitate an old Argentine reputation for foul play. 'I do not argue with referees,' he says and he's as good as his word for he hasn't received a red card in over a decade. He really seems quite old-fashioned and Mr Clean is also Mr Constant for both club and country.

PLAYER FACT FILE

Name: Javier Adelmar Zanetti
Position: Defender
Caps: 136
Goals: 5
Team: Internazionale
Date of birth: 10 August 1973
Height: 178 cm/5 ft 10 in
Weight: 75 kg/165 lb
Previous clubs: Banfield, Talleres RE
International debut: 16 November 1994 v Chile
Previous World Cups: 1998, 2002

STYLE GUIDE
Zanetti is a softly spoken defender-cum-midfielder who makes his mark with consistent and reliable performances. For his country, he plays at right back, using his long experience to know when to switch between defence and attack. Even as a veteran, he has the stamina to surge past opposing defenders into advanced crossing positions and then to hare back to his defensive duties. He has a powerful right foot and scores the occasional long-range goal.

> ## " He's an international of the highest class who possesses all the attributes. "

MARK HUGHES, FORMER
MANCHESTER CITY MANAGER

Zanetti sought his fortune by heading for Europe, moving to Inter Milan (Internazionale) in 1995. 'Inter means a lot to me,' he says. 'It was the first team to open the doors of European football. I was very young when I came here and I think not many teams could have had so much faith and patience with a boy in his early twenties from the very first day like Inter did with me. I will always be grateful for that. For some reason I have always felt at home here at Inter and this is why I have never thought of leaving.'

At first the Italians nicknamed him *Il Trattore* ('the Tractor'). An agricultural style of play soon became more refined and, on earning the captain's armband in 1999, he became *Il Capitano*. He has led the team to four Serie A titles and has played in over six hundred matches, which is more than any other non-Italian born player.

Zanetti first played for Argentina in 1994 under the management of Daniel Passarella and was a regular at the 1998 and 2002 World Cups. He played in the qualification rounds for 2006, but was controversially ignored by José Pekerman. A recall came against France in 2007 under Alfio Basile and he provided the assist for Javier Saviola to score the only goal of the game. He was vice-captain for the Copa América 2007, having previously appeared in the 1995, 1999 and 2004 tournaments. Zanetti has remained a regular under Diego Maradona, though not as *Il Capitano* because that job has gone to Javier Mascherano.

OPPOSITE *Firm but fair: Javier Zanetti (left) tangles with Paraguay's midfielder Claudio Morel Rodriguez during a drawn World Cup qualifier in 2008.*

 ONE TO WATCH

Jesús Dátolo

Jesús Dátolo is an attacking left-sided midfielder who was in his mid-twenties before making his international debut. He served a long apprenticeship in Argentine club football before doing the Argentine football shuffle and moving to Europe. He thrived at Napoli during the 2008–09 season and his pace and eye for goal caught Maradona's attention. Cue for a try-out substitution in a friendly in Russia in August 2009, when he scored his first goal after twenty seconds on the pitch. Less than a month later, he was up against Brazil in front of the home crowd in the Estadio Gigante de Arroyito in Rosario. Dátolo found the net with a thirty-metre shot in a 1–3 loss that could have been disaster for his country but pushed a hitherto minor player towards a level of recognition he must have thought would elude him.' In January 2010 he was granted a transfer to Olympiacos so that he could play more regularly in the build up to the World Cup finals.

NIGERIA

GROUP B

Nigeria are the also-rans of African football. However, 2010 could be their year as they approach South Africa armed with a clutch of premier talents familiar to anybody who has watched the English Premiership: Danny Shittu, Joseph Yobo, Mikel, Nwankwo Kanu, Yakubu Aiyegbeni and Obafemi Martins.

On paper, Nigeria appear to be the best team in Africa, better surely than Ghana or South Africa and with the edge on arch-rivals Cameroon and the more fancied Côte d'Ivoire. Yet Nigeria haven't lifted a trophy since winning the African Nations Cup in 1994. They made World Cup appearances in 1994 and 1998, coming close to reaching the quarter-finals, but in 2002 they were outgunned in a group that contained England, Sweden and Argentina. They failed to qualify for the 2006 World Cup.

Nigeria took it to the wire for 2010 qualification. The player they must thank for that is Mozambique's Dário, whose shock goal against Tunisia on 11 November 2009 allowed Nigeria to sneak past the Tunisians and through to qualification with a 3–2 away win in Kenya. Nigeria's scorers in that emotional victory were Obafemi Martins and Yakubu Aiyegbeni. After the match, manager Shaibu Amodu said: 'I will say kudos and congratulations to the players for making it happen because they are the heroes of today. We fought and worked hard for it. It could have been difficult for us here if we didn't have the experience, the resilience and the determination. This is a typical Nigerian side that is motivated to be there because we believe that we deserve to be there.'

The manager dipped deep into the lexicon of his trade and it now remains for Amodu to improve on the organization of players in order to exploit properly the defensive brilliance of Joseph Yobo; the classy midfield work of Mikel; and in attack the temperamental flair of Obafemi Martins and the laid-back trickery of Kanu. Will the Super Eagles fly or will they remain as waddling wannabes ready only to snatch another defeat from the beak of victory?

ABOVE *Nigeria's fans stayed loyal throughout to a team whose hopes were all but lost until the final day of qualification, when Nigeria won in Kenya and Tunisia lost in Mozambique.*

ABOVE *Obafemi Martins (9) is a familiar face to English Premiership fans – he scored 28 times for Newcastle before moving to Wolfsburg. Seen here with Peter Odemwingie, he scored twice in Nigeria's 3–2 defeat of Kenya that secured a World Cup place in South Africa.*

POSSIBLE SQUAD

Goalkeepers

Dele Aiyenugba (Bnei Yehuda), **Vincent Enyeama** (Hapoel Tel Aviv), **Greg Etafia** (Moroka Swallows)

Defenders

Onyekachi Apam (Nice), **Uwa Elderson Echiéjilé** (Rennes), **Obinna Nwaneri** (Sion), **Chidi Odiah** (CSKA Moscow), **Danny Shittu** (Bolton Wanderers), **Taye Taiwo** (Marseille), **Joseph Yobo** (Everton)

Midfielders

Dele Adeleye (Sparta Rotterdam), **Femi Ajilore** (Groningen), **Sani Kaita** (Kuban Krasnodar), **Mikel John Obi** (Chelsea), **Seyi Olofinjana** (Hull City), **Ayila Yussuf** (Dynamo Kyiv)

Forwards

Yakubu Aiyegbeni (Everton), **Joseph Akpala** (Club Brugge), **Michael Eneramo** (Espérance), **Nwankwo Kanu** (C) (Portsmouth), **Obafemi Martins** (Wolfsburg), **Victor Obinna** (Málaga), **Peter Odemwingie** (Lokomotiv Moscow)

ROUTE TO THE FINALS

AFRICA QUALIFYING GROUP B – FINAL TABLE

Team	P	W	D	L	F	A	Pts
Nigeria	6	3	3	0	9	4	12
Tunisia	6	3	2	1	7	4	11
Mozambique	6	2	1	3	3	5	7
Kenya	6	1	0	5	5	11	3

FINALS GROUP B

Nigeria play		Date	Venue
	Argentina	12 June	Johannesburg (Ellis Park)
	Greece	17 June	Mangaung/Bloemfontein
	Korea Republic	22 June	Durban

VITAL STATISTICS

World ranking 22nd Keeper and defence 6/10
Midfield 7/10 Attack 6/10

Strengths and weaknesses The team sheet suggests an undeniably strong side. The weakness lies in a Nigerian talent to generate a shambles where order would seem the more obvious way.

How far will they go? Nigeria's chances are impossible to call. While the record book suggests otherwise, this team could forge further ahead than any other African team. A good outside punt for the quarters and beyond.

LEFT *Nigeria v Kenya, World Cup qualifying match, Nairobi, 14 November 2009: (back row, left to right) Mikel, Nwaneri, Eneramo, Yakubu, Olofinjana, Yobo; (front row) Apam, Odemwingie, Ajilore, Echejilé, Enyeama.*

Mikel

John Michael Nchekwube Obinna is a member of the Igbo (or Ibo) people and the second half of his original name means hope (Nchekwube) of his father's heart (Obinna). Mikel has grown into the hope of all Nigerian hearts, for he has the calm touch to lead his country into uncharted football territory.

> " I would like one of my African brothers or an African country to win the World Cup but I can see a European country winning it. "
>
> MIKEL

the 2005 Under 17 World Championships in Finland, the Nigerian FA misspelled one of his given names as Mikel. When he moved to Chelsea in 2006, he had become Mikel John Obi or John Obi Mikel, which he later refined down to a kind of cosmopolitan brand name: Mikel. He's a self-made man whose label reflects the way he plays his football: straightforward, memorable, modern.

Mikel's qualities have long been apparent. He trained with Chelsea for a week in the winter of 2004 and José Mourinho, the then manager, said: 'Everybody was in love, not just me. The players were amazed at a young boy with such quality.' Mikel starred in the 2005 World Youth Championship where Nigeria lost the final to Argentina 2–1. By then, he was apprenticed to Lyn Oslo in Norway and had also attracted the attention of Manchester United. The public scrap for the 18 year old's signature between Chelsea and United showed how highly he was regarded – as did the £16 million Chelsea paid when they eventually got their man.

Mourinho redirected Mikel's attacking instincts towards more defensive midfield duties. He groomed his young star as a replacement for the ageing Claude Makélélé and when the French old master left Chelsea in 2008, Mikel had already stepped into his boots. As with Makélélé, Mikel scores very few goals but this does not worry his current Chelsea boss. Carlo Ancelotti, a former Italian international midfielder who was noted for his cool, has this self-regarding assessment: 'With regards to playing characteristics, Mikel seems really like me. He has very good quality to play in front of the defence and from this position passes a lot of play for the team. It is not so easy and not so important for him to score.'

The only minus point to Mikel's game is a short temper, though he does seem to have learned that red cards are the reward for the red mists of rage. Opposing managers might instruct their attackers to wind up the big man but, as a widely experienced 23 year old, Mikel has probably gathered enough maturity to stay within the rules of the game. Nigerians are certainly hoping Mikel is up to his biggest test yet. He's the glue in their team of disparate talents.

LEFT *Mikel's muscular determination is shown here as he forces his way past Emmanuel Ake during Nigeria's 3–2 defeat of Kenya. The win ensured Nigerian representation in South Africa and gave Mikel his chance to shine at a World Cup finals. His African fans hope he will harness his skill and energy to the national cause and show the form and commitment that has made him a Chelsea stalwart.*

PLAYER FACT FILE

Name: John Michael Nchekwube Obinna
Position: Midfielder
Caps: 34
Goals: 2
Team: Chelsea
Date of birth: 22 April 1987
Height: 188 cm/6 ft 2 in
Weight: 86 kg/190 lb
Previous clubs: Lyn Oslo
International debut: 17 August 2005 v Libya
Previous World Cups: None

STYLE GUIDE
Mikel has sure feet and a big footballing brain. His powerful physique, his range of passing and his cool head at the competitive heart of the football pitch make him the perfect fit for the holding midfield role. He pulls the levers in the Nigerian and Chelsea engine rooms, first disrupting opposition attacks then spreading the play.

KOREA REPUBLIC

GROUP B

The Korea Republic team has a tradition of frantic play matched in intensity by the noise of its equally frantic fans. The country is now poised for a seventh successive World Cup appearance and fervently hopes to exceed the achievements of eight years ago.

As co-hosts with Japan of the 2002 World Cup, the South Koreans' most notable footballing hour came under Guus Hiddink. He led the Taeguk Warriors to tumultuous victories against Italy and Spain on the way to a glorious 1–0 semi-final defeat against Germany. In Germany 2006, Dick Advocaat was in charge but the Dutch managerial touch failed when Korea Republic did not make progress beyond the group stages. The 2010 World Cup campaign saw a change of tack with the appointment of a Korean manager, Huh Jung-Moo.

Huh makes the most of the experience of players who are familiar with European club football and then blends that know-how with more youthful home-nurtured talent. He led his team through a patchy, if unbeaten, qualifying run that began with a 4–0 home victory against Turkmenistan. High hopes were replaced by anxiety and criticism of lacklustre performances following draws against Korea DPR played in Shanghai and at home against Jordan. Three victories followed including the 1–0 defeat of arch-rivals Korea DPR that saw the two Korean nations finish jointly at the top of the table.

Korea Republic will be a team to beat, especially if star players fulfil expectations in high energy, high pressure counter-attacking line-ups. Look out for Park Ji-Sung, who has announced this will be his last World Cup. He has had a freer playing role under Huh than he enjoys with Manchester United. In the national side, Park Ji-Sung adds flair to his dependable game and he scored a decisive headed goal in Iran to earn his country a vital qualifying point.

Park Chu-Young is another one to watch. Now in his mid-twenties, he is in his prime and has figured for his AS Monaco club and his country as a creative and agile forward who passes the ball with cunning and who can score from both free kicks and open play.

ABOVE *Huh Jung-Moo plays a cheerful managerial role as Park Ji-Sung leads a celebration crawl after scoring the equalizer in his side's 1–1 World Cup qualifier draw with Iran in Seoul.*

ABOVE *A sweet victory against his team's most bitter rivals: Kim Dong-jin raises his arms in triumph after the late, single goal by fellow substitute Kim Chi-Woo that earned South Korea victory in their World Cup qualifier against North Korea, 1 April 2009.*

POSSIBLE SQUAD

Goalkeepers

Jung Sung-Ryong (Seongnam Ilhwa), Kim Young-Kwang (Ulsan Hyundai Horang-i), Lee Woon-Jae (Suwon Samsung Bluewings)

Defenders

Hwang Jae-Won (Pohang Steelers), Kang Min-Soo (Jeju United), Kim Dong-Jin (Zenit St Petersburg), Kim Kun-Hoan (Yokohama F. Marinos), Lee Gang-Jin (Busan I'Park), Lee Jung-Soo (Kyoto Sanga), Lee Young-Pyo (Al-Hilal), Oh Beom-Seok (Ulsan Hyundai)

Midfielders

Cho Won-Hee (Wigan Athletic), Choi Tae-Uk (Jeonbuk Hyundai Motors), Ki Sung-Yong (FC Seoul), Kim Chi-Woo (FC Seoul), Kim Jung-Woo (Seongnam Ilhwa), Lee Chung-Yong (Bolton Wanderers), Park Ji-Sung (C) (Manchester United)

Forwards

Bae Ki-Jong (Suwon Samsung Bluewings), Lee Keun-Ho (Júbilo Iwata), Park Chu-Young (AS Monaco), Shin Young-Rok (Bursaspor), Yang Dong-Hyun (Busan I'Park)

ROUTE TO THE FINALS

ASIA QUALIFYING FINAL GROUP 1 – FINAL TABLE

Team	P	W	D	L	F	A	Pts
Korea Republic	8	4	4	0	12	4	16
Korea DPR	8	3	3	2	7	5	12
Saudi Arabia	8	3	3	2	8	8	12
Iran	8	2	5	1	8	7	11
UAE	8	0	1	7	6	17	1

FINALS GROUP B

Korea Republic play		Date	Venue
	Greece	12 June	N. Mandela Bay/Pt Elizabeth
	Argentina	17 June	Johannesburg (Soccer City)
	Nigeria	22 June	Durban

VITAL STATISTICS

World ranking 52nd   Keeper and defence 6/10
Midfield 6/10   Attack 6/10

Strengths and weaknesses The team could be hampered by unrealistically high expectations. An all-round self-belief needs to be combined with guile if the team is to approach the successes of past World Cup campaigns.

How far will they go? It will be difficult, but not impossible, for this side to emerge from a group that includes Argentina and Nigeria.

RIGHT *Korea Republic (South Korea) v Korea DPR (North Korea), World Cup qualifying match, World Cup Stadium, Seoul, South Korea, 1 April 2009: (back row, left to right) Lee Woon-Jae, Kang Min-Soo, Hwang Jae-Won, Park Chu-Young, Cho Won-Hee, Ki Sung-Yong; (front row) Park Ji-Sung, Oh Beom-Seok, Lee Keun-Ho, Lee Chung-Yong, Lee Young-Pyo.*

Park Ji-Sung

The South Korean captain is a proven World Cup veteran whose vital goals have assured him a place in Korean history. He led Korea Republic through the 2010 qualifiers without a single defeat and a personal tally of five goals.

At the 2002 World Cup, Park Ji-Sung was a star in the host nation's advance to the semi-finals. He scored the match winner against Portugal when he controlled the ball with his chest, beating a defender to unleash a left-foot volley that advanced South Korea into the knockout stages. Fast forward four years to Germany and Park scored the equalizer in a group match against France, the eventual finalists.

Name: Park Ji-Sung
Position: Midfielder
Caps: 84
Goals: 11
Team: Manchester United
Date of birth: 25 February 1981
Height: 175 cm/5 ft 9 in
Weight: 75 kg/165 lb
Previous clubs: Kyoto Purple Sanga, PSV Eindhoven
International debut: April 2000 v Laos
Previous World Cups: 2002, 2006

STYLE GUIDE
Park is an indefatigable utility player who will take up a busy role to the centre, right and left of midfield or as a support striker. His pace, fitness and never-say-die attitude are enhanced with moments of great skill and his big-game experience has brought a greater composure in attack than his early form suggested.

LEFT Park Ji-Sung surging forward on a typical run taking him past Iran's Masoud Shojaei (18) in a World Cup qualifier in Tehran in February 2009. Park's determined captaincy and headed equalizer ensured Korea Republic came away with a vital point in a 1–1 draw.

RIGHT TOP Park Ji-Sung rises above Korea DPR's Lee Kwang-Chon during a bitterly contested World Cup qualifier in April 2009. Korea Republic won 1–0.

Park made his international debut as a defensive midfielder. Guus Hiddink, who managed South Korea in 2002 and subsequently took the South Korean star to PSV Eindhoven, converted Park into a more attack-minded player and instilled Park with a sense of belief. In his autobiography, Park says: 'Hiddink says you have great mentality and in the entire World Cup, I played with those words ringing in my ears. I kicked the ball and ran around the field clinging on to those words. For better or for worse, I am calm and quiet, so not many people take notice of me. If it was not for Coach Hiddink, I would not be where I am now. With the words "where I am now", I am not referring to me becoming famous or being able to purchase a spacious condo for my parents. I am referring to the fact that I learned to love myself more. Within a minute, what Coach Hiddink said to me changed my life forever.

I feel a bit shy thinking about what he would think after reading this, but he is my "master" and I owe him everything and I won't be able to repay it in my lifetime.'

Sir Alex Ferguson paid Eindhoven £4 million for him in 2005, intending that Park would become Manchester United's replacement for Ryan Giggs. Instead, he has been more ball winner than goal-poaching left wing. His nickname 'Three Lung Park' is testimony to his vigorous contribution at Old Trafford.

> ❝ **If his feet were covered with paint, he would paint the entire pitch.** ❞
>
> HYOUNG-OK SEO
> SOUTH KOREAN BROADCASTER

GREECE

GROUP B 🇬🇷

When Greece met Portugal in the 2004 European Cup final, they emerged as 1–0 winners and 'King Otto' of Greece assumed his place at the centre of Greek culture.

Otto Rehhagel is still in charge and has engineered his adoptive country their second World Cup appearance having had the good fortune to be in a lightweight qualifying group. The Swiss won the group and Greece had to sneak in via the play-offs.

The old German maestro has done it with guile rather than flair, plus a way with motivational one-liners such as: 'When I arrived the players were talented, but did not obey the rules. Once they understood they needed to, they could then express themselves' and 'Everyone's free to say what I want' and 'Verbals haven't won a game yet.' His close-marking tactical approach is summed up in his vivid phrase: 'I want to know the aftershave used by every opposing player.'

Under Rehhagel, team effort has been all. The manager is credited with honing the leadership skills of the captain, Giorgos Karagounis. The Panathinaikos midfield general is seen as a fit replacement for Thodoris Zagorakis who led the team to victory at Euro 2004. Goalkeeper Alexandros Tzorvas put in some outstanding performances during qualification, while attackers to watch for are Dimitris Salpigidis of Panathinaikos and Celtic's Georgios Samaras. Theofanis Gekas of Bayer Leverkusen was the top-scoring European with ten goals in the run-up to World Cup qualification.

Greek fans look back to 2004 when their famous captain was named the man of the tournament having put in the most tackles. It seems unlikely that those who have followed Zagorakis will tackle their way to success in South Africa. But with King Otto in charge, who knows?

BELOW LEFT *The Greek team bearing their manager Otto Rehhagel aloft, having left it to the play-offs to qualify. Will South Africa be too close to the sun?*

BELOW RIGHT *No, it's not Wayne Rooney. It is Greece's Dimitris Salpigidis showing his delight and relief after scoring against Ukraine in the play-offs.*

POSSIBLE SQUAD

Goalkeepers

Kostas Chalkias (PAOK), Michalis Sifakis (Aris), Alexandros Tzorvas (Panathinaikos)

Defenders

Georgios Galitsios (Olympiacos), Sotirios Kyrgiakos (Liverpool), Vangelis Moras (Bologna), Avraam Papadopoulos (Olympiacos), Sokratis Papastathopoulos (Genoa), Nikos Spiropoulos (Panathinaikos), Vasilis Torosidis (Olympiacos), Georgios Tzavelas (Panionios), Loukas Vyntra (Panathinaikos)

Midfielders

Giorgos Karagounis (C) (Panathinaikos), Kostas Katsouranis (Panathinaikos), Grigoris Makos (AEK Athens), Sotiris Ninis (Panathinaikos), Vasilis Pliatsikas (Schalke 04), Alexandros Tziolis (Panathinaikos)

Forwards

Angelos Charisteas (Nuremberg), Theofanis Gekas (Bayer Leverkusen), Kostas Mitroglou (Olympiacos), Dimitris Salpigidis (Panathinaikos), Georgios Samaras (Celtic)

ROUTE TO THE FINALS

EUROPE QUALIFYING GROUP 2 – FINAL TABLE

Team	P	W	D	L	F	A	Pts
Switzerland	10	6	3	1	18	8	21
Greece	10	6	2	2	20	10	20
Latvia	10	5	2	3	18	15	17
Israel	10	4	4	2	20	10	16
Luxembourg	10	1	2	7	4	25	5
Moldova	10	0	3	7	6	18	3

EUROPE PLAY-OFFS

14.11.09	Greece 0	0 Ukraine
18.11.09	Ukraine 0	1 Greece

FINALS GROUP B

Greece play		Date	Venue
	Korea Republic	12 June	N. Mandela Bay/Pt Elizabeth
	Nigeria	17 June	Mangaung/Bloemfontein
	Argentina	22 June	Polokwane

VITAL STATISTICS

World ranking 12th	Keeper and defence 6/10
Midfield 5/10	Attack 5/10

Strengths and weaknesses Discipline, defence and drudgery are what makes this team strong. A lack of world-class talent in an anonymous looking squad is a definite weakness.

How far will they go? The Greeks were 150-1 outsiders when they won Euro 2004. The odds are shorter now, but this isn't a team that neutrals expect (or want) to progress far.

LEFT *Greece v Ukraine, World Cup play-off, first leg, Olympic Stadium, Athens, 14 November 2009: (back row, left to right) Gekas, Moras, Katsouranis, Vyntra, Kyrgiakos, Tzorvas; (front row) Salpigidis, Karagounis, Samaras, Spiropoulos, Papastathopoulous.*

ENGLAND

GROUP C

A generation of talented and big match-hardened players plus a favourable first-round draw have given England a real chance in South Africa. Throughout a powerful qualifying campaign, the arguments for and against English World Cup optimism have filled the press and the airwaves.

FOR: Football was invented in England and the national team is the joint oldest in the world. England won the World Cup in 1966 and has maintained a consistent position as a top-ten world side with a presence at every tournament final since 1994. In Fabio Capello, the current team has a great manager who selects players from the best league in the world. Who could fail when talent down the spine of the team includes Rooney, Terry and Ferdinand, Gerrard and Lampard? The key players have immense experience and are playing at the top of their game. England's time has come.

AGAINST: English teams have been tactically inept since the Second World War. Aside from the fortunate home victory in the 1966 final, they've reached only one World Cup semi-final and find a natural limit at the quarter-final stages. No manager will change the fact that England are rubbish at penalty shoot-outs. The Premier League is bloated with TV money and reliant on overseas players. Even Wayne Rooney's brilliance won't carry a team all the way and nobody won anything with a pair of centre backs as star players. Forget Gerrard and Lampard because together they're less than the sum of their parts. And who's going to play in goal? Gordon Banks? This World Cup will be like the last one and the one before that and …

RIGHT *Wembley, 1 April 2009: Peter Crouch scores the opening goal in England's qualifying match against Ukraine. England's goal difference in the qualifying rounds is a good omen for the main event in South Africa.*

The argument will be settled in June. Meanwhile positive assessments of England's chances have gone beyond homegrown trumpet-tooting. Speaking before the Brazil v England friendly in November 2009, Kaká said: 'What seems to have changed about England is the arrival of a better collective awareness. The attitude is also stronger. They are definitely one of the teams to consider for the trophy in South Africa.'

Recent form certainly gives ground for optimism. England's best ever start to a World Cup qualifying campaign included a sweet 4–1 victory away to Croatia, who had qualified for Euro 2008 at England's expense. Theo Walcott scored a hat-trick and cemented his place in England plans. Nearly as sweet was a convincing 2–1 victory in a friendly against old rivals Germany.

It is true that goalkeeping is a problem, but whoever makes the cut between the sticks will be protected by a defence that has world-beaters in Ashley Cole, John Terry and Rio Ferdinand. There is an abundance of talent

BELOW *The backbone of England's team: Terry, Gerrard, Lampard and Rooney.*

in midfield and Capello has done better than either Sven-Göran Eriksson or Steve McClaren in combining the talents of Gerrard and Lampard. He has also developed Gareth Barry as a holding midfielder. In attack the force of Rooney and the finesse of Walcott are sure to make sparks and the surprise of the tournament could be Peter Crouch. Perhaps he'll emulate Geoff Hurst, another unfashionable attacker who, back in 1966, fired the hat-trick that brought the nation's only World Cup victory. So far.

> **❝ He is very well prepared from a tactical point of view, so he is going to be able to get the English team, with the great players they have got, to compete with the best in the world. ❞**
>
> MARCELLO LIPPI
> ITALY TEAM MANAGER
> ON FABIO CAPELLO

GREAT MATCH
2002 England 1–0 Argentina

World Cup, group stage
Sapporo Dome, Sapporo, Japan

England finally laid to rest the Indian sign Argentina had held over them for 15 years with a determined and fantastically organized victory. Man-of-the-match Nicky Butt put his Manchester United team-mate Veron in the shade, and Michael Owen provided a constant threat.

It was an early injury to Hargreaves that helped England gel. Sinclair replaced him and made inroads down the left, and Scholes moved into the centre where he drove the team forward. The goal came with just two minutes to go to half-time. Owen slipped around Pochettino, fell over his outstretched leg and referee Collina pointed to the spot. David Beckham, whose life had been made a misery after being sent off in the 1998 match, took a deep breath before hammering the ball past Cavallero.

Argentina camped themselves in England's half for the last thirty minutes of the game, but were frustrated by the midfield line and a brilliant Seaman save to deny Pochettino. Revenge was sweet – the blue-and-whites were all but boarding the plane home.

RIGHT *David Beckham in action during England's classic match against Argentina in 2002 – it was his penalty that secured England's victory. Assuming he's fit, Beckham is likely to make the squad for South Africa and then to feature as a super-sub. Could his final act as a player be one last penalty shoot-out goal?*

COACH **Fabio Capello**

Born 18 June 1946
Record: P21, W15, D2, L4

Fabio Capello is a winner. He has won a major league championship in seven of his 16 seasons as a coach and claimed domestic league titles with every club he has managed: AC Milan, Real Madrid, Roma and Juventus.

Capello is no easy-going Italian. He was as decisive in transferring the captaincy to Rio Ferdinand in February as he was in the more trivial affair of banning mobile phones at team meals. The unsmiling disciplinarian is an astute tactician whose overall approach has given everybody much to smile about. He has defused all hysteria with a string of well-organized victories that almost justifies the £6 million annual salary he's earned since taking the England job early in 2008.

Marcello Lippi, the manager of Italy and Capello's old friend and rival, got it about right when he spoke of Capello's appointment as England manager: 'Fabio is the type of man whose personality and charisma can bring the team together and make them all participate at the same time. He is very well prepared from a tactical point of view.'

RIGHT England v Croatia, World Cup qualifying match, Wembley Stadium, 9 September 2009: (back row, left to right) Heskey, Upson, Gerrard, Terry, Green, Lampard; (front row) Ashley Cole, Lennon, Johnson, Rooney, Barry.

POSSIBLE SQUAD

Goalkeepers

Robert Green (West Ham United), **David James** (Portsmouth), **Paul Robinson** (Blackburn Rovers)

Defenders

Wayne Bridge (Manchester City), **Wes Brown** (Manchester United), **Ashley Cole** (Chelsea), **Rio Ferdinand (C)** (Manchester United), **Glen Johnson** (Liverpool), **Joleon Lescott** (Manchester City), **John Terry** (Chelsea)

Midfielders

Gareth Barry (Manchester City), **David Beckham** (Los Angeles Galaxy/Internazionale), **Michael Carrick** (Manchester United), **Steven Gerrard** (Liverpool), **Frank Lampard** (Chelsea), **James Milner** (Aston Villa), **Shaun Wright-Phillips** (Manchester City), **Theo Walcott** (Arsenal)

Forwards

Peter Crouch (Tottenham Hotspur), **Jermain Defoe** (Tottenham Hotspur), **Emile Heskey** (Aston Villa), **Aaron Lennon** (Tottenham Hotspur), **Wayne Rooney** (Manchester United)

HOW THEY'LL LINE UP

Cautiously does it is the way of modern international football and the England manager is as modern and cautious as they come. The 4-4-2 set-up Fabio Capello often favours for England aims at a balance through the middle. Gareth Barry is deployed as a holding player to protect the back four, with Frank Lampard or Steven Gerrard acting as playmaker. The approach casts Emile Heskey or Peter Crouch or Jermain Defoe as the likely target man, playing off Wayne Rooney. England have also played 4-2-3-1, the more defensive formation Capello used at Real Madrid.

James

Johnson   Ferdinand   Terry   A Cole

Gerrard   Barry   Carrick   Lampard

Rooney   Crouch

ROUTE TO THE FINALS

MATCHES PLAYED

06.09.08	Andorra 0	2 England
10.09.08	Croatia 1	4 England
11.10.08	England 5	1 Kazakhstan
15.10.08	Belarus 1	3 England
01.04.09	England 2	1 Ukraine
06.06.09	Kazakhstan 0	4 England
10.06.09	England 6	0 Andorra
09.09.09	England 5	1 Croatia
10.10.09	Ukraine 1	0 England
14.10.09	England 3	0 Belarus

EUROPE QUALIFYING GROUP 6 – FINAL TABLE

Team	P	W	D	L	F	A	Pts
England	10	9	0	1	34	6	27
Ukraine	10	6	3	1	21	6	21
Croatia	10	6	2	2	19	13	20
Belarus	10	4	1	5	19	14	13
Kazakhstan	10	2	0	8	11	29	6
Andorra	10	0	0	10	3	39	0

FINALS GROUP C

England play	Date	Venue
USA	12 June	Rustenburg
Algeria	18 June	Cape Town
Slovenia	23 June	N. Mandela Bay/Pt Elizabeth

VITAL STATISTICS

World ranking 9th   Keeper and defence 8/10
Midfield 8/10   Attack 8/10

Strengths and weaknesses The core of the team has been together since Euro 2004 and knows what to expect in hothouse atmospheres a long way from home. The defence will be sound and an on-form Rooney could make the tournament his own.

How far will they go? Possible winners, if only they can leap the quarter-final hurdle. But before that, there's the first match against an in-form USA which will have old men recalling the World Cup defeat in 1950; and Algeria could be tricky; and Slovenia can defend and …

John Terry

Although John Terry is an inspirational leader and a brick wall of a centre back, his off-field persona eventually disqualified him from the England captain's job. With that, bang went his chance of being the first England captain to lift the World Cup since Bobby Moore.

Terry was made Chelsea captain at 23, having served an apprenticeship in the defensive arts when playing alongside the French World Cup winning pair of Marcel Desailly and Frank Leboeuf. He led Chelsea to two Premier League titles, in 2004–05 with the most clean sheets and the best defensive record in Football League history. That season he scored eight goals, including a late winner against Barcelona in the Champions League.

At the age of 25, he had seemed to have all the right credentials when the former England manager, Steve McClaren, gave him the England armband. Now the choice appears yet another aspect of McClaren's international management fiasco, another demonstration of naivety. 'Choosing a captain is one of the most important decisions a coach has to make. I'm certain I've got the right man in John Terry. I'm convinced he will prove to be one of the best captains England has ever had.' Not quite. England failed to qualify for Euro 2008 under Terry's leadership and perhaps the stigma of the Euro exit is why Fabio Capello tried several other players for captain before returning the job to Terry. He led England throughout the qualifiers but then had to relinquish the post in a flurry of headlines five months before the finals, in February 2010.

Terry made his full international debut in a friendly against Croatia in 2003. England won the game 3–1 and his main defensive partner in a stroll of a victory was the slightly more experienced Rio Ferdinand. It was the beginning of an enduring international partnership that makes the English defence one of the most feared in the world. With these two players in their prime, and with both anticipating South Africa 2010 as their final chance of an England final, opportunity and motivation could not be higher.

PLAYER FACT FILE

Name: John Terry
Position: Defender
Caps: 58
Goals: 6
Team: Chelsea
Date of birth: 7 December 1980
Height: 187 cm/6 ft 2 in
Weight: 90 kg/198 lb
Previous clubs: None
International debut: 3 June 2003 v Serbia and Montenegro
Previous World Cups: 2006

STYLE GUIDE
Faultless is the word often used in reports of matches in which John Terry has played. He is a centre back in the classic mould whose influence extends beyond his powerful tackle, his heading ability, his understanding of the game and his upfield forays for free kicks and corners. Whether captain or not, watch him talking to the players around him, cajoling and bullying and organising and making his presence felt.

> 66 He has surprised us all. Maybe he is a bionic man. 99
>
> AVRAM GRANT
> FORMER CHELSEA MANAGER

ABOVE *Wembley, 1 April 2009: Terry plays up to the fans after scoring against Ukraine.*

LEFT *Wembley, 9 September 2009: Terry giving his all during England's 5–1 win over Croatia. Their eighth consecutive win in qualifying ensured their passport to South Africa, banishing the demons of Euro 2008.*

Ashley Cole

There are two faces to England's left back: first, his feisty concentration and skill that make him arguably the best at his position in the world; and second his off-field reputation.

The young Ashley Cole was as precocious as he has been consistent. In 2000, he pushed aside the Brazilian international Sylvinho to claim an Arsenal place. After a mere 19 Premiership appearances, he made his international debut in a World Cup qualifier against Albania. In that initial playing year he also won his first FA Cup final medal, something he went on to win a record five times.

> " Ashley is one of the best left backs in the world but I believe his best is yet to come. "

CARLO ANCELOTTI
CHELSEA MANAGER

In 2003, Cole was a vital component of the Arsenal defence that lasted a whole Premiership campaign without losing a match. His selected highlights include a few goals as well, such as the one in 2003 against FC Dynamo Kiev that kept Arsenal in the Champions League and the penalty shoot-out goal that secured one of his collection of FA Cup medals against Manchester United in 2005. On his move to Chelsea in 2006, Arsenal fans behaved predictably in shifting Cole from hero to zero, while his off-field reputation was hardly improved by an autobiography that left many fans feeling queasy after some of its revelations.

It's lucky for Cole that he can do his talking on the pitch; and lucky for England fans that there is a top-drawer left back of such long international pedigree. Sven-Göran Eriksson had the foresight to play Cole in his first competitive match in a win against Albania that helped take England through to Korea/Japan 2002. Cole's attacking ability down the left flank remained a constant in Eriksson's game plans at Euro 2004, after which he was picked for the all-star squad. Cole played in every England game in the 2006 World Cup, then continued as a first choice on the team sheets during Steve McClaren's brief reign.

Cole's form and fitness have been maintained and he'll be a key figure in Fabio Capello's plans for South Africa 2010.

FAR LEFT AND ABOVE *Ashley Cole has the gift of concentration. His prowess at left back has earned him an assured place in England's line-ups whether controlling the ball at speed, putting in one well-timed tackle after another or running deep into opposition territory.*

Rio Ferdinand

Rio Ferdinand played in the 2002 and 2006 World Cup finals. His experience, composure and speed have made him one of the first on the England team sheet for the best part of a decade. So it's no surprise that Fabio Capello made him captain in February 2010.

Ferdinand is a players' player and two retired Manchester United defenders voice a consensus. Gordon McQueen says he has 'not seen a better defender' and Peter Schmeichel, the most famous of the Man U goalies, proclaims: 'Rio is the best centre back in the world.'

When needs must, Ferdinand is a traditional stopper who will give strikers a tough time, then hoof the ball upfield to clear his lines. However, a more cultured technique is what distinguishes him and his

> **Four years ago, subconsciously we didn't see ourselves beating Brazil. Now we believe in ourselves.**
>
> RIO FERDINAND

BELOW AND RIGHT *Rio Ferdinand displaying his attacking and defensive skills during England's 5–1 win against Kazakhstan in October 2008: (below) scoring the opening goal and (right) keeping a firm eye on a headed clearance.*

PLAYER FACT FILE

Name: Rio Gavin Ferdinand
Position: Defender
Caps: 76
Goals: 3
Team: Manchester United
Date of birth: 7 November 1978
Height: 189 cm/6 ft 2½ in
Weight: 77 kg/170 lb
Previous clubs: West Ham United, AFC Bournemouth, Leeds United
International debut: 15 November 1997 v Cameroon
Previous World Cups: 2002, 2006

STYLE GUIDE

Tactically astute and athletically mobile, Rio Ferdinand is the complete modern centre back. Team awareness reinforces his playing skills and he's formed outstanding partnerships with Nemanja Vidić for Manchester United and Sol Campbell for England. His current pairing with John Terry makes this England defence a rock on which most attacks will founder. As captains, Ferdinand and Terry are interchangeable.

ability to make the telling pass helps England play the international game of building from the back. He also pops up in the box at set pieces to knock in the odd goal as he did in the World Cup qualifying game against Kazakhstan.

Ferdinand was barely 19 when he got his first full England cap in 1997. He developed at West Ham and Leeds and joined Manchester United in July 2002 for £30 million. Since then he has helped his club to five Premiership titles and one Champions League title. There's another side to the story because the young Rio's brilliant career could have fizzled when, as a teenager, he was left out of the 1998 England squad following a charge for drink driving. Then he missed a drugs test and was banned for eight months and couldn't play at Euro 2004. But now he has turned 30, his life seems as measured as his playing style.

South Africa is probably the last chance for Ferdinand to cement his reputation as one of the world's best ever defenders. Injuries have reduced his appearances under the Capello regime and he had a couple of poor matches during qualification. However, if he's fully fit, it is quite possible that 11 July 2010 could be the day when he adds an England World Cup winner's medal to the hatful of club medals he has already earned. His role model must now be Sir Bobby Moore, and if Ferdinand emulates him and lifts the World Cup for England, he'll soon be dropping on one knee to be told: 'Arise, Sir Rio.'

Steven Gerrard

There are few better sights in football than Steven Gerrard marshalling an attack and mixing astute prodded passes with raking cross-fielders. And all the while is the exciting possibility that he'll find the net himself, as he showed at the last World Cup when he was England's top scorer.

'Stevie G MBE' is a one-club man who has played in just about every position for Liverpool and scored in four major finals, something no other English player has done. He will make himself a national hero if he can do for England what he has done for his home town.

Who would deny him a place in Merseyside folklore for the way he led Liverpool's comeback against AC Milan in the 2005 Champions League final? During a six-minute stretch in the second half, Liverpool clawed back a three-goal deficit to draw 3–3 after extra time, with Gerrard scoring one of the goals. Liverpool's third goal was from a penalty after Gerrard was brought down in Milan's penalty box.

> **" He is, in my opinion, the best midfielder in the world, and has a track record for delivering on the big occasions. "**
>
> GRAHAM TAYLOR
> FORMER ENGLAND MANAGER

PLAYER FACT FILE

Name: Steven George Gerrard
Position: Midfielder
Caps: 77
Goals: 16
Team: Liverpool
Date of birth: 30 May 1980
Height: 185 cm/6 ft 1 in
Weight: 82 kg/181 lb
Previous clubs: None
International debut: 31 May 2000 v Ukraine
Previous World Cups: 2006

STYLE GUIDE

Steven Gerrard is a Roy of the Rovers style of player. He has the will and the energy to drive a team to victory and the power and pace to go with a never-say-die attitude. He is versatile and most often used in central midfield, though he can drift right or left, or move up the pitch as an auxiliary striker. He needs a free role to play at his inspirational peak – a role the England manager has largely denied him.

The pressing question for England fans is how often Gerrard will be pushing forward to repeat something like this for England in South Africa. The smart answer is that the way Fabio Capello uses him means Gerrard is not often enough in the penalty area to even be fouled.

Gerrard is usually cast in a subdued role in international games where he is not the boss on the pitch controlling the tempo of play. Within the England camp, Gerrard is in a bigger pond than at Liverpool and the feted club captain must give precedence to John Terry, Rio Ferdinand and perhaps also to his fellow midfielder Frank Lampard.

The Lampard/Gerrard question is key and the pair still hasn't proved they can mesh their centrally based forward-looking skills. That said, Gerrard is a big-game player with masses of international experience, not least his impressive contributions during England's serene progress through the World Cup qualifying rounds.

ABOVE *Gerrard goes between Hryhory Yarmash (16) and Anatoliy Tymoshchuk (4) during England's World Cup qualifier against Ukraine at Wembley on 1 April 2009.*

LEFT *Celebrating after scoring England's fourth goal against Croatia in September 2009.*

David James

On 7 February 2008, David James was picked for Fabio Capello's first match in charge and played his first full game in England's goal since 2005. He kept a clean sheet and the manager demonstrated an Italian lack of football ageism in selecting an old pair of safe hands.

Capello picked a man who, late in his career, had spent holidays training with the Miami Dolphins American football team. What must have impressed the assiduous Capello was the way James consulted sports psychologists to give him the edge at penalty kicks. These things can make all the difference.

David James is the most vivid of men. He has found fame for his comedy haircuts, Armani modelling contracts, art collecting, his collection of Action Men, his public effort to stop smoking, his *Observer* newspaper column, and a compulsion for computer games that he said had affected his concentration in the Liverpool goal. Throughout a two-decade career, he has worn a smile in defiance of the convention that on-field emotion must see the grimace of effort bracketed only by ecstasies of rage and celebration.

PLAYER FACT FILE

Name: David Benjamin James
Position: Goalkeeper
Caps: 49
Goals: 0
Team: Portsmouth
Date of birth: 1 August 1970
Height: 196 cm/6 ft 5 in
Weight: 90 kg/198 lb
Previous clubs: Watford, Liverpool, Aston Villa, West Ham United, Manchester City
International debut: 29 March 1997 v Mexico
Previous World Cups: 2002, 2006

STYLE GUIDE
Athleticism and timing makes David James unsurpassed as a shot-stopper. However, rushes of blood to the head can have him haring out of the penalty area when he should stay put or lunging at crossed balls that are best cleared by defenders. He has kept working at his game though, and has earned the right to call himself England's number one goalkeeper.

LEFT AND RIGHT *The broad-shouldered, lion-hearted David James is the England team's elder statesman. He is a man who has been around long enough to know when to give his younger colleagues some comfort and encouragement and when to yell at them with the instructions on exactly how to organize themselves in defence.*

James's stop-start international career began with a friendly against Mexico in 1997. After David Seaman's final international in 2002, James was England's number one. He played throughout Euro 2004 but was dropped later that year following an error in a 2–2 World Cup qualifier against Austria. His nadir came a year later as halftime substitute when he conceded all the goals in Denmark's 4–1 thrashing of England. James looked set for his pension and memories of Liverpool in the 1990s as one of the Spice Boys along with Steve McManaman, Jamie Redknapp and Robbie Fowler. Liverpudlians dubbed him Calamity James because of the errors that eventually saw him sold to Aston Villa in 1999. But he's very far from being a football joke: he has made more Premier League appearances than any other footballer, and has the most clean sheets in Premiership history.

A couple of clean sheets could clinch it for England in South Africa and top off a distinguished career that Fabio Capello so wisely revived. And a well-anticipated World Cup final penalty block could remain burned in the national consciousness for more years than David James has kept goal.

> **" David James has improved as a goalkeeper but the one thing he hasn't improved on is his judgement. "**
>
> ALAN HANSEN
> FORMER SCOTLAND INTERNATIONAL
> AND TV PUNDIT

Frank Lampard

His manager thinks he's the best player in Europe; if he plays to his potential, Lamps could light up South Africa. Heartbroken after the last World Cup, the Chelsea midfielder has matured as a player and will be determined to return with a winner's medal.

Lampard is an officer type, with an IQ of over 150 that puts him in the most intelligent 0.1 per cent of the population. His service record reveals a midfield strategist who, from commanding positions at the centre of the park, plays an elegant, unruffled game creating the time and space to initiate attacks.

Lampard's goal scoring is an added extra, but was always expected from the man who stepped into the England side as Paul Scholes' successor. At Chelsea, Lampard is the local hero who has fired more goals for his club than any other midfielder. Internationally he started well, scoring nine for the England under-21s. He got three goals in four matches as England made it to the quarter-finals at Euro 2004 and fans voted him England Player of the Year in 2004 and 2005.

Things then started to go wrong for national hero Lamps. Despite playing every minute of England's 2006 World Cup and shooting more frequently than any other England player, Lampard failed to score. England supporters booed him during England's Euro 2008 qualifying match against Estonia in October 2007 and he took some of the blame when England failed to qualify for the tournament.

For Lampard, it was hello to adversity for the boy who was born into a footballing dynasty – father Frank also played for England, and Harry and Jamie Redknapp are uncle and cousin. When Fabio Capello took over the England managership in 2008, Lampard found himself playing international catch-up. He responded slowly but surely with his first international goal in two years in a 4–0 win over Slovakia in March 2009. Equally important was the assist for a Wayne Rooney goal.

Now that Lampard is matching his international showings with those for Chelsea, the big question is the one left unanswered from the last World Cup. Can he and Steven Gerrard play productively in the same team?

LEFT *The standing foot perfectly in place, Frank Lampard is pictured performing one of his specialities and scoring a penalty in the home qualifier against Croatia at Wembley in September 2009. Watch for him watching the sky each time he scores.*

PLAYER FACT FILE

Name: Frank James Lampard
Position: Midfielder
Caps: 76
Goals: 20
Team: Chelsea
Date of birth: 20 June 1978
Height: 184 cm/6 ft ½ in
Weight: 90 kg/198 lb
Previous clubs: West Ham United, Swansea City
International debut: 10 October 1999 v Belgium
Previous World Cups: 2006

STYLE GUIDE

Consistent and superbly fit, Frank Lampard is a goal-scoring midfielder with an accurate pass and a well-timed tackle. Despite the benefits of deploying him as an advanced attacking midfielder, managers like to exploit his stamina and usually instruct him to work as a box-to-box midfielder.

 ONE TO WATCH

Glen Johnson

Glen Johnson is a versatile right back who, like so many of the England team, began his career at West Ham. He moved to Chelsea in 2002, the first big buy of Roman Abramovich's ownership. Competition from Paolo Ferreira and Geremi for the Chelsea right-back slot meant his career stalled and he spent two years at Portsmouth before moving to Liverpool at the end of the 2009 season.

Johnson has been more fortunate in the rivalry for an England place with the competition coming from an ageing and injured Gary Neville and from Luke Young. However, it wasn't until Fabio Capello's appointment that Johnson blossomed in an England shirt. The new manager's immediate revival of Johnson's international career has given this efficient full back a run of games to bring confidence to the player and stability at the right of the team's defence.

Wayne Rooney

The hopes of a nation rest on Wayne Rooney's muscular young shoulders. He is the undisputed English footballer of his generation – without a Rooney on form, England will find themselves struggling in South Africa.

Rooney's strength and balance achieve an odd grace and his sheer physicality animates teammates and crowds alike. His exciting talent and extraordinary energy have illuminated so many big games, it's hard to credit that he's not yet 25. Despite relentless press exposure and unremitting pressures of expectation, Rooney's will to win seems as fresh as when he made his England debut against Australia in 2003 and then quickly emerged as the star of Euro 2004.

An injured foot marred Rooney's (and England's) chances of significant World Cup progress in 2006. Four years ago, the nation became experts on broken metatarsals while Rooney struggled for fitness. Rooney was on less than peak form as England laboured towards a quarter-final confrontation with Portugal where he was sent off for stamping on a defender and being winked at by Ronaldo. England went out on penalties.

An older, wiser Rooney will be able to redeem himself in South Africa. With three Premier League titles and the 2008 Champions League among his club honours, he is already an Old Trafford legend who has paid back the £28 million it took to prise him from Everton. At Manchester United he has moved to centre forward and it is likely that in South Africa he will stay up front in the spearhead role and go flat out to score rather than acting as a marauding provider behind the main striker.

In a recent interview, Rooney was asked to name his favourite player. 'Maradona,' he replied. 'He's definitely the best player there's ever been in my eyes. He had pace, great skill and an unbelievable desire to win.' The assessment applies to Rooney too. Under his shirt he has a tattoo that reads: 'Just Enough Education To Perform.' Well, England expects this one man to deliver the performance of a lifetime in South Africa.

BELOW AND RIGHT *The ball seems to stick to Wayne Rooney's foot. As top scorer in the European qualifying zone, he will be a marked man in South Africa – he has the talent, strength and ambition to take England all the way to the final.*

PLAYER FACT FILE

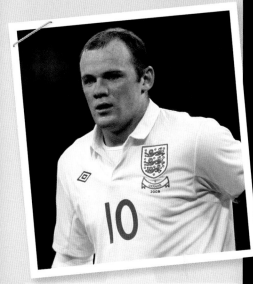

Name: Wayne Mark Rooney
Position: Striker
Caps: 57
Goals: 25
Team: Manchester United
Date of birth: 24 October 1985
Height: 178 cm/5 ft 10 in
Weight: 83 kg/183 lb
Previous clubs: Everton
International debut: 12 February 2003
v Australia
Previous World Cups: 2006

STYLE GUIDE

The complete soccer package is wrapped
in Rooney's chunky bullock-like frame. He
rides tackles bravely to terrify defences with
rollicking runs into shooting positions. The
passing and the movement are clever too.
His control at speed is phenomenal, he has
the wit to pull off the trickiest of lobs and the
power to volley with either foot. The physical
balance is not always matched by emotional
equilibrium and his full-pelt aggression and
commitment is always liable to tip into
tantrums and swearing. It's fun to watch
but lip readers, look away.

Theo Walcott

The school sprint champion began his international football career at a cracking pace – after all, having signed a Nike sponsorship deal aged only 14, he has always had a nice pair of trainers.

Theo Walcott became England's youngest player aged 17 years 75 days in a 3–1 defeat of Hungary. By then, Sven-Göran Eriksson had included him in the 2006 World Cup squad as back-up to Wayne Rooney and Michael Owen ahead of Darren Bent, Andy Johnson, Dean Ashton and Jermain Defoe. Eriksson's choice was controversial

Name: Theo James Walcott
Position: Striker
Caps: 8
Goals: 3
Team: Arsenal
Date of birth: 16 March 1989
Height: 175 cm/5 ft 9 in
Weight: 68 kg/150 lb
Previous clubs: Southampton
International debut: 30 May 2006 v Hungary
Previous World Cups: 2006

STYLE GUIDE

Walcott's blistering pace scares the defenders he runs at. When he cuts in from the right, goalkeepers quake in anticipation of powerful shots that leave them confused because they're delivered with so little backlift. If he goes to the byline, central defenders have grown wary of Walcott's accuracy with a cross.

LEFT *The old icon David Beckham enters the field of play to give icon-to-be Theo Walcott a pat on the head for the hat-trick he has just scored against Croatia. As England pulled off a famous qualifying victory it was right feet forward with the maestro meeting the young pretender; guile meeting speed; the substitute wearing number 17 meeting the new number 7.*

ABOVE *Theo Walcott can hit as he runs and is shown above firing in a right-foot shot during the World Cup qualifying match against Andorra in June 2009. Joleon Lescott and a sparse Wembley crowd are looking on.*

but never foolish and the teenage prodigy came good for Fabio Capello when, in 2008, he became the youngest England hat-trick scorer in the 4–1 win over Croatia in Zagreb.

Walcott was equally quick out of the blocks at club level. At 15, he was Southampton's youngest ever reserve. He set another Southampton record when he joined the first team aged 16 years 143 days. At the beginning of 2006, he went to Arsenal for £12 million, making him the most expensive 16 year old. The story quickly went round that Walcott had the pace to outsprint Thierry Henry on the training ground, and the following August he made his Premiership debut in the first game in the new Emirates Stadium.

There have been blips during Walcott's gilded progress. A shoulder injury has hampered him and both post-Eriksson England managers have insisted he is put through the normal paces. Steve McClaren insisted Walcott played for the England Under-21s, claiming he was 'toughening up' on his squad selections. Walcott's response was to become the youngest player to score for the Under-21 team and to carry on scoring in ways that drew more comparisons with Thierry Henry. In 2009, Capello continued the under-21 apprenticeship, despite fears that junior and senior squad appearances would lead to burnout and injury.

Walcott's status as national treasure elect was confirmed when he paraded around London carrying the 2008 Olympic flame. That would be as nothing compared to a 2010 World Cup victory cavalcade. By July, Walcott's tag as England's most talented teenager will be out of date – so will the 20 year old break beyond the tape of adulthood as a national hero?

> 66 **Theo is awesome. He frightens the life out of defenders and gives the team an awful lot, defensively as well as going forwards.** 99
>
> JOHN TERRY

USA

GROUP C

America's fittest and best gravitate to American football, baseball or athletics rather than to the poor sporting relation called 'soccer'. Yet the national side approaches a sixth successive World Cup finals ranked 14th in the world.

That ranking reflects their form in the 2009 Confederations Cup, a campaign that included a 2–0 semi-final victory over Spain, thus ending Spain's 35-game unbeaten run and a 15-game winning streak. There was no shame in losing the final 2–3 to a full-strength Brazil, particularly after leading 2–0 at half-time. In fact, the United States have often proved that big reputations are there to be punctured. Their 1–0 victory against England in the 1950 World Cup was one of football's greatest upsets, and they reached the quarter-finals of the 2002 World Cup. However, American optimism was deflated in the 2006 World Cup when they were drawn in the 'group of death'.

The immediate future is with the efficient collective that the American manager Bob Bradley has moulded since taking the job on in 2006. He has drawn on the country's youth system to prepare a squad combining overseas players with up-and-comers from Major League Soccer. Bradley belongs to the school that holds that winning needn't be pretty. He emphasizes the collective and likes to keep things compact and tight in midfield.

Some feel this is the best team the United States has yet sent to a World Cup. Much will depend on striker Landon Donovan, midfielder Clint Dempsey, full back Jonathan Spector and goalie Tim Howard. They come from a country where seven million people play organized football. However, size isn't everything and there is no longer any expectation that North American innovation will remodel football as the South Americans did in the 1930s and the Hungarians in the 1950s. Instead they'll play a high-paced huffing-up-and-down-the-pitch game reminiscent of the English first division in the 1980s.

In South Africa there will be brash displays of passion and toughness from red-clad fans known as the American Outlaws, or Sam's Army. They wear US-flag bandanas over their faces and will make a noise to rival the racket of the *vuvuzela* horns.

ABOVE *Semi-detached: the USA's rugged manager, Bob Bradley, showing little emotion during his side's 2–0 Confederations Cup semi-final win against Spain in Bloemfontein.*

ABOVE *Final joy: Landon Donovan leaps to celebrate his 27th-minute goal against Brazil in the Confederations Cup final. Clint Dempsey (8) had already scored in an astonishing showdown that Brazil eventually won with three goals in the second half.*

RIGHT *USA v Brazil, Confederations Cup final, Ellis Park Stadium, Johannesburg, South Africa, 28 June 2009: back (left to right) DeMerit, Howard, Onyewu, Spector, Bocanegra, Dempsey; (front) Clark, Altidore, Feilhaber, Davies, Donovan.*

POSSIBLE SQUAD

Goalkeepers

Brad Guzan (Aston Villa), Tim Howard (Everton), Troy Perkins (Vålerenga)

Defenders

Carlos Bocanegra (C) (Rennes), Jonathan Bornstein (Chivas USA), Jimmy Conrad (Kansas City Wizards), Jay DeMerit (Watford), Frankie Hejduk (Columbus Crew), Oguchi Onyewu (AC Milan), Jonathan Spector (West Ham United)

Midfielders

DaMarcus Beasley (Rangers), Michael Bradley (Borussia Mönchengladbach), Ricardo Clark (Houston Dynamo), Clint Dempsey (Fulham), Benny Feilhaber (AGF), Stuart Holden (Houston Dynamo), Robbie Rogers (Columbus Crew), José Francisco Torres (Pachuca)

Forwards

Jozy Altidore (Hull City), Conor Casey (Colorado Rapids), Kenny Cooper (1860 Munich), Charlie Davies (Sochaux), Landon Donovan (Everton)

ROUTE TO THE FINALS

CONCACAF FINAL STAGE – FINAL TABLE

Team	P	W	D	L	F	A	Pts
USA	10	6	2	2	19	13	20
Mexico	10	6	1	3	18	12	19
Honduras	10	5	1	4	17	11	16
Costa Rica	10	5	1	4	15	15	16
El Salvador	10	2	2	6	9	15	8
Trinidad & Tobago	10	1	3	6	10	22	6

FINALS GROUP C

USA play		Date	Venue
	England	12 June	Rustenburg
	Slovenia	18 June	Johannesburg (Ellis Park)
	Algeria	23 June	Tshwane/Pretoria

VITAL STATISTICS

World ranking 14th   Keeper and defence 6/10
Midfield 6/10   Attack 6/10

Strengths and weaknesses A team of fighters will tussle for every ball and dominate possession against glitzier rivals. However, goals are what count and, when it comes to scoring, the USA will struggle.

How far will they go? Along with England, the USA is the team most likely to move from Group C to the second round.

Clint Dempsey

Dempsey grew up in Texas before becoming a four million dollar Fulham man. Well known to England fans, he's a tough customer whose combat-assault style on the pitch once had him playing through the pain of a broken jaw. He's nothing if not intense.

Now in his mid-twenties, Dempsey has curbed the temper that on a couple of occasions had his younger self suspended for violent conduct. His all-round game puts him at the heart of many US moves and he's the closest the country has to a footballing superstar. As a boy, he studied Maradona on the television and started learning the basics of his trade playing with local Mexican immigrant children. He went on to attend college as a health and exercise major and then turned professional as an attacking central midfielder with New England Revolution. His move to Fulham at the end of 2006 established him as a regular Premiership midfield battler with the ability to score vital goals.

> **❝ I got on my job an' made the game ferocious; I was born with the drive I got that from no coaches. ❞**
>
> THE RAPPER DEUCE
> CLINT DEMPSEY

Name: Clinton Drew Dempsey
Position: Midfielder
Caps: 59
Goals: 17
Team: Fulham
Date of birth: 9 March 1983
Height: 185 cm/6 ft 1 in
Weight: 84 kg/185 lb
Previous clubs: New England Revolution
International debut: 17 November 2004 v Jamaica
Previous World Cups: 2006

STYLE GUIDE

Dempsey is a versatile player in midfield for Fulham and further forward in attack for his country. He's happiest approaching the goal from the wing using his extravagant dribbling skills. His midfield tenacity and brave diving headers in crowded penalty areas are other trademarks of his varied contributions.

Dempsey has been an international since he was 19 and has set a couple of records: he scored the only goal by a US player in the 2006 World Cup; and he scored the fastest goal in US qualifying history with a first-minute sliding shot that began an 8–0 rout of Barbados. He hit form in the 2009 Confederations Cup, scoring goals in the quarters, the semi and the final. He was awarded the man of the match for his performance in the semi-final and got his last goal of the tournament against Brazil, from a Jonathan Spector cross in the tenth minute.

Outside football, Dempsey is into hip-hop music and adopted the alias of Deuce when he joined other Texan rappers XO and Big Hawk to record a song called *Don't Tread On Me*. North America's most famous footballing export is not the sort of man anybody would tread on lightly; the folks back home are hoping he'll take them a step further to World Cup success than the United States has managed so far.

ABOVE AND LEFT *Dempsey takes delight at having broken Spanish hearts in the USA's famous Confederations Cup semi-final victory against Spain in summer 2009. His opportunistic goal beat Iker Casillas at the near post and was the second goal of a 2–0 victory that alerted the soccer world to the United States' potential.*

ALGERIA

GROUP C

Known as *Les Fennecs* (The Desert Foxes) or the *Moharibou Essahra* (Desert Warriors), Algeria were once the hope of Africa.

In the 1982 World Cup they recorded a famous 2–1 victory over West Germany, eventual finalists. They were back in World Cup action in 1986, and won the African Nations Cup in 1990, but then they faded. Algerian qualification for 2010 couldn't have been closer – or much nastier. Their qualifying matches against arch-rivals Egypt spawned riots that spread from North Africa into Marseille. The necessity for a play-off was the result of a statistical freak that left both teams level in their group on points (13), goal difference (5) and goals scored (9). The play-off was in neutral Sudan and required 15,000 police to keep the peace among 30,000 spectators.

Algeria 3 Egypt 1; Algeria 0 Egypt 2; Algeria 1 Egypt 0 are scorelines burned into the minds of bitter opponents whose rivalry has long spilled over into hooliganism and bloodshed. But then football in Algeria has always been more than just a game. In the 1950s, it acquired explicit political focus when the Algerian team was formed in defiance of French colonial power. FIFA supported the French government in announcing that any team playing the Algerian FLN (Front de Libération Nationale) would be expelled from the World Cup. Who said football isn't about politics?

Since recognition in 1962, Algeria have gone through 34 managers, and current success may be due to the relative stability of having had Rabah Saâdane in charge for three years. Saâdane, a former Algeria defender, has moulded a team that is more European than African in style, more the fox than the warrior. Cautious 4-4-2 formations put defence at a premium. Anything exciting is likely to flow through the versatile midfielder Karim Ziani or Rafik Saifi, a 35-year-old goal poacher.

BELOW LEFT *Karim Ziani, Algeria's midfield dynamo, battles to retain the ball in the play-off against Egypt on 14 November 2009.*

BELOW RIGHT *Four days later, on neutral territory, Algeria secured a place in South Africa. They were given a rapturous welcome when they returned home.*

POSSIBLE SQUAD

Goalkeepers

Faouzi Chaouchi (ES Sétif), Lounès Gaouaoui (ASO Chlef), Mohamed Ousserir (CR Belouizdad)

Defenders

Réda Babouche (MC Algiers), Nadir Belhadj (Portsmouth), Madjid Bougherra (Rangers), Rafik Halliche (Nacional Madeira), Abdelkader Laïfaoui (ES Sétif), Slimane Raho (ES Sétif), Anthar Yahia (Bochum), Samir Zaoui (ASO Chlef)

Midfielders

Yacine Bezzaz (Strasbourg), Hameur Bouazza (Blackpool), Khaled Lemmouchia (ES Sétif), Yazid Mansouri (C) (Lorient), Karim Matmour (Borussia Mönchengladbach), Mourad Meghni (Lazio), Hassan Yebda (Portsmouth), Karim Ziani (Wolfsburg)

Forwards

Rafik Djebbour (AEK Athens), Abdelkader Ghezzal (Siena), Kamel Ghilas (Hull City), Rafik Saïfi (Al-Khor)

ROUTE TO THE FINALS

AFRICA QUALIFYING GROUP C – FINAL TABLE

Team	P	W	D	L	F	A	Pts
Algeria	7	5	1	1	10	4	16
Egypt	7	4	1	2	9	5	13
Zambia	6	1	2	3	2	5	5
Rwanda	6	0	2	4	1	8	2

PLAY-OFF

18.11.09	Algeria 1	0 Egypt

FINALS GROUP C

Algeria play		Date	Venue
	Slovenia	13 June	Polokwane
	England	18 June	Cape Town
	USA	23 June	Tshwane/Pretoria

VITAL STATISTICS

World ranking 28th	Keeper and defence 6/10
Midfield 5/10	Attack 5/10

Strengths and weaknesses Algeria are strong on organization and are drilled to mount a resolute defence. They are weaker on flair and are over-reliant on Ziani's midfield probing and Saïfi's sharpness in front of goal. Keep these two quiet and Algeria will disappear.

How far will they go?
Once the most promising of African teams, Algeria are unlikely to survive an opening group that pits them against England, USA and Slovenia.

اتصالات etisalat

الراعي

LEFT *Algeria v Egypt, World Cup qualifying match, Cairo International Stadium, Egypt, 14 November 2009: (back row, left to right) Halliche, Meghni, Yahia, Gaouaoui, Bougherra; (front row), Matmour, Mansouri, Saïfi, Ziani, Belhadj, Lemmouchia.*

SLOVENIA

GROUP C

Slovenia give nothing away. They conceded only four goals in qualifying from a group that included hard nuts Poland, the Czech Republic and Slovakia.

Sweetest of all were the play-off games against Russia in November 2009. In the first leg, an 88th-minute close-range header from Nejc Pečnik halved Russia's lead and provided the crucial away goal that meant Zlatko Dedič's single goal in the return leg was more than enough.

Much of the success is down to the way coach Matjaž Kek has organized the defence and midfield. A club-level centre half with managerial experience in Austria, Kek said: 'Our style is not down to any individual player, but the team as a whole. We prepare thoroughly for matches and analyse the opposition's style of play beforehand. I'm so pleased that we accomplished our plan.'

Slovenia's opponents in South Africa should be warned that painstaking preparation and a strict adherence to plans have created a formidably disciplined collective. Teams facing Slovenia must staunch the flow of passes from Dedič and keep Köln forward Milivoje Novakovič under control. He scored five goals in qualifying.

Slovenia's form since the team was created after the break-up of Yugoslavia in 1991 is of qualified success. They got to the 2002 World Cup without losing a match, recording six wins and six draws. However, they lost all three games at the finals. Two years later they were at Euro 2004 and now they have once again fought through to a big stage. They're not to be written off.

Italy will treat Slovenia with respect having lost to them 0–1 in a 2006 World Cup qualifier. And England players will recall that it took a dodgy penalty for England's 2–1 win against them in a September 2009 friendly. This is not a side to be taken lightly.

BELOW LEFT *Matjaž Kek is a master tactician with the determination to create a tough national side that is greater than the sum of its parts.*

BELOW RIGHT *Zlatko Dedič performs a one-man war dance after scoring the single play-off goal in the match that knocked Russia out of the World Cup.*

POSSIBLE SQUAD

Goalkeepers

Jasmin Handanovič (Mantova), Samir Handanovič (Udinese), Aleksander Šeliga (Sparta Rotterdam)

Defenders

Mišo Brečko (Köln), Boštjan Cesar (Grenoble), Luka Elsner (Domžale), Branko Ilič (FC Moscow), Bojan Jokič (Sochaux), Matej Mavrič (TuS Koblenz), Marko Šuler (Gent)

Midfielders

Andraž Kirm (Wisła Kraków), Andrej Komac (Maccabi Tel Aviv), Robert Koren (C) (West Bromwich Albion), Rene Krhin (Internazionale), Darijan Matič (Rapid Bucureşti), Nejc Pečnik (Nacional), Aleksander Radosavljevič (Tom Tomsk), Dalibor Stevanovič (Vitesse), Anton Žlogar (Omonia)

Forwards

Valter Birsa (Auxerre), Zlatko Dedič (Bochum), Zlatan Ljubijankič (Gent), Milivoje Novakovič (Köln)

ROUTE TO THE FINALS

EUROPE QUALIFYING GROUP 3 – FINAL TABLE

Team	P	W	D	L	F	A	Pts
Slovakia	10	7	1	2	22	10	22
Slovenia	10	6	2	2	18	4	20
Czech Republic	10	4	4	2	17	6	16
Northern Ireland	10	4	3	3	13	9	15
Poland	10	3	2	5	19	14	11
San Marino	10	0	0	10	1	47	0

EUROPE PLAY-OFFS

14.11.09	Russia 2	1 Slovenia
18.11.09	Slovenia 1	0 Russia

FINALS GROUP C

Slovenia play		Date	Venue
	Algeria	13 June	Polokwane
	USA	18 June	Johannesburg (Ellis Park)
	England	23 June	N. Mandela Bay/Pt Elizabeth

VITAL STATISTICS

World ranking 33rd	Keeper and defence 6/10
Midfield 5/10	Attack 5/10

Strengths and weaknesses While this team can cope with pressure, the Slovenians could find it difficult coping with the technicalities of goal scoring against top-notch opposition.

How far will they go? They have the resilience and a defensive miserliness that could see them through to the second round. Slovenia in the quarters, however, would count as an upset.

LEFT *Slovenia v San Marino, World Cup qualifying match, Stadio Olympico, Serravalle, Italy, 14 October 2009: (back row, left to right) Samir Handanovič, Cesar, Novakovič, Šuler, Dedič, Birsa; (front row) Radosavljevič, Kirm, Brečko, Jokič, Stevanovič.*

GERMANY

GROUP D

Germany made heavy work of winning a featherweight World Cup qualifying group. But don't write off this side of Bundesliga journeymen. German national sides have a long record of being more than the sum of ordinary parts. Maybe this team has the potential to reveal some extraordinary footballing arts.

German fans mount a good case that their side is on a World Cup winning trajectory, pointing out that they came third as hosts in 2006, second at Euro 2008, and so a first place in South Africa must therefore follow. Consider the statistics going further back in time. Germany have won the World Cup three times, behind Brazil (five titles) and Italy (four titles) and have finished as runners-up four times, two more than any other side. There have been 11 semi-final showings and at least a quarter-final finish for the past 14 World Cups.

Statistically based assertions aside, there are reservations about a German international team that is becoming one of the also-rans of world football. Their last World Cup final victory was in 1990 when the former German star Franz Beckenbauer announced that a united Germany would be unstoppable for years to come. It hasn't happened that way. At club level, the united Germany has not matched the mid-1970s Bundesliga dominance of European football. Aside from Michael Ballack, the international squad plays its football for German teams and has not been honed by the intensity of Champions League knockout rounds. That lack of experience must filter through to the international side. One way or another, over the past two decades *die nationalmannschaft* ('the national team') has come to seem a normal international football side.

The current squad is more diverse than in the past, with several players of Turkish or Polish descent. Much more surprising is the move to a free and open style of play which has made the clichés of ruthless German efficiency outdated. Two successive managers have built a team around the attack-minded midfield guile of Michael Ballack. He is the star player but, good as he is, he's an engine-room talent rather than a world-beater who sweeps all before him in the mould of Beckenbauer.

LEFT *Rising star Mesut Özil vaults a challenge from Russian midfielder Konstantin Zyryanov during a World Cup qualifier in October 2009, which Germany won 1–0.*

RIGHT *Lukas Podolski (right) celebrates with Bastian Schweinsteiger after scoring during the World Cup qualifying match against Liechtenstein, 28 March 2009.*

*Philipp Lahm,
Andreas Beck, Miroslav
Klose, Mesut Özil,
Michael Ballack and
Bastian Schweinsteiger
in front of their fans in
Hanover, 5 September
2009. They are
celebrating one of two
Klose goals that earned
them a comfortable 4–0
victory over Azerbaijan,
edging them closer to a
place in South Africa.*

Ballack has commented on a lack of overall quality and says: 'Drive and motivation are our keys to success. We don't have the extra touch of class enjoyed by others.' And perhaps the backbone has gone missing. Until his suicide in autumn 2009, Robert Enke was emerging as goalkeeping successor to Jens Lehmann and Oliver Kahn. His death left the way open for the lesser known presences of René Adler, Timo Hildebrand and Manuel Neuer. Although Per Mertesacker is a strong central defender and will get support from the up-and-coming Serdar Tasci, this defence won't be forming a bulwark to intimidate top-level strikers. In midfield Ballack plus Mesut Özil and Bastian Schweinsteiger are

more than competent, but are they the world's best? Ditto for an attack that only shines when both Miroslav Klose and Lukas Podolski are on their top form.

Until recently, in a break with a long tradition, team management was inconsistent. By 2004 Germany were looking for their third new coach in six years, having had only six coaches in the previous 75 years. Jürgen Klinsmann, a star striker who had never held any coaching jobs before, led the 2006 campaign before handing over to his assistant Joachim Löw who was given the security of a contract to include this 2010 World Cup. So, it's worth repeating that Germany were third in the 2006 World Cup and second at Euro

GREAT MATCH
1954 West Germany 3–2 Hungary

World Cup final
Wankdorf Stadium, Berne, Switzerland

In Germany they still refer to it as the 'Miracle of Berne'. The result meant so much more than a football match should. It gave a beaten people back their pride and led to an upswelling of joy only the fall of the Berlin Wall has since matched. It would also be the springboard for the German domination of European football for the next fifty years.

Having only just been allowed back to the World Cup by FIFA, few gave the Germans a chance against the 'Magnificent Magyars' who had gone 32 games unbeaten, boasted the likes of Puskas and Hidegkuti, and had already beaten them 8–3 in the group stage. But the Germans had regrouped around a core of Kaiserslauten players and had slowly improved as they progressed through the tournament. With the news that Puskas was to play even though only half-fit, all they needed now was a minor miracle.

Hungary led 2–0 after only eight minutes, and the match seemed to be following the script, but the Germans dug in and their flair player Helmut Rahn came into his own, crossing for Max Morlock to get a goal back and slamming home an angled volley for the equalizer on 35 minutes. For the rest of the game, they were pinned back, relying on the heroics of keeper Toni Turek. Then, with just five minutes remaining, a cross somehow landed at the feet of Rahn who calmly slotted it home. West Germany were back on the football map – and they had no plans to leave.

BELOW *Max Morlock sliding home West Germany's first goal in the astonishing World Cup final comeback that saw Hugary concede a two-goal lead.*

2008. A reestablishment of managerial traditions helped this upswing in achievement and when there is continuity, the ifs and buts can be put aside and the Germans could once again win the World Cup.

> **Without speed you do nothing. Speed in the mind, speed in the technique and also one hundred per cent concentration on tactics.**
>
> JOACHIM LÖW

COACH **Joachim Löw**

Born 3 February 1960
Record: P45, W31, D8, L6

Joachim Löw was the unseen technician behind the Jürgen Klinsmann charisma. They'd met as opposing players in the 1980s, became friends on coaching courses in the 1990s and Klinsmann recruited Löw as assistant when he became German coach in 2004. Löw, an attacking midfielder in his playing days, is regarded as the superior tactician and his was the attacking blueprint that took Germany to the 2006 semi-finals.

In 2006 Klinsmann resigned a national hero. Cue for Jogi Löw to step into the limelight. Ten years of club management in Germany, Austria and Turkey plus his successful assistant's role qualified him for promotion. The German FA was already familiar with his rigorous training methods and his desire to integrate young players into the national side. He started on a winning streak of five victories, without his side conceding a goal in 418 minutes of play. He had a successful Euro 2008, with Germany eventually losing 0–1 to Spain in the final.

RIGHT *Germany v Finland, World Cup qualifying match, HSH Nordbank Arena, Hamburg, Germany, 14 October 2009: (back row, left to right) Hitzlsperger, Adler, Friedrich, Westermann, Gómez, Ballack; (front row) Trochowski, Podolski, Lahm, Beck, Cacau.*

ROUTE TO THE FINALS

MATCHES PLAYED

06.09.08	Liechtenstein 0	6	Germany
10.09.08	Finland 3	3	Germany
11.10.08	Germany 2	1	Russia
15.10.08	Germany 1	0	Wales
28.03.09	Germany 4	0	Liechtenstein
01.04.09	Wales 0	2	Germany
12.08.09	Azerbaijan 0	2	Germany
09.09.09	Germany 4	0	Azerbaijan
10.10.09	Russia 0	1	Germany
14.10.09	Germany 1	1	Finland

EUROPE QUALIFYING GROUP 4 – FINAL TABLE

Team	P	W	D	L	F	A	Pts
Germany	10	8	2	0	26	5	26
Russia	10	7	1	2	19	6	22
Finland	10	5	3	2	14	14	18
Wales	10	4	0	6	9	12	12
Azerbaijan	10	1	2	7	4	14	5
Liechtenstein	10	0	2	8	2	23	2

FINALS GROUP D

Germany play	Date	Venue
Australia	13 June	Durban
Serbia	18 June	N. Mandela Bay/Pt Elizabeth
Ghana	23 June	Johannesburg (Soccer City)

VITAL STATISTICS

World ranking 6th
Midfield 7/10

Keeper and defence 6/10
Attack 7/10

Strengths and weaknesses If long term World Cup pedigree is a strength, Germany are strong; if players with top club experience counts as a strength, then they are not quite so strong. Manager Joachim Löw's reputation as master tactician will undergo destruction testing in South Africa.

How far will they go? A good bet for the quarter-finals, a decent punt for the semis, but there's surely not quality enough for Germany to go all the way. Not this time.

HOW THEY'LL LINE UP

Löw has retained Klinsmann's attacking formats and added a return to older values. 'Most important is speed and technique,' he says. 'Without speed you do nothing. Speed in the mind, speed in the technique and also one hundred per cent concentration on tactics.' In essence the tactics hark back to Germany's glory days, though without the quality of player. As ever, there is strength and height at the back, and a determined midfield laced with enough flair to provide chances up front. Ballack and Özil are playmakers while Schweinsteiger has a mobile role to give Podolski and Klose the openings they need.

POSSIBLE SQUAD

Goalkeepers

René Adler (Bayer Leverkusen), **Manuel Neuer** (Schalke 04), **Tim Wiese** (Werder Bremen)

Defenders

Andreas Beck (1899 Hoffenheim), **Arne Friedrich** (Hertha Berlin), **Andreas Hinkel** (Celtic), **Marcell Jansen** (Hamburg), **Philipp Lahm** (Bayern Munich), **Per Mertesacker** (Werder Bremen), **Marcel Schäfer** (Wolfsburg), **Serdar Tasci** (Stuttgart), **Heiko Westermann** (Schalke 04)

Midfielders

Michael Ballack (Chelsea), **Christian Gentner** (Wolfsburg), **Thomas Hitzlsperger** (Stuttgart), **Aaron Hunt** (Werder Bremen), **Mesut Özil** (Werder Bremen), **Bastian Schweinsteiger** (Bayern Munich), **Piotr Trochowski** (Hamburg)

Forwards

Cacau (Stuttgart), **Mario Gómez** (Bayern Munich), **Miroslav Klose** (Bayern Munich), **Lukas Podolski** (Cologne)

Michael Ballack

Michael Ballack was nicknamed 'Little Kaiser' when he began his playing career with Chemnitzer FC in 1995. He has been captain of Germany since 2004 and has the clout to insist on wearing the number 13 shirt whichever side he plays for.

Jürgen Klinsmann's first move as manager of Germany was to make Ballack captain, and he moulded the lesser talents available to him around his star midfielder. Joachim Löw maintained the approach and both managers have been rewarded with a hatful of goals and match-winning leadership.

Despite the talent and the accolades, Ballack has a reputation for choking when the pressure is most intense. Critics point to two seasons when he missed out on four trophies. In 2002, Bayer Leverkusen were second in the Bundesliga, German Cup and the Champions League and Germany lost to Brazil in the 2002 World Cup final. In 2008, Chelsea were second in the League Cup, Premier League and Champions League and Germany, now captained by Ballack, lost to Spain 1–0 in the Euro 2008 final.

All that must be set against a record of leadership and goal scoring for clubs and country that has brought a cupboard full of trophies and acccolades. He was Bundesliga winner with Bayern Munich in 2003, 2005 and 2006, and German Cup winner from 2003 to 2006. At Chelsea he has won the FA Cup in 2007 and 2009 and the League Cup in 2007. He was German Footballer of the Year in 2002, 2003 and 2005; the UEFA Club Midfielder of the Year in 2002; and he has been selected as one of FIFA 100, Pelé's choice of the 'greatest living footballers'.

> **❝ Ballack creates his own space. He's got a languid style and looks like he is not bothered at times but ... his range of passing is great. ❞**
>
> LEE DIXON
> TV PUNDIT AND FORMER ARSENAL DEFENDER

PLAYER FACT FILE

Name: Michael Ballack
Position: Midfielder
Caps: 97
Goals: 42
Team: Chelsea
Date of birth: 26 September 1976
Height: 189 cm/6 ft 2½ in
Weight: 89 kg/196 lb
Previous clubs: Chemnitzer FC, 1. FC Kaiserslautern, Bayer Leverkusen, Bayern Munich
International debut: 28 April 1999 v Scotland
Previous World Cups: 2002, 2006

STYLE GUIDE
Skill and strength are wrapped up in Michael Ballack. He has a Brazilian-like repertoire of shooting and passing skills, and he is comfortable hitting the ball with either foot. His preferred position is as an attacking midfielder, though he can drop back to play more destructively and make fierce but well-timed tackles.

Ballack is an all-rounder who says of himself: 'I'm a flexible player, I can play offensively or defensively, but wherever I play I always want to score.' And the statistically superstitious will note that Germany has never lost a game when Ballack has scored. The same goes for Miroslav Klose, Ballack's fellow thirty-something colleague on whom Germany is also relying.

BELOW *Michael Ballack strikes a classic football pose with a perfectly poised strike of the ball. When he plays for his country, the captain's armband and the number 13 shirt have become his own personal trademarks.*

Miroslav Klose

Miroslav Klose is Germany's 21st-century goal-scoring talisman. His World Cup goal-getting is impressive and he's the only player to have scored five in consecutive tournaments. If he repeats the feat a third time, he'll be in reach of Ronaldo's record tally of 16 World Cup goals.

Having trained as a carpenter, Klose is unusual among modern footballers in having completed an apprenticeship in another trade. He therefore began his playing career late and nearly began the international part of it as a Pole. He was born in Silesia and qualified for selection through his father's German nationality. His mother is Polish, his wife is Polish, the family language is Polish and he has said that had Polish officials been faster in seeking his services, he'd be playing for Poland now.

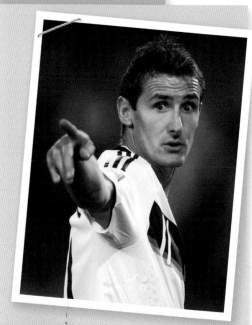
STYLE GUIDE

Some would dismiss Miroslav Klose as a goal-hanging heading machine. That's to ignore a player who has the instincts and football intelligence to consistently find the right scoring positions. And if a chance isn't on, he's got a fine record of assists. All that and he has a useful right foot as well.

As César Luis Menotti, former Argentina coach, says: 'There is more football in him than is believed by people who only associate him with his heading ability. I have seen details that I thought were remarkable: the way he shakes off opponents, shields the ball, prepares goal chances.'

Efficient German officials ensured that Klose's professional football life has been solidly German. There was talk after his five-goal success in the 2006 World Cup of a move from Werder Bremen to Barcelona or Juventus but he remained in Germany with a move to Bayern Munich at the end of the 2007 season. That summer the German coach Joachim Löw promoted Klose to stand-in captain in a 2–0 Euro-qualifier victory over Wales. In the 2008 European tournament, Klose played in an emotional game against Poland. He proved his loyalties were not divided with two passes that put Lukas Podolski through for both German goals. He scored in the quarter-final and semi-final against Portugal and Turkey but didn't score against Spain in the final. Germany lost.

Klose's slight physique means he doesn't look the part of a battering-ram centre forward. However, all German fans have thrilled to his unerring heading ability and his signature front-flip celebration after scoring. Knowledgeable fans point out the number of passes he makes to help his teammates score and the fact that three of the five goals Klose scored at the last World Cup came from his right foot. There's more to come from a modern man on whom old nationalistic ideas sit lightly and who says he's best thought of as a European, rather than a German or a Pole.

LEFT AND ABOVE Moscow, 10 October 2009: Miroslav Klose rides an agricultural challenge from the striker Pavel Pogrebnyak during Germany's crucial qualifying match against Russia. Klose scored the only goal, proving once again that he's a fantastic number 11 whichever way anybody looks at it. The witness to the veteran's famous celebration flip (left) is Germany's young gun Mesut Özil.

> **❝ There is more football in him than ... his heading ability. I have seen details that I thought were remarkable. ❞**
>
> CÉSAR LUIS MENOTTI
> FORMER ARGENTINA COACH

Philipp Lahm

Philipp Lahm is a Lilliputian figure in the Brobdingnagian ranks of German defenders but his standing is huge. German fans are aflutter when this extraordinarily versatile player swerves in from the left to fire a shot with his more forceful right foot.

Lahm's talent was apparent from an early age and he signed on for Bayern Munich when he was 11, playing in the junior sides as a defensive midfielder, right midfielder or right fullback. On moving to VfB Stuttgart for a couple of years, he was deployed at left back, and he remained in this position when he returned to Bayern in 2005. In the 2007 season Bayern followed Lahm's wishes and moved him to the right, buying Marcell Jansen as a new left back. Injuries to Jansen resulted in Lahm staying put out left. That is where he has gained his reputation for being one of the best fullbacks in the world, a fact

PLAYER FACT FILE

Name: Philipp Lahm
Position: Defender
Caps: 63
Goals: 3
Team: Bayern Munich
Date of birth: 11 November 1983
Height: 170 cm/5 ft 7 in
Weight: 61 kg/135 lb
Previous clubs: VfB Stuttgart
International debut: 18 February 2004 v Croatia
Previous World Cups: 2006

STYLE GUIDE

Lahm is an overlapping left back whose style mixes steady defending with penetrative runs up the wing. Upfield, he has the dribbling skills to worm beyond the last defender and deliver an accurate cross. However, his trademark attacking move is cutting in towards the centre and having a pop at goal.

LEFT *Lahm's last-minute winner took Germany to the Euro 2008 final, leaving Turkey to rue their misfortune after some inspired football.*

Serdar Tasci

Serdar Tasci is one of the key young players Joachim Löw has promoted to bring internal competition to an ageing squad and give his defence some much-needed steel. The 23 year old is a right-footed centre back who was born in Germany to Turkish parents. He came up through the ranks at Stuttgart and has been playing for them in the Bundesliga since August 2006. Early in his career he opted to play for Germany rather than Turkey and Löw rewarded him with a senior international debut in 2008 in a friendly against Belgium. Tasci's unfussy and effective performances earned him more international appearances throughout the World Cup qualifying rounds.

recognized by his nomination for the UEFA Team of the Year in the seasons he has been fit (2004, 2006 to 2008), putting him alongside Michael Ballack as most nominated German player.

FIFA made him left back of the year in 2008 in recognition of his play during Euro 2008. He clinched the semi-final against Turkey with a last-gasp goal: with the game at 2–2, Lahm played a high-speed one-two off Thomas Hitzlsperger to take the ball into the penalty area and fire past the Turkish keeper at the near post. It gave him the confidence to go forward in the final against Spain, though he was at fault when a communication breakdown with his goalie Jens Lehmann allowed Fernando Torres to get behind him and chip in the game's only goal.

That goal denied Lahm the international winner's medal he wants to put alongside three Bundesliga medals, his World Cup third-place medal from 2006 and his second-place medal at Euro 2008.

Lukas Podolski

The key to Germany's progress in South Africa could lie in the partnership between striker Lukas Podolski and Miroslav Klose.

Podolski was born in Poland but his heart is in Cologne where his family moved when he was aged two. He signed for FC Köln at the age of 10 and at 18 made Bundesliga history when he scored 10 goals in his first 19 games. It didn't prevent Köln's relegation and he remained top scorer in see-saw seasons of promotion and a second relegation. Bayern Munich snap up top German players and Podolski was duly snapped up. Three unhappy seasons later and he returned home to re-sign for Köln.

> **❝ I have two hearts – a German one and a Polish one. ❞**
>
> LUKAS PODOLSKI

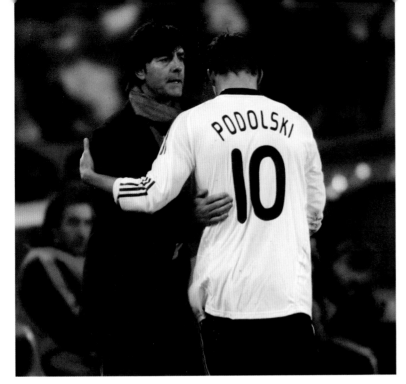

LEFT *Löw asserts his authority by parking Podolski on the bench during Germany's match againt Wales, 15 October 2008.*

BOTTOM LEFT *Podolski turning sharply to get in a left-foot shot and score his second goal during a friendly against Côte d'Ivoire in November 2009.*

PLAYER FACT FILE

Before the deal was concluded in 2009, Podolski sought assurance from his national coach Joachim Löw that a return to Cologne would not harm his international chances. Internationally, Podolski had an odd start. When he came to prominence in his late teens he expressed an interest in playing for Poland but the manager, Paweł Janas, didn't recognize potential when he saw it and rejected the approach, saying 'We have much better strikers in Poland.' Thus Germany found one of their very best strikers in Podolski.

Podolski made his debut for Germany aged 19 and was the squad's youngest player at Euro 2004. In the 2006 World Cup he partnered Miroslav Klose in attack, scoring a goal against Ecuador and both goals in the 2–0 quarter-final win over Sweden. He was named the World Cup's Best Young Player. His international career continued to develop and in the first Euro 2008 match he scored both goals in the victory over Poland. As a mark of respect for his country of birth, his celebrations were undemonstrative.

Despite a tumultuous time when his Bayern stint was drawing to a close, Podolski performed well for his country during the 2010 qualifiers with the opening two goals in Germany's game against Liechtenstein and the opener in the 2–1 home win over Russia. A blemish on his progress came in a game against Wales when he had an on-pitch altercation with Michael Ballack. The manager, Joachim Löw, used the incident to assert his authority and immediately substituted Podolski. After the match Löw explained: 'If the captain gives a player a tactical instruction, then that player must obey. That is absolutely clear. Lukas has to listen to an experienced player like Michael Ballack.'

Name: Lukas Podolski
Position: Striker
Caps: 69
Goals: 37
Team: Köln
Date of birth: 4 June 1985
Height: 182 cm/5 ft 11½ in
Weight: 82 kg/181 lb
Previous clubs: Bayern Munich
International debut: 6 June 2004 v Hungary
Previous World Cups: 2006

STYLE GUIDE

Defenders preparing to meet Lukas Podolski know they face a goal-every-other-game man who, on his day, oozes confidence. He's difficult to mark in an international position where he often advances in from left of midfield to add distribution skills to his pace, strength, balance and sharpness in front of goal.

Bastian Schweinsteiger

Bastian Schweinsteiger is a tousled blond with the flair to fashion goals and generally lift German teams to unexpected levels of footballing glamour. He plays with a cheery dash and will be eager to impose himself in South Africa.

As a boy, Schweinsteiger considered a career in ski-racing but plumped for football when, like many of Germany's most talented footballers, he signed for Bayern Munich's youth team. A pin-up star before he'd left his teens, the acclaim he earned for his skills went to his head and a promising career seemed to be skidding downhill in a series of well-publicized scrapes involving nightclubs, fast cars, and a lot more.

All was forgiven when he took Euro 2004 by storm with his trickery and a persistence that set up the opening goal for his Bayern colleague Michael Ballack. Schweinsteiger scored his first two international goals against Russia to start a surprising run in which Germany have not lost a game when he has scored.

RIGHT *Schweinsteiger nips in ahead of Portuguese defenders Paulo Ferreira and Ricardo Carvalho to score the first goal of the Euro 2008 quarter-final. Germany won 3–2 in a game where Cristiano Ronaldo was meant to have dominated but where Schweinsteiger, the opposite number seven, shined brightest.*

> ❝ **He just goes out there and gets on with it, and he's not put off if he tries something but loses the ball.** ❞
>
> MICHAEL BALLACK

Bastian Schweinsteiger has been first name on the German team sheet since the middle part of the decade and he has remained a controversial and eye-catching figure. In Euro 2008, he was sent off in Germany's group match against Croatia, which ended in a 2–1 defeat. He returned from suspension to score the first goal in a 3–2 semi-final victory over Portugal when he also delivered the free kicks from which Miroslav Klose and Michael Ballack scored. He scored the first goal in the 3–2 semi-final victory against Turkey.

Of late, the high scoring has fallen off as the goal-grabber prodigy has settled into the increasingly defensive midfield role more suited to the mature gentleman footballer in his mid-twenties. German fans have long recognized 'Basti' or 'Schweini' as a grafter and now that he's in his playing prime he presents himself in a more conservative way than in his youth, saying: 'I can be the playmaker, but I think that I'm better in a defensive role. I hate to see our opponents create chances and I'd rather break up play than make play.'

AUSTRALIA

GROUP D

Australia have emerged as a 21st-century footballing force with the Socceroos poised to travel across the Southern hemisphere for a second successive World Cup appearance. Aussie anticipation runs high.

A sports-mad nation is looking to go beyond the 2006 second-round milestone when Guus Hiddink's unfancied side finally succumbed to a dubious injury-time penalty awarded to Italy, the eventual champions. Pim Verbeek, another Dutch manager, has built on Hiddink's achievements and there is a growing swagger in the disciplined way the Australian team has approached games in the run-up to

South Africa. The ease of South African qualification has bolstered confidence, with Australia bossing its qualifying group. The team earned a maximum ten points from the opening five matches to ensure progression to the final qualifying round with a game to spare. The manager immediately looked ahead to South Africa and told his players: 'Our target is to do better than 2006.'

The majority of his Australia squads have comprised Europe-based players, and Verbeek has made it clear that in his opinion the local A-League is not yet up to World Cup standards. He has, however, assured the Australian media that he will sing the national anthem before each game in South Africa. Add real playing determination to the manager's assumed patriotism and Australia could go far.

Tim Cahill, the Everton star who has graduated from Socceroo super-sub to its chief playmaker, echoes the confidence of his fellow countrymen when he says: 'We can do better in South Africa as long as every player has the same mindset and belief to go out there and win. The quality is there. The players are getting better in the A-League, more players are in Europe. Of course we've got the chance of going one better if we can produce at the right time.'

LEFT *Sydney, Australia, 1 April 2009: Joshua Kennedy celebrates with teammates after scoring during the qualifying match between the Socceroos and Uzbekistan.*

RIGHT *Mark Schwarzer, Australia's talismanic goalkeeper, was on the field for every minute of Australia's eight matches of final qualifying and conceded only one goal.*

HOW THEY'LL LINE UP

The manager has a reputation as a dour results man rather than a stylist and he favours cautious line-ups featuring holding midfielders in support of a lone striker. The tempo of play is often slow and there is a heavy reliance on crosses. Much will depend on experienced players finding the form they have shown in the English Premiership – the best Australia can hope for is that Harry Kewell on the wing will provide the ammunition for Tim Cahill bursting in from midfield.

POSSIBLE SQUAD

Goalkeepers

Adam Federici (Reading), Brad Jones (Middlesbrough), Mark Schwarzer (Fulham)

Defenders

David Carney (FC Twente), Scott Chipperfield (Basel), Craig Moore (Brisbane Roar), Lucas Neill (C) (Everton), Jade North (Incheon United), Shane Stefanutto (North Queensland Fury), Luke Wilkshire (Dynamo Moscow), Rhys Williams (Middlesbrough)

Midfielders

Mark Bresciano (Palermo), Tim Cahill (Everton), Nick Carle (Crystal Palace), Jason Culina (Gold Coast United), Brett Emerton (Blackburn Rovers), Vince Grella (Blackburn Rovers), Harry Kewell (Galatasaray), Mile Sterjovski (Perth Glory)

Forwards

Alex Brosque (Sydney FC), Bruce Djite (Gençlerbirliği), Brett Holman (AZ Alkmaar), Joshua Kennedy (Nagoya Grampus)

ROUTE TO THE FINALS

MATCHES PLAYED

06.02.08	Australia 3	0 Qatar
23.03.08	China PR 0	0 Australia
01.06.08	Australia 1	0 Iraq
07.06.08	Iraq 1	0 Australia
14.06.08	Qatar 1	3 Australia
22.06.08	Australia 0	1 China PR
10.09.08	Uzbekistan 0	1 Australia
15.10.08	Australia 4	0 Qatar
19.11.08	Bahrain 0	1 Australia
11.02.09	Japan 0	0 Australia
01.04.09	Australia 2	0 Uzbekistan
06.06.09	Qatar 0	0 Australia
10.06.09	Australia 2	0 Bahrain
17.06.09	Australia 2	1 Japan

ASIA QUALIFYING GROUP 1 – FINAL TABLE

Team	P	W	D	L	F	A	Pts
Australia	8	6	2	0	12	1	20
Japan	8	4	3	1	11	6	15
Bahrain	8	3	1	4	6	8	10
Qatar	8	1	3	4	5	14	6
Uzbekistan	8	1	1	6	5	10	4

FINALS GROUP D

Australia play		Date	Venue
	Germany	13 June	Durban
	Ghana	19 June	Rustenburg
	Serbia	23 June	Nelspruit

VITAL STATISTICS

World ranking 21st **Keeper and defence** 6/10
Midfield 6/10 **Attack** 5/10

Strengths and weaknesses Top-drawer Dutch management has bred sides imbued with discipline and patience, but will that make up for shortfalls in individual skill and creativity?

How far will they go? While most Aussies believe their team is headed for the quarter-finals, they'll have to get past Ghana or Serbia to even make it to the second round.

COACH **Pim Verbeek**

Born 12 March 1956
Record: P24, W13, D7, L4

Pim Verbeek had an unspectacular Netherlands-based playing career before becoming a flying Dutch manager. He managed Japanese club teams before entering international coaching in South Korea, first as assistant to Guus Hiddink and then Dick Advocaat. He took the top South Korea job and guided the team to the 2007 Asian Cup semi-finals. He resigned but stayed in the Southern Hemisphere when he was offered the Australia manager's job at the end of 2007.

He has guided Australia to a third successive World Cup finals appearance. The playing style he fosters is pragmatic, and to those who say he forms dull teams he points out that he's a results man who lets the results do his speaking for him.

OPPOSITE *Australia v Japan, World Cup qualifying match, Melbourne Cricket Ground, Melbourne, Australia, 17 June 2009: (back row, left to right) Kennedy, Williams, Schwarzer, Sterjovski, Grella, Carle; (front row) Stefanutto, Cahill, Neill, Culina, North.*

Tim Cahill

A central midfielder who is also a natural and consistent goal scorer, Tim Cahill is the most talented Australian footballer of this or any other generation.

When Cahill pulls on his Australia shirt, he scores in every other game. He scored the first ever Australia goal at a World Cup in a match against Japan in 2006. The next year he was the first Australia player to score at an Asian Cup.

Cahill is a tough customer who spent the start of his club career at Millwall before moving to Everton at the end of 2007. That move saw him graduate from snapping midfielder to more full-on attacker and, despite featuring for only half the season, he finished his first Premiership campaign as Everton's top scorer. He is the only Everton player since Dixie Dean to score for Everton in three Anfield derbies.

Name: Timothy Joel Cahill
Position: Midfielder
Caps: 37
Goals: 19
Team: Everton
Date of birth: 6 December 1979
Height: 178 cm/5 ft 10 in
Weight: 68 kg/150 lb
Previous clubs: Millwall
International debut: 30 March 2004 v South Africa
Previous World Cups: 2006

STYLE GUIDE

Cahill is a free-scoring, box-to-box workhorse of a midfielder. His nickname is Tiny Tim but he performs way above his physique. He can muscle past defenders on surging 'Cahill Expressway' runs from midfield or battle it out with centre halves in the penalty area to score with his head.

LEFT AND TOP RIGHT *Cahill in action during Australia's World Cup qualifier against Japan in June 2009: (left) getting the better of Marcus Tulio Tanaka and (top right) celebrating his second goal, in a 2–1 victory, with teammate Lucas Neil.*

Harry Kewell

If you want Aussie flair, Harry Kewell is the one to watch. At 17 years 7 months, Kewell was the youngest player to represent his country and while with Liverpool he became the only Australia-born player to win a Champions League medal. South Africa 2010 will be the last chance for the 31-year-old Kewell to make further soccer history. However, he nearly didn't make it, because he seemed a spent force when he left Liverpool in 2008 after an injury-strewn five seasons. His career revived in Turkey with Galatasaray and club form assisted in the fight back to national prominence. Kewell has a forceful personality to go with his skill and speed and his maturity has been recognized. Unusually for a midfielder-cum-winger, he was appointed national team captain and he turned in some winning performances during the successful qualifying campaign. In South Africa this talented player will be going flat out to add to his list of career achievements.

Cahill was born in Sydney; his father is of Irish descent and his mother is Samoan. Having played for the Samoa youth team when he was 14 years old, he seemed to have scuppered his chances to qualify for his native Australia. After mounting a press and legal campaign that matched his determined playing style, Cahill persuaded FIFA to register him for Australia and he made his full international debut at the late age of 25. That was in a friendly against South Africa.

South Africa beckons once again, and Cahill will be a fully fledged star on his summer 2010 trip. When he scores – as he almost inevitably will – he'll treat the global TV audience to his famous celebration: the shirt badge goes into his mouth; he runs to the corner; he punches the corner flag in an exuberant release of aggression. In 2008, an alternative celebration earned him censure after he mimicked being handcuffed in tribute to his brother who had recently been jailed for grievous bodily harm.

One way or another, and most likely as a goal scorer, Tim Cahill is bound to hit the World Cup headlines.

SERBIA

GROUP D

Balkan politics meant that Serbians played for Yugoslavia until 2003, then for Serbia and Montenegro until the last World Cup, and only now as Serbia. National excitement could not be running higher.

It is a tradition of World Cup finals that Balkan teams arrive promising much and then fizzle out in unattractive combinations of mean defending and meagre goal scoring. The manager Radomir Antić, star of the current set-up, is someone who has the ability to break that grim footballing heritage. He can only do better than Germany 2006 when Serbia and Montenegro qualified strongly but disappeared in the finals with three defeats in three games.

Antić came out of retirement to take over his national team in 2008. Older British fans will remember him as Raddy Antić, the Luton Town defender who, in 1983, scored the last-gasp winner against Manchester City, his famous goal simultaneously saving Luton from relegation and condemning City to the drop. Antić's managerial career provided even more drama and he is the only person to have managed Barcelona, Real Madrid, and Atlético Madrid.

Political redefinition has resulted in Antić losing several old hands from Montenegro in a squad that has fewer players from the 2006 campaign than any other country and now has an entirely new attack. Serbia's two best-known players are the captain Dejan Stanković of Inter Milan and Nemanja Vidić of Manchester United. On his day, Stanković's midfield versatility and shooting power makes him a match winner. Vidić is the more reliable performer and his pacy positional sense qualifies him as one of the top defenders in the world.

Antić has the reputation of bringing on new talent. A couple of names to look out for when Serbia arrive in South Africa are Neven Subotić in defence, who plays for Borussia Dortmund and was brought up in the United States, and the skilful left winger Zoran Tošić, who is on the fringes of the Manchester United squad.

ABOVE *Raddy the player is a legend in Luton and Radomir the manager has many Spanish friends. Is Mr Antić the national coach on track to become a Hero of the Serbian people?*

ABOVE *Dejan Stanković vies for midfield control with the Ukraine's Yevgen Levchenko. In South Africa, the Inter Milan star could unlock defences and give Serbia's lesser-known forwards the chance to plunder a goal.*

RIGHT *Serbia v France, World Cup qualifying match, Belgrade, 9 September 2009: (back row, left to right) Stojković, Vidić, Luković, Miljaš, Ivanović, Stanković; (front row) Krasić, Jovanović, Kačar, Žigić, Obradović.*

POSSIBLE SQUAD

Goalkeepers

Vladimir Dišljenković (Metalurg Donetsk), Bojan Isailović (Cukarički Stankom), Vladimir Stojković (Getafe)

Defenders

Ivica Dragutinović (Sevilla), Branislav Ivanović (Chelsea), Aleksandar Kolarov (Lazio), Aleksandar Luković (Udinese), Ivan Obradović (Zaragoza), Antonio Rukavina (1860 Munchen), Neven Subotić (Borussia Dortmund), Nemanja Vidić (Manchester United)

Midfielders

Boško Janković (Genoa), Gojko Kačar (Hertha BSC), Miloš Krasić (CSKA Moscow), Zdravko Kuzmanović (Stuttgart), Nenad Milijaš (Wolverhampton Wanderers), Dejan Stanković (C) (Internazionale), Zoran Tošić (Manchester United)

Forwards

Milan Jovanović (Standard Liège), Danko Lazović (PSV Eindhoven), Marko Pantelić (Ajax), Miralem Sulejmani (Ajax), Nikola Žigić (Racing Santander)

ROUTE TO THE FINALS

EUROPE QUALIFYING GROUP 7 – FINAL TABLE

Team	P	W	D	L	F	A	Pts
Serbia	10	7	1	2	22	8	22
France	10	6	3	1	18	9	21
Austria	10	4	2	4	14	15	14
Lithuania	10	4	0	6	10	11	12
Romania	10	3	3	4	12	18	12
Faroe Islands	10	1	1	8	5	20	4

FINALS GROUP D

Serbia play		Date	Venue
★	Ghana	13 June	Tshwane/Pretoria
	Germany	18 June	N. Mandela Bay/Pt Elizabeth
	Australia	23 June	Nelspruit

VITAL STATISTICS

World ranking 20th	Keeper and defence 7/10
Midfield 6/10	Attack 5/10

Strengths and weaknesses Managerial flair and world-class defence will count for nothing unless midfield and attack are at their best.

How far will they go? The form book suggests that strong Balkan qualifiers become weak in the finals. So don't bet on this team to make it past Germany, Australia and Ghana into the second round.

Nemanja Vidić cemented his international reputation as part of the 'Famous Four' Serbian defence that conceded only one goal during the ten-game qualification campaign for the 2006 World Cup.

These international displays helped persuade Manchester United to pay Spartak Moscow £7 million for him in January 2006. Players and fans would all agree this was one of Sir Alex Ferguson's soundest investments. During the 2008–09 season, Vidić started every match in the Premiership-record run of 14 consecutive clean sheets. His defensive partnership with Rio Ferdinand has brought Manchester United three consecutive Premier League titles, the Champions League, the World Club Cup and two League Cup medals. Vidić won the Barclays Player of the Season award in 2009 and has been in Professional Footballers' Association team of the year sides from 2007 to 2009.

Sir Alex Ferguson compares Vidić to another top defender: 'Vida has the courage of Steve Bruce. Brucie would always stick his head in and ask the question of the forward: "Are you brave enough to stick your head in too?" '

Vidić occasionally sticks his head in for goals from set pieces but this is not his main strength. In South Africa, Serbia will look to him to put in consistently excellent challenges on the ground and in the air. Age and experience have brought out an organizer's streak in Vidić and he will also be important marshalling his side from the back and sliding through the telling pass to his midfielders.

'Vida' has become a Manchester United cult figure, and fans have a good line in Vida jokes: he does not sleep, he waits; when he ate an entire bottle of sleeping pills, it only made him blink; he once ate a whole cake before his friends could tell him there was a stripper in it; he puts the laughter in manslaughter; when Vidić exercises, the machine gets stronger.

PLAYER FACT FILE

Name: Nemanja Vidić
Position: Defender
Caps: 44
Goals: 2
Team: Manchester United
Date of birth: 21 October 1981
Height: 188 cm/6 ft 2 in
Weight: 84 kg/185 lb
Previous clubs: Red Star Belgrade, Spartak Moscow
International debut: 12 October 2002 v Italy
Previous World Cups: 2006

STYLE GUIDE

Vidić is a master of the perfectly timed last-ditch tackle. His undoubted aggression is kept under close control and he has one of the best disciplinary records of any international centre half. His game is more than that of efficient stopper because he is a smart distributor who can turn defence into immediate counter-attack.

> **Against Wigan I saw the best centre-half display I have seen for years in Nemanja Vidić. We have had a lot of standout performers, players who have all done well, but Vidić is exceptional.**

SIR ALEX FERGUSON
MANCHESTER UNITED
MANAGER

RIGHT *Nemanja Vidić (right) vies with Chelsea's Nicolas Anelka during Serbia's World Cup qualifier against France at Belgrade's Marakana Stadium, 9 September 2009.*

GHANA

GROUP D

Ghana, also known as the Black Stars, are star turns on their own continent having won the Africa Cup of Nations four times. This is their second successive appearance in the World Cup finals.

In 2006, Ghana was the only African side to advance beyond the group stages, with famous victories over the Czech Republic and the United States. The nation went wild with anticipation but fate didn't favour them for their star player, Michael Essien, was suspended and the draw put them up against Brazil, who won 3–0.

That team was the youngest of the 2006 World Cup with an average age of under 24. The key players are still in place and will go to South Africa older, wiser and better practised at club level. The main striker Matthew Amoah plays for Breda while defenders John Mensah and John Paintsil play for Sunderland and Fulham respectively. European club credentials are more impressive in midfield with the key duo of Michael Essien (Chelsea) and Sulley Muntari (Internazionale) having it in their power to dictate the pace of any game. Their inspirational captain, Stephen Appiah, a Juventus star before being transferred to Fenerbahçe, spent much of the qualifying campaign in dispute with the Turkish club, playing only in internationals.

Ghana has traditionally looked to Europe for managerial expertise, recently favouring Balkan hard-nuts to instil the discipline to make the most of the available skills. In 2006, Radomir Dujković led the side; in 2010 the man charged with melding disparate talents into a unit is Milovan Rajevac. Hopes are high for the way he has guided the side into an efficient 4-4-2 line-up that has pushed forward fearlessly during qualifying games.

In October 2009 Ghana won the FIFA Under-20 World Cup in Cairo, beating Brazil to become the first African side to win the tournament. Any team facing the senior team in South Africa will know they'll be in a game.

BELOW LEFT *Air Ghana: Sulley Muntari, a midfield flier for his country and for Internazionale.*

BELOW RIGHT *Fulham's John Paintsil waves the flag for Ghana during the African Nations Cup.*

POSSIBLE SQUAD

Goalkeepers

William Amamoo (Vasalunds IF), Richard Kingson (Wigan Athletic), George Owu (El-Masry)

Defenders

Eric Addo (Roda JC), Harrison Afful (Espérance Sportive de Tunis), Samuel Inkoom (FC Basel), John Mensah (Sunderland), John Paintsil (Fulham), Hans Sarpei (Bayer Leverkusen), Isaac Vorsah (TSG 1899 Hoffenheim)

Midfielders

Anthony Annan (Rosenborg), Stephen Appiah (C) (Bologna), Haminu Dramani (Kuban Krasnodar), Michael Essien (Chelsea), Laryea Kingston (Hearts), Sulley Muntari (Internazionale), Moussa Narry (Auxerre), Agyeman Prempeh Opoku (Al Wahda)

Forwards

Junior Agogo (Apollon Limassol), Emmanuel Agyeman-Badu (Recreativo de Huelva), Asamoah Gyan (Stades Rennais), Quincy Owusu-Abeyie (Spartak Moscow), Prince Tagoe (TSG 1899 Hoffenheim)

ROUTE TO THE FINALS

AFRICA QUALIFYING GROUP D – FINAL TABLE

Team	P	W	D	L	F	A	Pts
Ghana	6	4	1	1	9	3	13
Benin	6	3	1	2	6	6	10
Mali	6	2	3	1	8	7	9
Sudan	6	0	1	5	2	9	1

FINALS GROUP D

Ghana play		Date	Venue
	Serbia	13 June	Tshwane/Pretoria
	Australia	19 June	Rustenburg
	Germany	23 June	Johannesburg (Soccer City)

VITAL STATISTICS

World ranking 37th
Midfield 7/10
Keeper and defence 6/10
Attack 5/10

Strengths and weaknesses The side is more mature than the one that reached the second round in Germany. Also, partisan crowds can be expected to get behind one of the continent's best teams. However, Ghana's big-name players are clustered in midfield and doubts persist about defensive resilience and attacking flair.

How far will they go? Current odds suggest Ghana will come second in Group D. That would put them against England for a place in the quarters.

LEFT *Ghana v Zambia, International friendly, Brisbane Road, London, 12 August 2009: (back row, left to right) Owu, Paintsil, Dramani, Addo, Dicko; (front row) Essien, Afful, Annan, Agogo, Muntari, Inkoom.*

Michael Essien

Michael Essien's skill and commitment have made him a Chelsea local hero and a Ghana national hero. He is the lungs and the brain of his national side, and Ghana's official website lists him as the most internationally well-known Ghanaian after Kofi Annan, the former Secretary-General of the United Nations.

On the pitch, Essien's power and aggression has earned him the nickname 'The Bison'. Off the pitch and he's as likely to be in bed as anywhere else for he claims to build his energy with 14 hours' sleep a day. His box-to-box game demands maximum stamina as he moves up and down the pitch to maintain a tackling, passing, shooting presence. His managers value his contributions: José Mourinho, the man who brought Essien to Chelsea in 2005 for a then club record of £24.4 million, calls him 'multifunctional'; Claude Le Roy, the former Ghana manager, is more lyrical in his praise: 'Michael is not a normal player, he is from another planet.'

On planet football, Michael Essien will do as requested and function consistently above the norm. At Chelsea, he has often been instructed to sit deep and hold a position on the right of defence. That doesn't stop him scoring dramatic goals from outside the box, most notably the late equalizer against Arsenal which fans voted as Chelsea Goal of the Season for 2006–07. For Ghana, he's the main midfielder who occupies the centre of the park and is given more encouragement to advance into scoring positions. This nets him a goal every four games, typical of which was the long-range drive to secure Ghana's World Cup qualification in the 2–0 win against Sudan in September 2009.

Essien served a long international apprenticeship starting with a star role at the 2001 World Youth Championship in Argentina. By the 2006 World Cup in Germany he was central to Ghana's progress to the second round but was suspended for the second-round defeat against Brazil. In driving Ghana to the Africa Cup of Nations' 2008 semi-final, he was perhaps the tournament's most outstanding player – he approaches South Africa 2010 in his prime.

> **❝ It is clear to me that Michael Essien is one of the best midfield players in the world. ❞**
>
> LUIZ FELIPE SCOLARI
> FORMER BRAZIL, PORTUGAL
> AND CHELSEA MANAGER

PLAYER FACT FILE

Name: Michael Kojo Essien
Position: Midfielder
Caps: 74
Goals: 10
Team: Chelsea
Date of birth: 3 December 1982
Height: 178 cm/5 ft 10 in
Weight: 84 kg/185 lb
Previous clubs: Bastia, Lyon
International debut: 21 January 2002
v Morocco
Previous World Cups: 2006

STYLE GUIDE

Tough in the tackle, precise in the pass and with a shattering shot, Michael Essien is an all-round midfielder who excels in defence and attack. His style is one of controlled aggression and in most games he achieves his stated aim of 'unsettling' his opponents. Premiership fans who are used to watching him play for Chelsea admire a defence-minded midfielder who will occasionally advance from the right to unleash powerful goal attempts from distance. Ghana's supporters see him operate at the hub of the national side and expect the regular bursts he makes into the final third of the pitch.

NETHERLANDS

GROUP E

The *Oranjes* are known for 'total football', plus a wonderful roll call of past talent. It is a credible claim that the present Dutch stars can win what the Dutch have never won before.

BELOW *Winners. The team gathers to congratulate Eljero Elia (third from left) after he had scored the single goal that won the match against Scotland at Hampden Park in September 2009. Scotland were squeezed out of the play-offs and the Netherlands kept their unbeaten qualifying record intact.*

Johan Cruyff, Frank Rijkaard, Ruud Gullit ... names such as these prove that the Netherlands is a production line for soccer talent, much of it for export to high-paying customers around the world. Flying Dutchmen have consistently featured as flair players and managers for top European clubs. Guus Hiddink, Pim Verbeek and Dick Advocaat have gone one better and added to their reputations in the role of miracle-working managers for nations such as South Korea and Australia. The Netherlands has one of the world's most distinctive and sophisticated football cultures, and it is surely the best nation never to have won the World Cup.

Successive generations of world-stage nearly men have played a brand of precision-passing *totaalvoetbal* ('total football') that once had the Dutch team nicknamed Clockwork Orange. The *Oranjes* reached two finals in the 1970s against West Germany and Argentina but from the 1980s a tradition of misdirected player power went foot in boot with free-flowing skills. Dutch teams fought their managers and each other during decades of World Cup underachievement including a failure to qualify in 2002. In 2006 they lost 1–0 to Portugal in the second-round 'Battle of Nuremberg', a match that produced a record 16 yellow and 4 red cards.

GREAT MATCH
1993 Holland 2–0 England

World Cup, group qualifying stage
Feyenoord Stadium, Rotterdam, Netherlands

The contention of a game full of incident and disputed decisions began with Frank Rijkaard's first half disallowed goal which TV replays proved had been clearly onside.

Holland gradually outmuscled England's midfield and things reached a boiling point 15 minutes into the second half. Ronald Koeman's foul on David Platt prevented a goal-scoring chance and arguably merited a red card. Two minutes later, at the other end of the pitch, Paul Ince fouled Jan Wouters and was then booked for encroachment when Koeman took the free kick. Koeman curled the retaken free kick past David Seaman to put his side a goal up. Moments later, a Paul Merson shot hit the Dutch crossbar, and Dennis Bergkamp's goal after seven minutes' more breathless action finished the game.

Meanwhile Graham Taylor, the England manager, was being filmed on the touchline for the documentary *An Impossible Job*. The cameras documented Taylor's impotent fury when the referee failed to send Koeman off and then booked Ince. A new phrase became cemented into the language.

RIGHT *The figure sprawled face down at the bottom of the photo is David Platt. The bruiser in orange is Ronald Koeman who has just pinched the ball having clattered into Platt to deny the England midfielder a clear chance on goal.*

> **Pressuring is not the same as running forward with seven players. It's suicide. Your defence has to play one-on-one with heaps of space behind them.**
>
> BERT VAN MARWIJK

BELOW *Wesley Sneijder roars in to smash home goal number two in the Netherlands' 3–0 demolition of Italy at Euro 2008. Italy's Antonio Di Natale could only stand and watch. The Netherlands will be looking for more of the same in South Africa.*

There's a new Dutch name to consider, and one not much known outside his home country. Bert van Marwijk, appointed national team manager in 2008, is a straight-talking realist whose long career in football has largely been in the Netherlands. He led a talented group of players through a flawless winning run of qualifying games for the 2010 competition. In the process, van Marwijk has moved away from *totaalvoetbal* pitching his tactics in a more predictable and less fluid direction. The Dutch coach is a new sporting realist who puts industry ahead of artistry. 'Space is getting scarcer and the players are stronger and faster,' he says. 'Today's football teams are very well organized and disciplined. Wingers get double marking for instance. They have to take on two defenders now to cross the ball in and there's hardly time for a dribble or a one-to-one action.'

If all-out attack has become more difficult in the modern game, so too has defence. As van Marwijk points out, 'Twenty or thirty years ago, full backs were the lesser players of the team. Nowadays, there are no weak links anymore. With national teams, it's even harder since you don't get time to gel a good solid team together. Pressuring is not the same as running forward with seven players. It's suicide. Your defence has to play one-on-one with heaps of space behind them.'

The world's best theories depend on practitioners and with players like Dirk Kuyt, Nigel de Jong, Arjen Robben, Wesley Sneijder, Rafael van der Vaart and Robin van Persie at the peak of their game Holland's chances are good. Team spirit is high for van Marwijk (unlike many of his predecessors) does not believe in introducing the insecurities involved in squad rotation. He has stuck with a small squad which has obeyed a more fixed tactical approach than the classic losers who have gone before. 'This team needs to grow towards a peak performance,' van Marwijk says. 'We need to keep the sharpness consistent over at least seven games. That is what a big tournament requires. We need stability and consistency. Every game counts, whether it's a friendly, training match or the real deal. We don't want to play around or embarrass ourselves. You play how you train and you train how you play. Simple.'

COACH **Bert van Marwijk**

Born: 19 May 1952
Record: P16, W9, D5, L2

When Bert van Marwijk took up the Dutch managerial post after Euro 2008, he didn't seem to have the track record to replace the legendary Marco van Basten. His footballing achievements were relatively modest with one international cap as a winger and a UEFA Cup managerial medal with Feyenoord in 2002. There were doubts about his ability to deal with egos inflated by stardom and doubts about his tactical sophistication.

Van Marwijk turned out to have a wise footballing brain and his systematic approach has earned the success to dispel doubts. As the testing time in South Africa approaches, he's in a strong enough position to concede that coaching systems can't take a team all the way. 'You need players who can pace the game, so everybody complies. You learn that on the street. Today, players who can do this are immediately called brilliant players. Liverpool has only one player who can do it: Gerrard. Chelsea has Lampard. AC Milan has Pirlo. Xavi does it for Barca. In today's Oranje, I think typical street-players like van Bommel, Sneijder and van Persie still have that leadership. And I can still see them in the youth. Afellay, Wijnaldum, Daley Blind, Siem de Jong ...'

ROUTE TO THE FINALS

MATCHES PLAYED

10.09.08	FYR Macedonia 1	2 Netherlands
11.10.08	Netherlands 2	0 Iceland
15.10.08	Norway 0	1 Netherlands
28.03.09	Netherlands 3	0 Scotland
01.04.09	Netherlands 4	0 FYR Macedonia
06.06.09	Iceland 1	2 Netherlands
10.06.09	Netherlands 2	0 Norway
09.09.09	Scotland 0	1 Netherlands

EUROPE QUALIFYING GROUP 9 – FINAL TABLE

Team	P	W	D	L	F	A	Pts
Netherlands	8	8	0	0	17	2	24
Norway	8	2	4	2	9	7	10
Scotland	8	3	1	4	6	11	10
FYR Macedonia	8	2	1	5	5	11	7
Iceland	8	1	2	5	7	13	5

FINALS GROUP E

Netherlands play		Date	Venue
	Denmark	14 June	Johannesburg (Soccer City)
	Japan	19 June	Durban
	Cameroon	24 June	Cape Town

VITAL STATISTICS

World ranking 3rd	Keeper and defence 8/10
Midfield 7/10	Attack 7/10

Strengths and weaknesses There's as much raw talent in the Dutch training camp as in any previous World Cup campaign and the side could overcome a reputation as World Cup also-rans if it sticks to a duller set of tactics than in the past. The players must also avoid an old tendency to lose discipline and even fall out among themselves.

How far will they go? New defensive strengths could take the team to a semi-final appearance. First, there's a tough group because the Danes, the Japanese and the Cameroonians won't be overawed by Holland's star-studded squad.

HOW THEY'LL LINE UP

Bert van Marwijk has abandoned the old explosive 4-3-3 formations for a more cautious approach. 'The disappearance of Dutch School football is inevitable,' is the view he has acted on. In South Africa, he aims for midfield control to deny space in the centre of the pitch. His teams are drilled to stand off opposing back four passing players and to apply pressure when the ball reaches midfield. His players tend to step back when they lose possession, but try not to huddle up in their own box. The idea is for them to play compactly and maintain pressure by keeping the spaces tight.

POSSIBLE SQUAD

Goalkeepers

Maarten Stekelenburg (Ajax), Henk Timmer (Unattached), Michel Vorm (Utrecht)

Defenders

Khalid Boulahrouz (Stuttgart), Edson Braafheid (Bayern Munich), Giovanni van Bronckhorst (C) (Feyenoord), John Heitinga (Everton), Dirk Marcellis (PSV Eindhoven), Joris Mathijsen (Hamburg), André Ooijer (PSV Eindhoven), Gregory van der Wiel (Ajax)

Midfielders

Ibrahim Afellay (PSV Eindhoven), Mark van Bommel (Bayern Munich), Nigel de Jong (Manchester City), David Mendes da Silva (AZ), Stijn Schaars (AZ), Wesley Sneijder (Real Madrid), Rafael van der Vaart (Real Madrid)

Forwards

Ryan Babel (Liverpool), Klaas-Jan Huntelaar (Milan), Dirk Kuyt (Liverpool), Robin van Persie (Arsenal), Arjen Robben (Real Madrid)

BELOW *Netherlands v England, International friendly, Amsterdam Arena, 12 August 2009: (back row, left to right) Kuyt, Stekelenburg, Mathijsen, Heitinga, Ooijer; (front row) van Persie, de Jong, Schaars, van der Vaart, Robben, Braafheid.*

Dirk Kuyt

He netted three goals in the 2010 World Cup qualifiers and, in a drawn summer 2009 friendly against England, snapped up a Rio Ferdinand back pass to bag another. England be warned.

Every Premiership fan knows that Dirk Kuyt's line is not really scoring but to make the opposition's life difficult. Kuyt's own rating of his best match was Holland's World Cup qualifying clincher over the Czech Republic in 2006, a game in which he didn't score but instead had the Czech defence reeling as he set up both goals.

Kuyt is the son of a fisherman and would have followed his father's trade had he not scaled football's heights. He made his international debut in 2004 and was in the starting line-up for most of the 2006 World Cup qualifiers before struggling for a place during the finals. That summer, Kuyt was a star catch for Liverpool when Feyenoord sold him for a reported £9 million. Since then, he has been a regular for club and country, skating up and down the right wing, favoured for his crossing and angled runs in attack, for his tireless tackling and for his selfless tracking back.

PLAYER FACT FILE

Name: Dirk Kuyt
Position: Forward
Caps: 59
Goals: 13
Team: Liverpool
Date of birth: 22 July 1980
Height: 184 cm/6 ft
Weight: 77 kg/170 lb
Previous clubs: Utrecht, Feyenoord
International debut: 3 September 2004 v Liechtenstein
Previous World Cups: 2006

STYLE GUIDE

Kuyt is a striker who can play on the right or down the middle. His work rate alone ensures he is a danger in the box, taking advantage of situations where the keeper has blocked or parried a shot and the ball is loose. He is always ready for the second ball when it drops.

RIGHT *The direct play of Dirk Kuyt makes him a winner. He is pictured here putting in a tackle on England's Gareth Barry during a friendly at the Amsterdam Arena in summer 2009.*

He casts himself as the people's friend with his Dirk Kuyt Foundation to help disadvantaged children and his habit at the end of games of visiting each corner of the pitch to applaud the fans. Perhaps he fishes for compliments, perhaps he applauds because he knows it's such hard work just watching him. Yet for all his frenetic activity, Kuyt has a cool head and is a penalty specialist calm enough to have scored from two spot kicks in a 2–1 Merseyside derby.

The Dutch have a long tradition of failure at penalty shoot-outs and at Euro 2000 missed a total of five penalties in the final against Italy. That still rankles. If Kuyt can help save Holland from another such fiasco, the applause will be loud enough to drown the noise of a North Sea gale.

> **"You could call him Mr Duracell, because of the way he plays, always running and always on the go. "**
>
> RAFAEL BENÍTEZ
> LIVERPOOL MANAGER

Arjen Robben

Has boots – will travel – and travel at speed. Arjen Robben belongs firmly to the Johan Cruyff and Marc Overmars tradition of thrilling left-sided Dutch players.

Robben is at the top of his game and yet, like his countryman Wes Sneidjer, he faced rejection when Real Madrid bought Kaká and Ronaldo in summer 2009. The former Chelsea and PSV Eindhoven star wasn't about to jeopardize his World Cup chance by warming a substitute's bench in Spain and immediately transferred to Bayern Munich for €25 million. He scored twice on his Bundesliga debut.

Robben was born in 1984 and – like the rest of the Dutch team – was too young to witness Dutch *totaalvoetbal*. He was educated in a less fluid and more systematic tradition of play called the Coerver Method after the Dutch football coach Wiel Coerver. This approach holds that excellent play can be taught and the young Robben was drilled in the basics of individual ball control and teamwork. Coerver's analysis is that top-flight football comprises a series of movements involving a small number of players: one on one; one on two; two on two; and so on. Practising and linking these component moves makes for an efficient footballing mechanism. Coerverism is big in Japan and the styles will meet in the group match on 19 June.

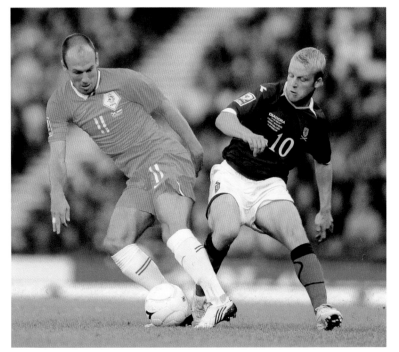

PLAYER FACT FILE

Name: Arjen Robben
Position: Forward
Caps: 45
Goals: 11
Team: Bayern Munich
Date of birth: 23 January 1984
Height: 180 cm/5 ft 11 in
Weight: 75 kg/165 lb
Previous clubs: Groningen, PSV Eindhoven, Chelsea, Real Madrid
International debut: 6 September 2003 v Austria
Previous World Cups: 2006

STYLE GUIDE
Typically, Robben makes forceful advances from left midfield to the byeline but he is comfortable as an inside left, or second striker, or even on the right. Whatever position he takes up, he has a devastating turn of speed.

LEFT *Arjen Robben retains possession and swerves away from Scotland's Steven Naismith during the World Cup qualifier in Glasgow.*

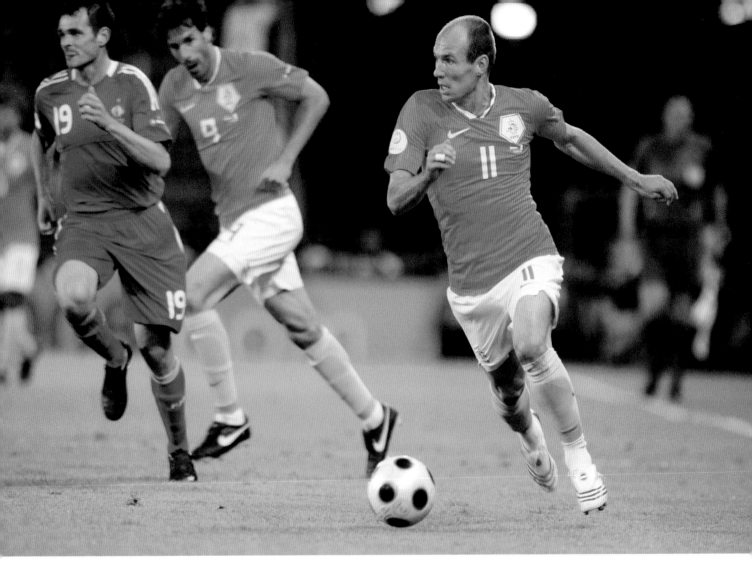

Coerverism is football recast in the terms of management theory and there's something of the young executive about Robben as he sets about another day's businesslike toil on the pitch. He has a face that seems made for a collar and tie and there's an earnestness to even his most exciting passages of play. The sheer focus has reaped dividends for his country. At the 2006 World Cup against Serbia and Montenegro, Robben scored the winning goal and was man of the match. He received the award a second time against Côte d'Ivoire.

It's tough at the top and at Euro 2008 Robben had to battle against Robin van Persie for his place on the left. Both are versatile players and the current manager, Bert van Marwijk, accommodated each man in the last two World Cup qualifying games against Scotland and Norway. It's a fair bet that both will figure in the *Oranje* starting line-ups in South Africa. It's a fair bet, too, that Arjen Robben, the serious boy who stayed on at school to finish his studies, will eventually turn from flying Dutch winger to flying Dutch manager.

> ❝ **Robben is the best winger in the world.** ❞
>
> RUUD GULLIT
> NETHERLANDS INTERNATIONAL
> 1981–94

Wesley Sneidjer

It must be odd to be one of the best footballers in the world – good enough, indeed, for your fellow countrymen to liken you to Dennis Bergkamp – and yet to face rejection.

That's what happened to Wesley Sneijder in the summer of 2009 when Real Madrid bought Kaká for £56 million and Ronaldo for £80 million. Sneijder fell from being Real's number ten to numero zero. Cue for José Mourinho's Internazionale to snap up Sneijder for a knockdown fee of around £15 million; cue also for Sneijder to prove he's still up with the best.

> " The last Dutch number ten at Inter was Bergkamp. He was an amazing player with lots of qualities ... and ... I hope I can do something of what he did. "
>
> WESLEY SNEIJDER

FAR LEFT AND LEFT *Wesley Sneijder demonstrated his physical balance and his eye for the ball throughout a Netherlands qualification campaign that saw them winning all eight games and conceding a mere two goals.*

On moving from Spain to Italy, he immediately played a role in the 4–0 derby win over AC Milan and then, in October 2009, scored his first Internazionale goal, a 92nd-minute winner in the 2–1 victory over Udinese. Sneijder, in short order, found himself a new home in Italy and earned himself another number ten shirt.

Back in Sneijder's native Holland, the Bergkamp comparison still stands. Think of the former Dutch master with added fight and running. Both are dead-ball specialists who can hit inspired passes in open play and advance from midfield into scoring positions. Both can hit spectacularly intuitive volleyed goals. Like Bergkamp, Sneijder honed his talents through the Ajax youth system and played for his local team before moving overseas. And, like Bergkamp, he's a natural-born midfield general who wears the *Oranjes* number ten shirt.

Wesley Sneijder made his Netherlands debut before his 19th birthday and within a year was scoring goals in the Euro 2004 qualifying matches. He appeared twice as substitute in the Netherlands' final run to the 2004 semi-finals and started all four games for the Netherlands at the 2006 FIFA World Cup in Germany. At Euro 2008, Sneijder marked his 24th birthday with a remarkable goal in the 3–0 rout of Italy, receiving a headed ball from Dirk Kuyt and volleying it with an acrobatic grace past Gianluigi Buffon.

For *Oranjes* following their fancied side through their South Africa 2010 adventure, only more of Sneijder's best will be good enough.

PLAYER FACT FILE

Name: Wesley Benjamin Sneijder
Position: Midfielder
Caps: 56
Goals: 12
Team: Internazionale
Date of birth: 9 June 1984
Height: 170 cm/5 ft 7½ in
Weight: 67 kg/148 lb
Previous clubs: Ajax, Real Madrid
International debut: 30 April 2003 v Portugal
Previous World Cups: 2006

STYLE GUIDE

Wesley Sneijder is an attacking midfielder who is equally comfortable kicking with left or right foot. His passing range is imaginative and he's capable of opening out a pitch that appears crowded with a single through ball. Though small, he is strong in possession and he hits a mean free kick.

Robin van Persie has played on the left and right wing for his country. While van Persie's stylish versatility recalls the *totaalvoetbal* of an earlier era, a barely controlled volatility also makes him something of a Dutch throwback.

Van Persie's 2010 World Cup place seemed in jeopardy when Bert van Marwijk was appointed national coach. The pair fell out at Feyenoord, when van Marwijk was van Persie's manager, and the rift culminated in 2004 when Arsenal secured a star player's services for a knockdown £2.75 million.

Despite injuries, the move to Arsenal has been a success. He was voted Arsenal's player of the season in 2009 and his control and skill have had Arsenal fans comparing him to Dennis Bergkamp. There is no higher praise. As another sublimely talented Dutch player to pull on the Arsenal shirt, van Persie really proved himself in January 2009 when he either scored or assisted every Arsenal goal that month.

Name: Robin van Persie
Position: Midfielder
Caps: 41
Goals: 14
Team: Arsenal
Date of birth: 6 August 1983
Height: 183 cm/6 ft
Weight: 71 kg/157 lb
Previous clubs: Feyenoord
International debut: 4 June 2005 v Romania
Previous World Cups: 2006

STYLE GUIDE

An elegant and explosive player, van Persie is an attacking midfielder who is a skilled provider with the ability to score spectacular goals. A trademark van Persie manoeuvre is to move from left to right of the pitch and then to cut inside to fire in a shot with his favoured left foot. He is also a dead-ball expert whose calmness at penalties, free kicks and right-sided corners is offset by the flares of bad temper that have given him a patchy disciplinary record.

LEFT *Robin van Persie goes eye to eye with Scotland's Darren Fletcher during the final game of Holland's unbeaten run of World Cup qualifiers.*

RIGHT *Van Persie spatchcocks Sweden's goalkeeper, Andreas Isaksson, for a headed goal in a friendly match.*

'Robin has a great left foot and is a great passer with excellent vision,' says Arsène Wenger, his club manager. Wenger has nurtured van Persie's talents as a goal scorer and that has benefited his country too. Van Persie scored a headed goal in a World Cup qualifying match against Scotland, which had Dutch fans wondering whether van Persie should be taking corners or receiving them.

Assuming that Bert van Marwijk can keep his talented charge under control, events in South Africa 2010 should answer the question of whether Robin van Persie will go down in Dutch football history as a goal provider or goal grabber. Or perhaps both.

> " He can play on the left side of midfield, as a creative player behind the main strikers or as a target man. "
>
> ARSÈNE WENGER
> ARSENAL MANAGER

DENMARK

GROUP E

ABOVE *6 June 2009: striker Nicklas Bendtner (left) shares the moment as jubilant Thomas Kahlenberg celebrates his winning goal against Scandinavian rivals Sweden.*

The Danes are said to be the happiest nation in the world. They play a happy brand of football to match and will be supported in South Africa by an army of cheerful fans.

Denmark won the 1992 European Cup final and reached the World Cup quarter-finals against Brazil in 1998. These triumphs are long gone. The team did not qualify for the last European or World Cups and it has been a long time since football fans have been able to anticipate the spectacle of watching this attractive team punch above its weight. That said, England supporters might recall friendly matches that had the Danes beating England 4–1 in 2005 (the biggest margin of defeat since 1980) and 3–2 in 2003.

The roll-call of former Danish stars who have played relaxed football with a smile includes Allan Simonsen, brothers Michael and Brian Laudrup, Peter Schmeichel and Morten Olsen. Olsen, the team captain who played 102 games for Denmark between 1970 and 1989, has been the Denmark manager since 2000.

The Olsen Gang has generally favoured an attacking style, exploiting the midfield passing skills of Christian Poulsen to unleash the speed of Jesper Grønkjær and Dennis Rommedahl on the wings. All are aged 30 or above and much will depend on two younger players who have done well in the English Premiership. Daniel Agger is a reliable defender for Liverpool and Arsenal fans know all about the attacking skills of the tall and powerful Nicklas Bendtner. Both are products of Olsen's insistence on youth coaching and part of a 'red thread' of talent that has been nurtured in Danish national youth teams.

Another thing to watch for in South Africa are the cheerful and easy-going Danish fans, also known as *roligans*. *Rolig* is Danish for calm and the gentle pun pokes fun at the rabid hooligan. Denmark is a civilized nation that values style and continuity over results and was prepared to wait for Olsen to lead his team in the successful qualifying campaign for World Cup 2010. Whatever happens, Olsen will retire in 2010 and his likely replacement is his long-time assistant Michael Laudrup.

ABOVE *Winger Dennis Rommedahl, Danish Footballer of the Year in 2007, vies for the ball with Sweden's Olof Mellberg.*

POSSIBLE SQUAD

Goalkeepers

Stephan Andersen (Brøndby), Jesper Christiansen (Copenhagen), Thomas Sørensen (Stoke City)

Defenders

Daniel Agger (Liverpool), Anders Møller Christensen (OB), Michael Gravgaard (FC Nantes), Lars Jacobsen (Blackburn Rovers), Simon Kjær (Palermo), Kristian Bak Nielsen (Heerenveen), Simon Poulsen (AZ)

Midfielders

Thomas Augustinussen (Red Bull Salzburg), Martin Bergvold (Livorno), Thomas Kahlenberg (VfL Wolfsburg), William Kvist (Copenhagen), Christian Poulsen (Juventus), Jakob Poulsen (AGF), Michael Silberbauer (Utrecht)

Forwards

Nicklas Bendtner (Arsenal), Martin Bernburg (Brøndby), Martin Jørgensen (Fiorentina), Morten Nordstrand (Groningen), Dennis Rommedahl (AFC Ajax), Jon Dahl Tomasson (C) (Feyenoord)

ROUTE TO THE FINALS

EUROPE QUALIFYING GROUP 1 – FINAL TABLE

Team	P	W	D	L	F	A	Pts
Denmark	10	6	3	1	16	5	21
Portugal	10	5	4	1	17	5	19
Sweden	10	5	3	2	13	5	18
Hungary	10	5	1	4	10	8	16
Albania	10	1	4	5	6	13	7
Malta	10	0	1	9	0	26	1

FINALS GROUP E

Denmark play		Date	Venue
	Netherlands	14 June	Johannesburg (Soccer City)
	Cameroon	19 June	Tshwane/Pretoria
	Japan	24 June	Rustenburg

VITAL STATISTICS

World ranking 26th   Keeper and defence 6/10
Midfield 6/10   Attack 6/10

Strengths and weaknesses Consistent management has achieved a stability that could have this team go far. Too much, however, rests on the talents of a few ageing players.

How far will they go? The Danes will have to surpass themselves if they are to beat the Netherlands and Cameroon into the next round.

LEFT Denmark v Sweden, World Cup qualifying match, Rasunda Stadium, Stockholm, Sweden, 6 June 2009: (back row, left to right) Sørensen, Agger, Bendtner, Kjær, Kahlenberg, Kvist; (front row) Jørgensen, Rommedahl, Jacobsen, Jakob Poulsen, Christian Poulsen.

Christian Poulsen

Christian Poulsen is nothing if not a trier. He's a national favourite, though less cheerful in his playing style than Denmark's *roligans*, the anti-hooligan travelling fans.

In fact there's a touch of the troublemaker in Poulsen, for he presents himself as the hard face of Danish football and as a player who is scared of no player or reputation. His countrymen are no softies either and recognize him as a winner, whose presence is Denmark's greatest hope in South Africa.

An un-Christian mean streak to the rough-cut Dane's raw competitiveness has spilled over into aggressive indiscipline, notably in an all-Scandinavian spat when he punched the Swedish striker Markus Rosenberg in the stomach. This sparked off crowd trouble, the match was forfeited to Sweden, and Denmark were fined and forced to play their next four home Euro 2008 qualification matches away from Copenhagen. A three-game suspension added to Poulsen's patchy disciplinary record.

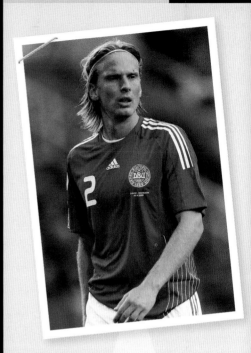

LEFT AND RIGHT *Poulsen imposing himself on Deco during Denmark's World Cup qualifying match against Portugal on 5 September 2009 at the Parken Stadium in Copenhagen . . . and receiving the red-card treatment against Sweden during Euro 2008.*

Nonetheless, Poulsen has remained an automatic and popular choice for his country. His two-footed passing ability supplements the physical stuff and, though able to operate in deep right-sided positions, he usually plays at the centre of the park. Denmark's tactics revolve around his charismatic presence and he was key to an early World Cup qualification from a strong group that included Portugal and Sweden.

A European career as a football nomad in Germany, Spain and Italy has helped to build Poulsen's international career. As a young man he turned down the chance of Premiership football in Birmingham in favour of a four-year stint in the Bundesliga with FC Schalke 04. He then helped Sevilla win the 2007 UEFA Cup and moved to Juventus in 2008. Not everything has run smoothly in Poulsen's career because he fell out of favour at Juventus and had to show the determined side of his character when he resisted his manager's attempts to transfer him and was subsequently reinstated in the Serie A team.

> **66 My dream is to surprise the public and show them that rather than being the unpolished player they perceive me as being I am in fact technically very sound. 99**
>
> CHRISTIAN POULSEN

JAPAN

Having won the Asian Cup three times, Japan is the most successful national Asian team and is now looking forward to their fourth World Cup finals in a row.

ABOVE *Takeshi Okada (in suit, right) proved that attack pays when Japan beat Uzbekistan 1–0 in Tashkent in June 2009 to qualify for South Africa.*

Japan's long-term form on the global stage suggests that significant progress beyond the opening rounds would be a big surprise. There will be goalkeeping heroics from the veteran captain Seigo Narazaki; expect solid and gritty defensive displays led by Yuji Nakazawa; the midfield will impress; and there will be pace in attack. What there won't be, unless the form book is torn up, are goals. Goals are always a problem for Japan and qualification relied on strong defence in 1–0 victories over Uzbekistan and then Bahrain, despite the new manager, Takeshi Okada, moving to a more attack-minded 4-3-3 formation in the latter game.

Japan has turned inwards in the push for footballing success in 2010. Most players are home-based in the J-League and experiments with three successive foreign managers (Philippe Troussier 2000–02, Zico 2002–06 and Ivica Osim 2006–08) ended with the appointment of Takeshi Okada. He had had the job during the 1998 World Cup, and his record is that of a defensive minded disciplinarian who finds it difficult to make room for unpredictable talents.

Japan's hopes rest on an unpredictable and fluid midfield, inspired by the accuracy and invention of Shunsuke Nakamura's left foot. During the later qualifying stages, Japan's only current international star was out of favour with Okada. A return to form for Celtic earned Nakamura a recall for the Kirin Cup tournament, which Japan won in May 2009. The following month Nakamura moved from Celtic to Espanyol. Okada, who had attracted criticism from the Japanese press for his dull tactics, said: 'I have realized anew that Nakamura's presence, the accuracy of his play and the fact that he is a player with very high ability to read how the game develops.' If Japan is to realize the hopes raised by its solid record, much will rely on the correct deployment of Nakamura's talents.

ABOVE *Shunsuke Nakamura, Japan's star player, can dictate the pace of play with his trusty left foot.*

RIGHT *Japan v Australia, World Cup qualifying match, Melbourne Cricket Ground, Melbourne, Australia, 17 June 2009: (back row, left to right) Konno, Hashimoto, Abe, Tanaka, Narazaki; (front row) Kengo Nakamura, Nagatomo, Okazaki, Uchida, Matsui, Tamada.*

POSSIBLE SQUAD

Goalkeepers

Eiji Kawashima (Kawasaki Frontale), **Seigo Narazaki** (Nagoya Grampus Eight), **Ryōta Tsuzuki** (Urawa Red Diamonds)

Defenders

Yuichi Komano (Jubilo Iwata), **Yasuyuki Konno** (FC Tokyo), **Tomoaki Makino** (Sanfrecce Hiroshima), **Yuto Nagatomo** (FC Tokyo), **Yuji Nakazawa (C)** (Yokohama F. Marinos), **Marcus Tulio Tanaka** (Urawa Red Diamonds), **Atsuto Uchida** (Kashima Antlers), **Satoshi Yamaguchi** (Gamba Osaka)

Midfielders

Yuki Abe (Urawa Red Diamonds), **Yasuhito Endō** (Gamba Osaka), **Hideo Hashimoto** (Gamba Osaka), **Daisuke Matsui** (Grenoble), **Kengo Nakamura** (Kawasaki Frontale), **Shunsuke Nakamura** (Espanyol), **Naoki Yamada** (Urawa Red Diamonds)

Forwards

Shinzo Koroki (Kashima Antlers), **Masashi Oguru** (Tokyo Verdy), **Shinji Okazaki** (Shimizu S-Pulse), **Keiji Tamada** (Nagoya Grampus Eight), **Kisho Yano** (Albirex Niigata)

ROUTE TO THE FINALS

ASIA QUALIFYING FINAL GROUP 1 – FINAL TABLE

Team	P	W	D	L	F	A	Pts
Australia	8	6	2	0	12	1	20
Japan	8	4	3	1	11	6	15
Bahrain	8	3	1	4	6	8	10
Qatar	8	1	3	4	5	14	6
Uzbekistan	8	1	1	6	5	10	4

FINALS GROUP E

Japan play		Date	Venue
	Cameroon	14 June	Mangaung/Bloemfontein
	Netherlands	19 June	Durban
	Denmark	24 June	Rustenburg

VITAL STATISTICS

World ranking 43rd   Keeper and defence 6/10
Midfield 5/10   Attack 4/10

Strengths and weaknesses The team will be strongest on discipline and weakest on scoring. An in-form midfield could present problems for more star-studded teams.

How far will they go? As the weakest team in a strong group, they won't go far in South Africa.

CAMEROON

GROUP E

Les Lions Indomptables set an African record in reaching the World Cup for the sixth time. It revived memories of earlier exuberant promise.

Cameroon was the first African team to reach the World Cup quarter-finals (in 1990) and the manner of their success suggested that a new African style might be about to imprint itself on football. It hasn't happened yet, though the Lions remained stylish – teams took to the field wearing sleeveless shirts in 2002, then a one-piece playing kit a year later. Illegal, said FIFA, on both occasions. There had been no legislating against Roger Milla's talent and his swaying dance round the corner flag when he scored his goals in the 1980s and 1990s.

Milla was the face of African football at the time, playing on into his forties, and it was a side of oldsters that lurched into the early rounds of qualifying for South Africa 2010, managing just one point after two matches. Cue for a new manager, Paul Le Guen, a French import who started work in July 2009. He appointed Samuel Eto'o as captain in place of the veteran defender Rigobert Song. Late in the day, Le Guen brought on an entirely new face, putting the 19-year-old Nicolas N'Koulou in defence in the emphatic 2–0 win against Morocco that capped off World Cup qualifying. The manager showed further commitment to youth in the likes of Alexandre Song, Landry N'Guémo, Franck Songo'o and Stéphane Mbia.

Their current style is a bit plodding. Aside from the free-scoring Eto'o, Cameroon's big-name European exports are defensive and midfield grafters. They put in well-muscled performances for Le Guen's run of four successive victories, games that were won with hard labour and not much flair. That said, Cameroon could spring a surprise in South Africa. But don't mention penalties: a Gary Lineker penalty decided the fate of their quarter-final appearance in 1990, while every Cameroonian remembers their World Cup qualifier against Egypt in 2006 when an injury-time spot kick would have clinched a passage to Germany. The only man brave enough to step up for it was the left back Pierre Womé. He missed, and retired from the national team soon afterwards.

ABOVE *Paul Le Guen's late appointment to the Cameroon managerial hotseat brought immediate success and looks like a marriage made in heaven.*

ABOVE *Jean Makoun looks indomitable as he eyes the ball during the tense play-off match against Morocco in November 2009.*

POSSIBLE SQUAD

Goalkeepers

Souleymanou Hamidou (Kayserispor), **Idriss Carlos Kameni** (RCD Espanyol), **Joslain Mayhebi** (Beitar Jerusalem)

Defenders

Benoît Assou-Ekotto (Tottenham Hotspur), **Sébastien Bassong** (Tottenham Hotspur), **Henri Bedimo** (Châteauroux), **André Bikey** (Burnley), **Geremi** (Newcastle United), **Nicolas N'Koulou** (Monaco), **Rigobert Song** (Trabzonspor)

Midfielders

Aurélien Chedjou (Lille), **Achille Emana** (Real Betis), **Daniel Ngom Kome** (Tenerife), **Jean Makoun** (Lyon), **Georges Mandjeck** (Kaiserslautern), **Stéphane Mbia** (Marseille), **Landry N'Guémo** (Celtic), **Alexandre Song** (Arsenal), **Somen Tchoyi** (Red Bull Salzburg)

Forwards

Paul Alo'o Efoulou (Nancy), **Samuel Eto'o (C)** (Internazionale), **Albert Meyong** (Sporting Braga), **Pierre Webó** (RCD Mallorca)

ROUTE TO THE FINALS

AFRICA QUALIFYING GROUP A – FINAL TABLE

Team	P	W	D	L	F	A	Pts
Cameroon	6	4	1	1	9	2	13
Gabon	6	3	0	3	9	7	9
Togo	6	2	2	2	3	7	8
Morocco	6	0	3	3	3	8	3

FINALS GROUP E

Cameroon play	Date	Venue
Japan	14 June	Mangaung/Bloemfontein
Denmark	19 June	Tshwane/Pretoria
Netherlands	24 June	Cape Town

VITAL STATISTICS

World ranking 11th   Keeper and defence 6/10
Midfield 5/10   Attack 5/10

Strengths and weaknesses Cameroon are robust in defence and can pounce through Eto'o in attack. Last-gasp managerial reorganization saw them through the qualifiers, but there doesn't seem to be enough backbone for the team to progress far.

How far will they go? The final group game on 24 June is against the Netherlands when the strongest team will most likely emerge as winner of Group E.

LEFT *Cameroon v Morocco, World Cup qualifying match, Fes, Morocco, 14 November 2009: (back row, left to right) Kameni, Rigobert Song, Webó, Assou-Ekotto, Alexandre Song, Eto'o; (front row) Geremi, N'Koulou, Emana, N'Guémo, Makoun.*

Samuel Eto'o

Ten goals in qualification and a newly assumed national captaincy have further cemented the reputation of Samuel Eto'o. He's part of the Cameroonian national scene and, though born in 1981, has been around long enough to seem a veteran.

Samuel Eto's first cap came a day before his 16th birthday on 9 March 1997, in a 5–0 loss to Costa Rica. The following year, in France 1998, he became the youngest player – at 17 years 3 months – to appear in a World Cup finals. He is the leading scorer in the history of the African Nations Cup, with 16 goals. He has won three African Player of the Year awards and finished third in the 2005 FIFA World Player of the Year, making him only the second African to be voted into the top three.

Name: Samuel Eto'o Fils
Position: Forward
Caps: 94
Goals: 44
Team: Internazionale
Date of birth: 10 March 1981
Height: 180 cm/5 ft 11 in
Weight: 75 kg/165 lb
Previous clubs: Real Madrid, Leganés, Espanyol, RCD Mallorca, Barcelona
International debut: 9 March 1997 v Costa Rica
Previous World Cups: 1998, 2002

STYLE GUIDE
The sinewy and athletic Samuel Eto'o is always going for goal. His direct approach is allied to skills on the ground and in the air, and there is an unquenchable commitment that harnesses his speed and strength to maximum effect.

LEFT AND ABOVE RIGHT *Samuel Eto'o put in an all-round performance to earn his country an unexpected South African ticket in the 2–0 play off victory against Morocco. He's pictured (left) whooping it up after scoring the second goal and (right) giving a captain's ticking off to Achille Emana, who was substituted in the 68th minute.*

Eto'o is as well known at club level. He scored over a hundred goals in five seasons with Barcelona, where he made the highest number of appearances by an African player in La Liga. He's the joint third highest scorer in Barça's history, and the second player (the first being Raúl) to have scored in two Champions League finals. Those matches stamped the name of Eto'o onto the parts of the English national consciousness labelled Arsenal and Manchester United. In 2006, the Arsenal goalie Jens Lehmann was sent off for fouling Eto'o on the edge of the penalty area. Arsenal lost their lead to a second-half Eto'o equalizer and lost the game 2–1. In 2009, Eto'o scored the opener in the Champions League final against Manchester United.

Then, in one of the most surprising transfers of summer 2009, came a swap with Eto'o leaving Barcelona for Internazionale and Zlatan Ibrahimović heading in the opposite direction. In Italy, the Eto'o goals kept flowing and if his goal-every-other-game career average is maintained in South Africa, Samuel Eto'o will be on his way to joining Roger Milla as a Cameroonian national monument.

> **❝ Soccer is so crazy that things can turn around at any moment. We have to keep calm heads even if our hearts are hot. ❞**
>
> SAMUEL ETO'O

ITALY

The current World Cup holders belong in the formidable Italian tradition of fielding teams that perform consistently at the top level. The *Squadra Azzurra* has been at 14 of the 16 World Cup finals and has succeeded in lifting the cup in 1934, 1938, 1982 and 2006. Only Brazil has done better. And this time round they have the luck of the draw having got the easiest rivals of all the seeds.

The enduring paradox of Italian sides is that they feature teamwork above individual talent and yet accommodate individual brilliance. Successive well-drilled teams always know how to stifle the opposition and, if they can't win, they will bore everyone to death with 0–0 draws. At the 2006 World Cup, Gianluigi Buffon, the goalie, was unbeaten for seven and a half hours of play. Italy conceded only two goals, one an own goal by Cristian Zaccardo and the second from Zinédine Zidane's penalty kick for France in the 1–1 stalemate of a final match.

The Italian game is not entirely about grim discipline. Members of this Italian squad understand each other's playing styles because Italian players compete in the same league. Serie A is rich enough to retain most of Italy's best players and those players have a familiarity with each other to work intuitively and switch the tempo of play to accelerate out of self-willed midfield quagmires into lightning attacks. And if all else fails, there's a collective cool for the penalty shoot-out.

RIGHT *Berlin, 9 July 2006: the Italian players celebrate as Fabio Cannavaro lifts the World Cup trophy aloft following victory in a penalty shoot-out against France.*

After the 2006 World Cup triumph, Marcello Lippi quit as manager and was replaced by Roberto Donadoni. Lippi was reappointed in the wake of Italy's poor showing at Euro 2008 and if his 2010 side sticks to its defensive form there will be a near repeat of these stats from 2006: a modest tally of 12 tournament goals scored by a total of ten players, four of them defenders. Tactics provided the interest. Italy played several different formations during the World Cup with five players in midfield in the group stages and four forwards in semi-final extra time.

When Italy tired in the final, Lippi substituted the forward Francesco Totti with the defensive midfielder Daniele De Rossi. According to Lippi, the shifts in approach were feasible because the 'Italian players are the best tactically in the world. That's an honest opinion. I'm not saying that it's the best-looking football but it's the hardest because, whatever team you play, you are always going to have great difficulty when playing them.'

The final part of the recipe for success is that the team is kept on its toes as youth is constantly mixed in with experience. One fresh name to look out for in South Africa is the Internazionale defender Davide Santon, who made his debut for Italy in June 2009 and has been compared to Paolo Maldini by Lippi.

BELOW Paolo Rossi – villain turned hero – shields the ball from Junior during Italy's classic encounter with Brazil in the 1982 World Cup.

GREAT MATCH
1982 Italy 3–2 Brazil

World Cup, second round, group stage
Estardio Sarria, Barcelona, Spain

With in-form Brazil only needing a draw to qualify for the semi-finals, Italy had it all to do in this final group game. The *Azzurri's* poor form in the first round was blamed on striker Paolo Rossi just returning from a lengthy ban over a betting scandal. However, Rossi found his feet after just five minutes and put the Italians in front. A few minutes later Zico fed Socrates to shoot past Dino Zoff for the equalizer. On 25 minutes Rossi scored again, punishing a Brazilian defensive mistake, and Italy went into the break 2–1 ahead.

Twenty minutes into the second half Brazil's Falcao pulled it back to 2–2, a result that would have been enough to see the South Americans through. But almost immediately Rossi scored a third, his hat-trick, to put the Italians back in front.

The final few minutes were breathtaking with both sides having goals ruled out and the 40-year-old Italian keeper Dino Zoff making several remarkable saves. In the end the Italians held on to win, and went on to beat Poland in the semi-final and Germany in the final to claim their third World Cup victory.

> **Those eyes are sometimes burning with seriousness, sometimes twinkling, sometimes warily assessing you – and always they are alive with intelligence.**

ALEX FERGUSON
ON MARCELLO LIPPI

BELOW *Daniele De Rossi celebrates after scoring against Georgia during Italy's qualifying match on 10 September 2008 in Udine. De Rossi scored both goals in a laboured victory.*

Lippi on team ethos and England

Lippi's managerial approach to coaching begins and ends with the team ethos. In his book *A Game of Ideas: Thoughts and Passions from the Sidelines*, he writes: 'A group of the best players do not necessarily make for the best team.' He compares a successful team to a healthy family whose mutual relationships are strong, and like all paterfamilias he pays lip service to the idea that individual members must be free to express themselves. But they can't be more free than the main man and Lippi dislikes the prima donna *galáctico* (superstar). He insists players adhere to the game plan and play for each other, not for themselves.

When Lippi's name was in the hat for the England job that went to Fabio Capello he was asked by the media if he would like to coach England. 'Yes, I would, but I did not put myself forward and nobody ever called me. For me it was already an honour that for a few days my name was close to the English national team.' He remained at home, until he was reappointed Azzurri manager in summer 2008.

'English footballers are very, very good,' Lippi says, 'but unfortunately there are not many of them. If I had a team with a lot, a lot of money I might consider buying Rooney, Gerrard and Lampard. I believe English football is really, really strong, great in defence, midfield, attack. They only need to become a team.'

COACH **Marcello Lippi**

Born 11 April 1948
Record: P48, W27, D16, L5

By his own estimation, the charismatic Marcello Lippi had 'an honourable, but not brilliant' playing career. He began footballing life as a central defender for Sampdoria, didn't play for his country and waited until middle age to make his mark. In a decade spent managing Juventus, he won five Serie A championships plus the European Cup. And in 2006, Lippi was in charge of Italy and became the only man to have lifted both the European and the World Cup.

Players can only defer to such a record and they respect a caution underpinning a flexible approach where the players available determine tactics. Lippi is also a motivator whose skill is in eliciting the best possible performances from seasoned professionals.

Unlike most national coaches, Lippi has only ever worked in his country of birth. Yet nobody would claim this has given Lippi a limited or parochial or localized view of the way football should be played. Over the years he has proved himself a pragmatist dedicated most to the notion of producing winning teams. He is certainly not bound by a rigid tactical approach and he has the charisma to unite disparate talents and earn the respect of a range of players. He's one major reason the Italians might do well again this time round.

ROUTE TO THE FINALS

MATCHES PLAYED

06.02.08	Cyprus 1	2 Italy
10.09.08	Italy 2	0 Georgia
11.10.08	Bulgaria 0	0 Italy
15.10.08	Italy 2	1 Montenegro
28.03.09	Montenegro 0	2 Italy
01.04.09	Italy 1	1 Republic of Ireland
05.09.09	Georgia 0	2 Italy
09.09.09	Italy 2	0 Bulgaria
10.10.09	Republic of Ireland 2	2 Italy
14.10.09	Italy 3	2 Cyprus

EUROPE QUALIFYING GROUP 8 – FINAL TABLE

Team	P	W	D	L	F	A	Pts
Italy	10	7	3	0	18	7	24
Republic of Ireland	10	4	6	0	12	8	18
Bulgaria	10	3	5	2	17	13	14
Cyprus	10	2	3	5	14	16	9
Montenegro	10	1	6	3	9	14	9
Georgia	10	0	3	7	7	19	3

FINALS GROUP F

Italy play		Date	Venue
	Paraguay	14 June	Cape Town
	New Zealand	20 June	Nelspruit
	Slovakia	24 June	Johannesburg (Ellis Park)

VITAL STATISTICS

World ranking 4th
Midfield 8/10

Keeper and defence 8/10
Attack 7/10

Strengths and weaknesses The team is managed by a maestro who picks from a pool of Serie A talent whose teamwork is unparalleled. The weakness is that success has generated a burden of expectation…

How far will they go? … and the expectation is that the reigning world champions and the second best team in the tournament's history are bound to go far. How could they fail to reach a semi-final in 2010? Will New Zealand or Slovakia get in their way?

HOW THEY'LL LINE UP

Marcello Lippi might be an old-style centre half but he's not one of those coaches who think the ball should be in the air for half the game. He favours patient passing across the width of the pitch and he fields teams that hold the ball before bursting into attack. Nonetheless, Lippi has stayed true to his playing days in building his teams from the back. Any manager would have Buffon in goal and make Fabio Cannavaro his captain. Cannavaro will draw on nearly two decades of playing experience to command the team from his centre-half vantage point.

POSSIBLE SQUAD

Goalkeepers

Marco Amelia (Palermo), Gianluigi Buffon (Juventus), Morgan De Sanctis (Sevilla/Napoli)

Defenders

Fabio Cannavaro (C) (Juventus), Giorgio Chiellini (Juventus), Domenico Criscito (Genoa), Alessandro Gamberini (Fiorentina), Fabio Grosso (Juve), Nicola Legrottaglie (Juventus), Davide Santon (Internazionale), Gianluca Zambrotta (Milan)

Midfielders

Alberto Aquilani (Liverpool), Mauro Camoranesi (Juventus), Daniele De Rossi (Roma), Gennaro Gattuso (Milan), Claudio Marchisio (Udinese), Simone Pepe (Udinese), Andrea Pirlo (Milan)

Forwards

Alberto Gilardino (Fiorentina), Vincenzo Iaquinta (Juventus), Fabio Quagliarella (Napoli), Giuseppe Rossi (Villarreal), Luca Toni (Bayern Munich)

BELOW *Italy v Bulgaria, World Cup qualifying match, Olimpico Stadium, Turin, Italy, 9 September 2009: (back row, left to right) Chiellini, Zambrotta, Gilardino, Grosso, Iaquinta, Buffon; (front row) Marchisio, De Rossi, Camoranesi, Pirlo, Cannavaro.*

Fabio Cannavaro

Can Italy's captain and most-capped player make it two in a row and take the *Azzurri* to victory in South Africa? Or will his fourth World Cup campaign prove to be one too many?

Despite age and a recent history of serious injury, Fabio Cannavaro has been quite open in his determination to captain Italy through the 2010 World Cup. He has his manager's support in the endeavour. 'Cannavaro is without question the absolute number one defender in the world,' is what Marcello Lippi says of the veteran captain who is about to embark on a fourth World Cup finals campaign.

Cannavaro has been there and done it with honours including winner's medals for the 2006 World Cup, the 1999 UEFA Cup, 1999 Italian Cup and the Spanish La Liga in 2007 and 2008. In 2006 he was voted European and World Footballer of the Year and Italian Serie A Footballer of the Year. And then there are the two revoked Serie A titles from 2005 and 2006 that were stripped away following the Juventus match-fixing scandal.

> **" Cannavaro is without question the strongest defender, and the absolute number one in the world. "**
>
> MARCELLO LIPPI

The long list of previous clubs proves Cannavaro more of a footballing nomad than most of his Italian colleagues, and he lost popularity with his Italian fanbase when he quit Juventus for Real Madrid, following his coach Fabio Capello to Spain in a €7 million deal. He found success only to return to Juventus at the end of the 2009 season in order to prepare for what must be his last World Cup campaign.

Cannavaro's career highlight came on his 100th international game when he lifted the 2006 World Cup. The victorious captain had played it hard but fair throughout and there can be few defenders who could match his 2006 record of not receiving a yellow or red card during the eleven and a half hours that he played in the tournament. Cannavaro has commanded the national team since 2002 and is Italy's most capped player of all time. What remains for him now is to bow out of the international arena with two captain's World Cup winner's medals in a row.

LEFT *Sofia, 11 October 2008: Cannavaro, a rock in defence, beats Dimitar Berbatov to the ball in Italy's qualifying match against Bulgaria..*

Gianluigi Buffon

Gianluigi Buffon, of Italy and Juventus, is one of the greatest goalkeepers in the history of the game. The record books confirm what is obvious to any committed football fan who has witnessed Buffon demonstrating the mad and risky art of goalkeeping.

When Buffon was awarded his first Italy cap at the age of 19 during a World Cup qualifer play-off against Russia in 1998, he broke the rule that goalkeepers must wait until reaching their mid-twenties before international call-up. And he broke another unwritten football rule saying that goalkeepers don't make captains when he led Italy for Euro 2008 after injury ruled out Fabio Cannavaro. He transferred from Parma to Juventus in 2001, for a world-record goalkeeper's fee of €52 million. He earned the UEFA most valuable player and best goalkeeper awards in 2003, and Pelé identified him as one of the top 125 greatest living footballers in March 2004. During the 2006 World Cup finals, Buffon kept five clean sheets and denied a goal to all attackers who faced him in open play for an astonishing 453 minutes.

A commitment to the cause is what has provided the platform for Buffon's formidable list of achievements. After Juventus was demoted from Serie A to the Cadetti league as punishment for illegal betting, Buffon stayed true to the team where he has spent the bulk of his career. He played down his loyalty, merely commenting, 'Serie B is a division I have never won and I want to try to do this.' True to his word, he helped Juventus make an immediate return to the Italian top flight and added an Italian second division winner's medal to a crowded trophy cabinet that still has room for a second World Cup winner's medal.

> **❝ One of the greatest living footballers. ❞**
>
> PELÉ

RIGHT *Gianluigi Buffon in the thick of it keeping the Brazilians at bay during a Confederations Cup match in June 2009.*

PLAYER FACT FILE

Name: Gianluigi Buffon
Position: Goalkeeper
Caps: 100
Goals: 0
Team: Juventus
Date of birth: 28 January 1978
Height: 191 cm/6 ft 3 in
Weight: 83 kg/183 lb
Previous clubs: Parma
International debut: 29 October 1997 v Russia
Previous World Cups: 1998, 2002, 2006

STYLE GUIDE

It goes without saying that Buffon is the complete goalkeeping package. There is the calmness under pressure and the unswerving commitment to club and country. There's the bravery verging on a foolhardiness that seems unconcerned with personal injury. And then there's the skill, positional sense and anticipation of a consummate shot stopper and penalty saver. His tall figure dominates any penalty area, where his communication with defenders is such that he knows when to claim a cross and when to stay put and guard the back line.

 ONE TO WATCH

DAVIDE SANTON

Santon had an eventful 2009. In January he turned 18 and made his Internazionale debut; in March he took up defensive duties facing Ronaldo in a European Cup tie against Man U; and in the summer he got a Serie A winner's medal and made his international debut against Northern Ireland. Santon is an attacking right back who has attracted plaudits from those who matter in his life. His club manager José Mourinho praises his attitude and a tactical flexibility that allows him to switch to left field positions. His international boss Marcello Lippi (a mean defender in his playing days) compares the newcomer to Paolo Maldini and comments: 'Santon was predestined to be an international and now that I have seen him in real life, I can confirm that is exactly how it is. He is only a lad, yet he has a great personality, plays the game easily and has the capacity of fitting in.'

Gennaro Gattuso

The hard face of Italian soccer looks like his name sounds: rough. Gattuso's nickname 'Ringhio' means the growler or snarler, onomatopoeic words that accurately characterize a style of play that can verge on the brutal.

But there's brain as well as brawn to his game. Above all, he's a team man who has developed into a fine judge of when to move forward in support of his strikers and when to remain in defence. Early on in his career, at the age of 19, Gattuso proved he was his own man when he quit Perugia to join Glasgow Rangers, thus asserting his right to a

> **Either you do things seriously or you don't do them at all.**
>
> GENNARO GATTUSO

free transfer under the Bosman ruling. A run of 40 Scottish Premier League games helped mould his robust style and Gattuso says that Walter Smith, his manager at Rangers, has been the biggest influence on his career.

Having done a year in Scottish finishing school, Gattuso returned to Italy with Salernitana in 1998. Though the newly promoted team was relegated after a season, he caught AC Milan's eye and signed for them in 1999. The then Milan manager Carlo Ancelotti (now of Chelsea) used him as a ball-winning foil to Andrea Pirlo and in the process formed a decade-long partnership for club and country.

Gattuso is a battler at the deep end of football and a huge favourite with Italian fans who respond to the passion he brings to his terminator role. They're still talking about his exhibitionism after Italy lifted the World Cup in 2006, when, in a show of mad exuberance, he ripped his shorts off and danced ecstatically around the pitch. What has the growler got planned for South Africa?

PLAYER FACT FILE

Name: Gennaro Ivan Grozni Gattuso
Position: Midfielder
Caps: 70
Goals: 1
Team: AC Milan
Date of birth: 9 January 1978
Height: 177 cm/5 ft 9½ in
Weight: 77 kg/170 lb
Previous clubs: Perugia, Rangers, Salernitana
International debut: 23 February 2000
v Sweden
Previous World Cups: 2002, 2006

STYLE GUIDE
Gattuso is a tireless defensive midfielder who is sometimes advanced into a right-wing position. His style is marked by aggression and hard tackling, making intimidation a part of his game. For both club and country, he is Andrea Pirlo's water carrier.

FAR LEFT AND LEFT *Gattuso showing who is boss: (far left) sweeping aside the challenge from the Cyprus number ten in a World Cup qualifier and (left) tussling for the ball with Egyptian midfielder Mohamed Homos during a Confederations Cup match in South Africa.*

Andrea Pirlo

Variously known as *'fantasista'*, *'l'architetto'* and 'the metronome', Andrea Pirlo provides game-winning inspiration and – more importantly in the Italian scheme of play – a relentless defeat-avoiding rhythm.

He epitomizes a style so successful in its mix of efficiency and brio that it earned Italy the last World Cup. The team to negate Pirlo's power could be the team to take the next World Cup.

Pirlo began as an offensive midfielder until the AC Milan manager Carlo Ancelotti deployed him in a deeper role during the 2002–03 season. As a club then international defensive midfielder, he delivered defensive support with his powerful running and

RIGHT *Pirlo surges past the challenge of Bulgaria's Valeri Domovchiyski during a World Cup qualifying match in Turin in September 2009. Pirlo's muscular athleticism is at the heart of the Italian push to retain the World Cup in 2010.*

PLAYER FACT FILE

Name: Andrea Pirlo
Position: Midfielder
Caps: 64
Goals: 8
Team: AC Milan
Date of birth: 19 May 1979
Height: 177 cm/5 ft 9¾ in
Weight: 68 kg/150 lb
Previous clubs: Brescia, Internazionale, Reggina
International debut: 7 September 2002 v Azerbaijan
Previous World Cups: 2006

STYLE GUIDE

Andrea Pirlo looks like he was born in midfield, sometimes patrolling in front of the back four, more recently up and close to the attack. He keeps his game simple and rarely loses the ball, playing in an understated way that leaves him unnoticed until flashes of inspiration release attackers with a raking cross-field pass or a threaded ball behind a defender's heels.

trustworthy tackling. Of far greater advantage, his relatively withdrawn position gave him the room to pick out passes and set the pace of a game. This is how it was at the 2006 World Cup when the Italian manager Marcello Lippi called him 'a silent leader on the pitch [whose] feet do the talking for him'. Indeed, Pirlo's feet were so eloquent that he won the man of the match award in both the semi-final against Germany and the final against France.

In qualifying games for 2010, Pirlo has been pushed forward to his old position as a playmaker behind the strikers. This allows him less time on the ball but gives him greater scope to set up goal-scoring opportunities in the contested ground immediately ahead of him. And up in the thick of forward play is where we're likely to see Pirlo when he lines up for Italy in South Africa.

Whether as the anchor man or the playmaker, Pirlo will be in the thick of it entering the field of play looking languid and even lightweight until the whistle blows and he emerges as an energetic footballing heavyweight with the drive and vision to take his team to the top.

66 **Almost all Italy's attacks were channelled through Pirlo. With his technique and creativity, he became a key factor in their attacking play.** 99

FIFA REPORT
2006 WORLD CUP

PARAGUAY

GROUP F

Paraguay are little known and little fancied outside South America. Their footballing efficiency secured them an early ticket to South Africa ahead of more illustrious South American rivals – don't expect any thrills from them.

Paraguay's route to qualification for their fourth consecutive World Cup finals saw an initial surge to the head of their South American group above Brazil, only to lose ground with one point from a possible 12 during the first half of 2009. They then outgunned more fancied rivals and booked their place in South Africa courtesy of a 1–0 defeat of Argentina. Salvador Cabañas set the goal up for Nelson Haedo Valdez to score.

Summer 2010 could see Cabañas, Valdez and (knee injury permitting) Manchester City's Roque Santa Cruz emerge as Paraguayan names to sit alongside recent World Cup heroes such as Celso Ayala, Carlos Gamarra, Roberto Acuña and José Luis Chilavert. The more likely outcome, however, is that the *Albirroja* ('white and reds') will emulate the early exit from eight previous World Cup finals.

In 2007 Gerardo 'Tata' Martino became the national manager charged with rejuvenating an ageing squad. The Argentine had been a success managing Paraguayan club sides and has since fortified his reputation as a sound tactician. He has built on youth team successes from earlier in the decade, and his remoulded side relies on the tested attacking skills of Cabañas, Valdez and Santa Cruz. Behind them, Martino's other key players are Justo Villar in goal; Claudio Morel, Paulo da Silva, Julio César Cáceres in defence; and Édgar Barreto, Jonathan Santana, Enrique Vera and Christian Riveros in midfield.

Together, they have maintained Paraguay's reputation in South America for sound defence, aerial ability and powerfully built attackers. Strength is rarely a subsitute for raw skill and the missing ingredient is flair. A team that has never gone beyond the second round of the World Cup finals and has won the Copa América in only 1953 and 1979 doesn't appear to hold much promise for significant progress in South Africa. The football future doesn't look Paraguayan.

ABOVE *Gerardo Martino's Argentine managerial know-how guided the Albirroja to an unexpected qualification for the World Cup finals.*

ABOVE *Nelson Haedo Valdez, who partners Roque Santa Cruz in attack, roars in celebration after scoring against Venezuela during a World Cup qualifier.*

POSSIBLE SQUAD

Goalkeepers

Diego Barreto (Cerro Porteño), **Aldo Bobadilla** (Independiente Medellín), **Justo Villar** (Real Valladolid)

Defenders

Julio César Cáceres (Boca Juniors), **Marcos Cáceres** (Racing), **Denis Caniza** (C) (Nacional), **Miguel Samudio** (Libertad), **Paulo da Silva** (Sunderland), **Aureliano Torres** (San Lorenzo), **Darío Verón** (UNAM Pumas)

Midfielders

Édgar Baretto (Atalanta), **Víctor Cáceres** (Libertad), **Osvaldo Martínez** (Monterrey), **Néstor Ortigoza** (Argentinos Juniors), **Christian Riveros** (Cruz Azul), **Jonathan Santana** (Wolfsburg), **Enrique Vera** (LDU Quito)

Forwards

Jorge Achucarro (Newell's), **Édgar Benítez** (Pachuca), **Salvador Cabañas** (América), **Oscar Cardozo** (Benfica), **Roque Santa Cruz** (Manchester City), **Nelson Haedo Valdez** (Borussia Dortmund)

ROUTE TO THE FINALS

SOUTH AMERICA QUALIFYING GROUP – FINAL TABLE

Team	P	W	D	L	F	A	Pts
Brazil	18	9	7	2	33	11	34
Chile	18	10	3	5	32	22	33
Paraguay	18	10	3	5	24	16	33
Argentina	18	8	4	6	23	20	28
Uruguay	18	6	6	6	28	20	24
Ecuador	18	6	5	7	22	26	23
Colombia	18	6	5	7	14	18	23
Venezuela	18	6	4	8	23	29	22
Bolivia	18	4	3	11	22	36	15
Peru	18	3	4	11	11	34	13

FINALS GROUP F

Paraguay play		Date	Venue
	Italy	14 June	Cape Town
	Slovakia	20 June	Mangaung/Bloemfontein
	New Zealand	24 June	Polokwane

BELOW *Paraguay v Argentina, World Cup qualifying match, Defensores del Chaco Stadium, Asuncion, Paraguay, 9 September 2009: (back row, left to right) Santana, Villar, Verón, Julio César Cáceres, da Silva, Valdez; (front row) Vera, Riveros, Cabañas, Édgar Baretto, Torres.*

VITAL STATISTICS

World ranking 30th
Keeper and defence 6/10
Midfield 5/10
Attack 6/10

Strengths and weaknesses Paraguay are consistent in their inconsistency. On their day, they are strong in the air, solid in defence and powerful up front. On an off day, they crumble to lesser opposition.

How far will they go? Beating Slovakia is the key to joining Italy in the second round.

Roque Santa Cruz

Santa Cruz is a Paraguayan attacking talisman who scored three goals for the national side on his debut in the Copa América aged 17 in 1999. That year he also starred for Olimpia Asunción, helping them to a Paraguayan championship and winning the Paraguayan Footballer of the Year award.

The youthful promise resulted in a move to Bayern Munich where he stayed for eight years until 2007, helping his team win the German league and cup double, the UEFA Champions League and the Intercontinental Cup. He scored 38 goals in 143 games but eventually fell out of favour at Bayern following the arrival of Miroslav Klose and Luca Toni. Meanwhile, the German magazine *Kicker* had voted him the sexiest man taking part in the 2006 World Cup.

Blackburn Rovers' manager Mark Hughes had always rated the Paraguayan striker and the club paid Bayern £3.5 million for Santa Cruz in summer 2007. He repaid the investment with 19 goals in his debut season, the first against Middlesbrough after three touches of the ball when he came on as a substitute in the opening game of the 2007–08 season. He went on to notch his first hat-trick for Blackburn in a 5–3 loss to Wigan Athletic in 2007.

When Hughes left Blackburn in the summer of 2008 to manage Manchester City, Santa Cruz made no secret of his restlessness. After missing much of the second half of his 2008–09 season through a persistent knee injury, he eventually rejoined his old boss and – at five times what Hughes first paid him – became a Manchester City player for a fee of around £17.5 million.

> **❝ I know the talent Roque has. I know the attributes he has and I know what kind of guy he is. He is a driven guy. He is ambitious and he wants to win. ❞**
>
> MARK HUGHES
> SANTA CRUZ'S MANAGER AT
> BLACKBURN AND MANCHESTER CITY

Name: Roque Luis Santa Cruz Cantero
Position: Striker
Caps: 66
Goals: 20
Team: Manchester City
Date of birth: 16 August 1981
Height: 189 cm/6 ft 2 in
Weight: 80 kg/176 lb
Previous clubs: Olimpia Asunción, Bayern Munich, Blackburn Rovers
International debut: April 1999 v Mexico
Previous World Cups: 2002, 2006

STYLE GUIDE

Santa Cruz is a tall and powerfully built attacker with the strength to outmuscle his markers and the speed to turn any defence. His sheer brawn can sometimes disguise the silky touch that has made him a regular international since his late teens.

Santa Cruz's international career has followed a smoother trajectory with a total of seven goals in the 2002 and 2006 World

NEW ZEALAND

GROUP F

Blackburn captain Ryan Nelsen, Celtic's Chris Killen, West Brom's Chris Wood and Plymouth's Rory Fallon are heroes back home. After all, they play in the side that earned New Zealand a place in the 2010 World Cup finals.

The All Whites had an easier route to South Africa than any of the other 31 participants apart from the host nation. They didn't even have to meet Australia, who FIFA have transferred to the harder Asian group. Instead, New Zealand competed among Pacific tiddlers before beating Bahrain in a two-leg play-off that was settled by a single Rory Fallon headed goal. Don't tell the likes of enforced World Cup stay-at-homes such as, Republic of Ireland, Scotland, Belgium, Hungary, Sweden, Russia or Croatia.

Five clean sheets during qualification plus a Mark Paston penalty save in the second game against Bahrain all suggest a defensive resilience. With Ryan Nelsen as the star, that's the best we can expect. Still, World Cup attendance is some achievement for a nation where the main sporting draws are cricket and All Blacks rugby. The coach, Ricki Herbert, says: 'We've all worked hard, we all backed the system that we truly believe was good enough to win. This is about a group who believed and have never stopped believing, and their dream continues which is fantastic.' New Zealand's only other World Cup trip was a Spanish nightmare in 1982 with straight losses to Scotland, Brazil and the Soviet Union.

Fans of the underdog will be rooting for New Zealand in 2010. So too will some of Shrewsbury, for their star forward, Kris Bright, is on the fringes of the NZ squad and might soon be a name to put alongside Shrewsbury Town's other internationals, such as Mickey Thomas and Neville Southall.

BELOW LEFT *Rory Fallon, whose father coached New Zealand in the 1980s, leaps above the Bahrain defence to score the goal that took New Zealand through to the World Cup finals.*

BELOW RIGHT *Ryan Nelsen (left), captain of Blackburn and New Zealand, congratulates his goalie Mark Paston for his crucial penalty save in the second leg of the play-off with Bahrain.*

POSSIBLE SQUAD

Goalkeepers

James Bannatyne (Team Wellington), Mark Paston (Wellington Phoenix), Jacob Spoonley (Auckland City)

Defenders

Andrew Boyens (Red Bull New York), Tony Lochhead (Wellington Phoenix), David Mulligan (Wellington Phoenix), Ryan Nelsen (C) (Blackburn Rovers), Steven Old (Kilmarnock), Aaron Scott (Waitakere United), Ben Sigmund (Wellington Phoenix), Ivan Vicelich (Auckland City)

Midfielders

Andrew Barron (Team Wellington), Leo Bertos (Wellington Phoenix), Jeremy Brockie (North Queensland Fury), Tim Brown (Wellington Phoenix), Jeremy Christie (Waitakere United), Simon Elliott (San Jose Earthquakes), Michael McGlinchey (Central Coast Mariners)

Forwards

Kris Bright (Shrewsbury Town), Rory Fallon (Plymouth Argyle), Chris Killen (Celtic), Shane Smeltz (Gold Coast United), Chris Wood (West Bromwich Albion)

ROUTE TO THE FINALS

OCEANIA QUALIFYING ROUND 2 – FINAL TABLE

Team	P	W	D	L	F	A	Pts
New Zealand	6	5	0	1	14	5	15
New Caledonia	6	2	2	2	12	10	8
Fiji	6	2	1	3	8	11	7
Vanuatu	6	1	1	4	5	13	4

ASIA/OCEANIA PLAY-OFF

10.10.09		Bahrain 0	0 New Zealand
14.11.09		New Zealand 1	0 Bahrain

FINALS GROUP F

New Zealand play		Date	Venue
	Slovakia	15 June	Rustenburg
	Italy	20 June	Nelspruit
	Paraguay	24 June	Polokwane

VITAL STATISTICS

World ranking 77th	Keeper and defence 5/10
Midfield 3/10	Attack 4/10

Strengths and weaknesses The All Whites are the weakest team in the competition.

How far will they go? Let the odds tell the story: they are rank outsiders at anything between 750-1 and 1000-1.

LEFT *New Zealand v Bahrain, World Cup play-off, Westpac Stadium, Wellington, 14 November 2009: (back row, left to right) Brown, Killen, Smeltz, Paston, Lochhead, Fallon; (front row) Sigmund, Nelsen, Bertos, Vicelich, McGlinchey.*

SLOVAKIA

GROUP F

Slovakia's qualification for South Africa is one of the surprises of the 2010 tournament. Since Czechoslovakia became two nations in 1993, Slovakia have qualified for nothing while the Czechs were at the 2006 World Cup, the Euro 96 final and the Euro 2004 semi-final.

The Slovaks emerged from a tough qualifying group that lined them up against more fancied neighbours in the Czech Republic and Poland. In April 2009, they consolidated an unlikely position at the top of Group 3 by winning 2–1 on a visit to the Czech Republic. A new nation that had had to content itself with ice hockey went football crazy and, with only a point needed from the penultimate game against Slovenia, 160,000 people applied for a seat in the tiny Tehelné Pole Stadium in Bratislava. Fortunately, only 23,000 Slovaks could squeeze in to witness Slovakia's 2–0 slump against Slovenia. The Slovenes looked set to win the group until a soft own goal on a snowy night in Poland secured another famous Slovakia away victory to elevate them to the sunny uplands of South Africa.

The accolades went to the manager Vladimír Weiss, who was a Czechoslovakian and a Slovakian international. He has instilled discipline and belief into an ordinary bunch of players who, while good enough to play throughout Europe, would pass unnoticed in most airport lounges. South Africa could change all that and bring both personal and national recognition.

Robert Vittek, the attacker and sometime captain of his national side, says: 'Our greatest strength is our collective approach. We've shown it in every qualifier so far. Obviously, we have a number of skilled individuals too.' Among Slovakia's most skilful individuals are: Stanislav Sestak, who plays in Germany and scored six goals in five qualifying appearances; the solid Liverpool defender Martin Škrtel; the precocious Napoli midfielder Marek Hamsik, who has also been national captain; and the manager's nineteen-year-old son, also Vladimír Weiss, who is on Manchester City's books and made his international debut in the summer of 2009.

ABOVE *Vladimír Weiss's businesslike approach to managing Slovakia made his unfancied team, drawn in a qualifying group that included the Czech Republic, stand out from the crowd.*

ABOVE *Stanislav Šesták hit a run of scoring form in the qualifiers and is shown here celebrating a goal against Northern Ireland.*

POSSIBLE SQUAD

Goalkeepers

Ľuboš Kamenár (Nantes), Dušan Kuciak (Vaslui), Ján Mucha (Legia Warszawa)

Defenders

Marek Čech (West Bromwich Albion), Ján Ďurica (Lokomotiv Moscow), Peter Pekarík (Wolfsburg), Martin Petráš (Cesena), Kornel Saláta (Slovan Bratislava), Martin Škrtel (Liverpool), Radoslav Zabavník (free agent)

Midfielders

Marek Hamšík (C) (Napoli), Kamil Kopúnek (Spartak Trnava), Ján Kozák (Slovan Bratislava), Marek Sapara (Rosenborg), Miroslav Stoch (Twente), Zdeno Štrba (Skoda Xanthi), Vladimír Weiss (Manchester City)

Forwards

Filip Hološko (Beşiktaş), Martin Jakubko (FC Moscow), Erik Jendrišek (Kaiserslautern), Ján Novák (MFK Košice), Róbert Vittek (Lille), Stanislav Šesták (VfL Bochum)

ROUTE TO THE FINALS

EUROPE QUALIFYING GROUP 3 – FINAL TABLE

Team	P	W	D	L	F	A	Pts
Slovakia	10	7	1	2	22	10	22
Slovenia	10	6	2	2	18	4	20
Czech Republic	10	4	4	2	17	6	16
Northern Ireland	10	4	3	3	13	9	15
Poland	10	3	2	5	19	14	11
San Marino	10	0	0	10	1	47	0

FINALS GROUP F

Slovakia play		Date	Venue
	New Zealand	15 June	Rustenburg
	Paraguay	20 June	Mangaung/Bloemfontein
	Italy	24 June	Johannesburg (Ellis Park)

VITAL STATISTICS

World ranking 34th   Keeper and defence 6/10
Midfield 5/10   Attack 5/10

Strengths and weaknesses This powerful collective is in South Africa against all the odds and might therefore play without fear. On the other hand, the pressure might suppress what little flair there is.

How far will they go? They could sneak past Paraguay into the second round, though cautious punters will keep holding the folding.

LEFT *Slovakia v Northern Ireland, World Cup qualifying match, Windsor Park, Belfast, 9 September 2009: (back row, left to right) Vittek, Škrtel, Šesták, Mucha, Pekarík, Kopúnek, Štrba; (front row), Ďurica, Weiss, Zabavník, Stoch.*

BRAZIL

GROUP G

The world's best side plays the most beautiful version of the world's favourite sport. After being eliminated in the quarter finals in 2006, nothing less than a sixth title win will be good enough for Brazil.

Brazil's footballing record is unsurpassed. A stunning 2–0 victory in the nation's first competitive match against Exeter City in 1914 was but a prelude to World Cup winners' medals in 1958, 1962, 1970, 1994 and 2002 and the unique achievement of having played in every World Cup. It is a mystery how each decade produces yet another clutch of star Brazilian players who

meld their skills into stellar teams. There is magic in there too because Brazilian managers must forge a collective entirely out of globetrotting, jet-lagged mercenaries. Domestic Brazilian football is disorganized and does not attract the television revenues to pay the telephone-number salaries on offer in Europe. The commercial reality that clubs come before country became clear in 2006,

since when Brazil have played international friendlies at Arsenal's Emirates Stadium in London or in Sweden. Home for Brazil is now away, and it's a tribute to Dunga's management that his side won the 2007 Copa América and the Confederations Cup in 2009.

The current team is formed in Dunga's tough and mentally strong image. They play

BELOW LEFT *Robinho (left) and Juan (centre) celebrate a goal by Kaká (right) on Brazil's path to the 2010 World Cup finals.*

BELOW *The manager's faith in fiery striker Luís Fabiano paid off in 2009: he was top scorer in the Confederations Cup.*

for a manager with the nerve to have scored in a World Cup final penalty shoot-out and have responded to an approach that has put teamwork above individuality. A certain ruthlessness distinguishes Dunga's team from earlier Brazilian sides and his players take to the field with the confidence of playing to a tested game plan. They are set up in a classic Brazilian counter-attacking and set-piece format that sometimes concedes possession to lure the opposition into complacency.

This hasn't happened automatically. Dunga dumped the previous manager's 'Magic Square' attacking formation of Ronaldo, Adriano, Kaká and Ronaldinho. Of these, only Kaká has been a constant in his plans and no manager could overlook his kind of skill and temperament. The heart of defence wasn't too much of a problem either and Dunga swiftly appointed Lúcio captain. At right back he is spoilt for choice and able to choose between Dani Alvez and Maicon,

both of whom are assured a place in the squad. So too is Robinho, for one of Dunga's triumphs has been in converting a tempestuous and peripheral talent into a first-choice forward. He has also looked for players outside of Europe's dominant clubs, announcing all would be treated as equals, and the current team has many players he has brought forward, notably the goalkeeper Júlio César and the centre forward Luís Fabiano.

Brazil are favourites for the 2010 World Cup, though they will have to contend with the fact that no Confederations Cup winner has gone on to lift the trophy. Tough competition will come from a resurgent Holland, a confident Spain or England, the sturdily constant threats of Italy and Germany plus France, Brazil's bogey team. Brazil are by no means a shoo-in to lift the World Cup for a sixth time, but who would bet against them when football really does come home and Brazil hosts the 2014 World Cup?

ABOVE *Elano lifts the trophy as Brazil celebrate their 3–2 victory over the United States in the final of the Confederations Cup.*

ABOVE RIGHT *Robinho has thrived under Dunga and will be at his prime in South Africa.*

RIGHT *Edison Arantes do Nascimento – known universally as Pelé (the best ever number ten) – scores the opening goal of the 1970 World Cup final.*

> **I'm proud of my side's progress. They are high-quality players, very committed professionals, and they are true men. Every day they play, they give of their best and I am very happy for them.**
>
> DUNGA

GREAT MATCH
1970 Brazil 4–1 Italy

World Cup final
Azteca Stadium, Mexico City, Mexico

Besides being one of the most exciting World Cup finals ever played, Brazil's third world championship victory earned them the right to keep the Jules Rimet trophy forever. The legendary Pelé's last World Cup appearance proved to be one of the best displays of attacking football ever witnessed.

On top in the opening exchanges, Italy went behind when Pelé outjumped Burgnich to head in a cross from Rivelino after 17 minutes. Fittingly, it was Brazil's 100th World Cup goal. Italy equalized soon after when Boninsegna seized on a mistake by Clodoaldo and steered the ball home.

But the Italian cause was lost as the Brazilians scored three goals in 25 second-half minutes. First Gerson scored with a powerful left-footer from outside the box, then a back-header across goal by Pelé following a Gerson free kick allowed Jairzinho to put them further ahead. Matters were finally sealed when Pelé fed the onrushing Carlos Alberto to blast a right-foot shot past the hapless Italian keeper Albertosi.

COACH **Dunga**

Full name: Carlos Caetano Biedorn Verri
Born: 31 October 1963
Record: P52, W36, D11, L5

It is strange that as undopey a figure as Dunga should have a nickname that translates as 'Dopey', the jibe of an uncle who reckoned his nephew wouldn't grow tall and so likened him to one of the Seven Dwarfs. Dunga grew up to claim 91 caps as a defensive midfielder and captained Brazil to the 1994 final success. Before that triumph, his nickname had gone national when the Brazilian press dubbed a dismal 1990 World Cup as the 'Era Dunga' and excoriated a single player's slow and defensive style. Those in the know knew it was a truly Brazilian style dependent on anticipation, timing and keen passing. It is also the style of Dunga's Brazil.

When Dunga became Brazil manager following the 2006 World Cup quarter-final fiasco against France (in which Roberto Carlos was seen tying his bootlaces, leaving Thierry Henry unmarked to score the winning goal), he lacked experience at international management and seemed a stopgap. He made the job his own with an astute team reorganization that led to a 2009 Confederations Cup victory after a sequence of 8 victories and 16 games without defeat.

POSSIBLE SQUAD

Goalkeepers
Júlio César (Internazionale), Doni (Roma), Gomes (Tottenham Hotspur)

Defenders
Dani Alves (Barcelona), Alex Costa (Chelsea), Lúcio (C) (Internazionale), Luisão (Benfica), Maicon (Internazionale), Marcelo (Real Madrid), Miranda (São Paulo), André Santos (Fenerbahçe)

Midfielders
Anderson (Manchester United), Júlio Baptista (Roma), Elano (Galatasaray), Kaká (Real Madrid), Kléberson (Flamengo), Felipe Melo (Juventus), Ramires (Benfica), Gilberto Silva (Panathinaikos)

Forwards
Luís Fabiano (Sevilla), Nilmar (Villarreal), Robinho (Santos, on loan from Manchester City), Diego Tardelli (Atlético Minero)

BELOW *Brazil v Spain, Confederations Cup semi-final, Ellis Park Stadium, Johannesburg, South Africa, 25 June 2009: (back row, left to right) César, Silva, Lúcio, Maicon, Melo, Luisão; (front row) Fabiano, Santos, Kaká, Robinho, Ramires.*

HOW THEY'LL LINE UP

Brazil play a waiting game and are always able to accelerate from elegant back-pedalling to turn a throw-in deep in their own territory into an attacking chance. Patience is the watchword, with Brazilian tactics structured to yield possession, defend deeply and wait for counter-attacking opportunities. Maicon and Ramires initiate lightning moves to unleash the speed and invention of Kaká and Robinho. Opposition defenders are revealed as slow on the turn and concede free kicks. Cue for a cavalry of tall players jostling to reach precision deliveries in a simple version of the beautiful game that has yielded Brazil half their recent goals.

VITAL STATISTICS

World ranking 2nd
Keeper and defence 8/10
Midfield 9/10
Attack 9/10

Strengths and weaknesses Brazilian sophistication, patience and skill will see off most teams. If there is a weakness, it's a reliance on set pieces for goals but it will take high-order defensive skills for any rival to turn that to advantage. About one in three knockout matches in international tournaments ends with a penalty shoot-out. Brazil's record is unsurpassed.

How far will they go? Anything less than the final would be a failure.

ROUTE TO THE FINALS

MATCHES PLAYED

14.10.07	Colombia 0	0 Brazil
17.10.07	Brazil 5	0 Ecuador
18.11.07	Peru 1	1 Brazil
21.11.07	Brazil 2	1 Uruguay
15.06.08	Paraguay 2	0 Brazil
18.06.08	Brazil 0	0 Argentina
07.09.08	Chile 0	3 Brazil
10.09.08	Brazil 0	0 Bolivia
12.10.08	Venezuela 0	4 Brazil
15.10.08	Brazil 0	0 Colombia
29.03.09	Ecuador 1	1 Brazil
01.04.09	Brazil 3	0 Peru
06.06.09	Uruguay 0	4 Brazil
10.06.09	Brazil 2	1 Paraguay
05.09.09	Argentina 1	3 Brazil
09.09.09	Brazil 4	2 Chile
11.10.09	Bolivia 2	1 Brazil
14.10.09	Brazil 0	0 Venezuela

SOUTH AMERICA QUALIFYING GROUP – FINAL TABLE

Team	P	W	D	L	F	A	Pts
Brazil	18	9	7	2	33	11	34
Chile	18	10	3	5	32	22	33
Paraguay	18	10	3	5	24	16	33
Argentina	18	8	4	6	23	20	28
Uruguay	18	6	6	6	28	20	24
Ecuador	18	6	5	7	22	26	23
Colombia	18	6	5	7	14	18	23
Venezuela	18	6	4	8	23	29	22
Bolivia	18	4	3	11	22	36	15
Peru	18	3	4	11	11	34	13

FINALS GROUP G

Brazil play		Date	Venue
	Korea DPR	15 June	Johannesburg (Ellis Park)
	Côte d'Ivoire	20 June	Johannesburg (Soccer City)
	Portugal	25 June	Durban

Lúcio

Even Brazil must know how to defend and in Lúcio they have a widely experienced rock of a centre back. He thrived under the defensively minded regime of the previous Brazil manager Alberto Parreira and has been the first-choice captain since Dunga took over as manager in 2007.

Lúcio has been a fixture on the world scene for a decade. England fans might remember him for a mistake that allowed Michael Owen to score the opening goal in the 2002 World Cup quarter-final match. Brazilian fans probably recall an otherwise flawless campaign highlighted with a heroic stand in the final against Germany when he took the full impact of a free kick and yet stayed standing to complete playing all 630 minutes of the tournament.

PLAYER FACT FILE

Name: Lucimar Ferreira da Silva
Position: Defender
Caps: 88
Goals: 4
Team: Internazionale
Date of birth: 8 May 1978
Height: 188 cm/6 ft 2 in
Weight: 81 kg/177 lb
Previous clubs: Internacional (Brazil), Bayer Leverkusen, Bayern Munich
International debut: 15 November 2000 v Colombia
Previous World Cups: 2002, 2006

STYLE GUIDE

Lúcio is clean, brave and dependable. He's probably Brazil's best-ever centre half and his stylish and intelligent reading of the game have placed him at the heart of the national side since the victorious 2002 World Cup campaign. The defensive value is usually supplemented with direct runs into opposition territory where he shows ball-playing skills unusual for a central defender. Upfield journeys for set pieces earn him the odd headed goal. Typical was the tournament winner in the 2009 Confederations Cup final against the United States when he headed home an Elano corner-kick in the 84th minute.

LEFT *Lúcio scoring with his thunderous left foot in the 3–1 qualifier victory against Argentina in September 2009.*

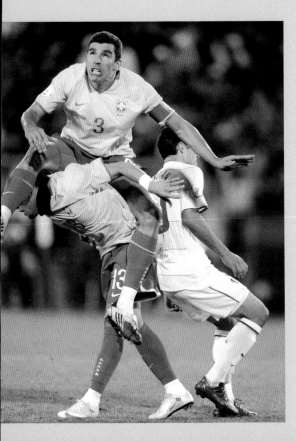

He is one of the cleanest players at the top level of the game. The 386 consecutive minutes that he played in the 2006 finals without fouling anybody is a World Cup final record that marks him out from more cynical kickers and hackers.

Lúcio is the genuine finished article. His classic centre half's heading and tackling skills have been influenced by ten years in European football. The positional sense that is invaluable for his country was honed in Germany where he has played the majority of his club football. At Bayern Munich he won three Bundesliga titles and three German Cups. A move to the Italian club Internazionale in summer 2009 can only have further refined the skills that still seem fresh, as Lúcio, now in the autumn of a distinguished career, approaches a third World Cup – but his first as captain.

He is looking forward and says: 'We're very proud that Brazil currently had the best attack and defence in the South American qualifiers. In the past there were always doubts surrounding the *Seleção*'s defensive system so this recognition makes us all very happy. On the other hand I know how it works with the Brazilian team: the pressure gets greater with every game.'

 ONE TO WATCH

Luís Fabiano

Luís Fabiano is a straightforward striker with pace and an accurate left foot who has recently taken a regular starting spot in Brazil's attack, leading the line alongside Robinho. Having earned his money with clubs like Rennes, Porto and now Seville, Fabiano exemplifies the way his manager has not simply gone for big-team players. His international career stalled in 2004 after a dozen games and he had to wait for Dunga's stewardship for his chance of World Cup renown. Dunga is taking a gamble because the 29-year-old new boy has a reputation for dirty play. He was once suspended for kicking an Argentine player near the neck and announcing he'd 'rather attack an Argentine than take a penalty'. Dunga's faith has been repaid with plenty of goals including a hat-trick in a friendly against Portugal and two goals in the Confederations Cup final.

Dani Alves

Daniel Alves is one of the best, most hard-tackling fullbacks in the world. He's also an attacker who sets off on swashbuckling upfield forays and who, during the moments of a game when Brazil are most likely to pounce, steps forward to deliver an explosive free kick.

> **Did I think that bringing Alves on might win the game for us? Absolutely. He's a dead-ball specialist and I knew we might get a chance to score that way. Fortunately, that's how it turned out and here we are in another final.**

PLAYER FACT FILE

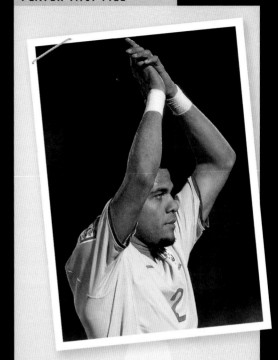

Name: Daniel Alves da Silva
Position: Defender
Caps: 32
Goals: 3
Team: Barcelona
Date of birth: 6 May 1983
Height: 173 cm/5 ft 8 in
Weight: 68 kg/150 lb
Previous clubs: Bahia, Sevilla
International debut: 10 October 2006
v Ecuador
Previous World Cups: None

STYLE GUIDE

Alves is a reliable and athletic attack-minded right wingback. His stamina and aggression have him mopping up in defence and then barrelling forward as a potent attacking force. He's also one to watch at free kicks.

Alves has travelled a long way from his birthplace in Juazeiro. He began playing with Bahia, his local club, before moving to Spain as a 19 year old in 2002. He is well known in Europe as a 2009 treble winner with Barcelona, although he had to endure the disappointment of missing the 2009 Champions League final due to a yellow-card suspension. Before joining Barcelona, he spent six years at Sevilla where he won UEFA Super Cup, Copa del Rey, the Spanish Super Cup and two UEFA Cups. During that time he was varuously linked to Chelsea and Liverpool before joining Barcelona in July 2008 for €34 million plus add-ons of €6 million. The deal made him the world's most expensive defender and, despite having agitated for a transfer, he managed some tears at the press conference to mark his departure from Sevilla. He said that he came to Sevilla as a boy and was now leaving them as a man.

His status in Brazil could be as a nearly man rather than as the world's most expensive defender. Alves marked a late arrival as an international superstar in the 2007 Copa América final when he entered play as a substitute to set up Brazil's second goal and score their third in a 3–0 defeat of Argentina. He further enhanced his international standing as a substitute in the 2009 Confederations Cup semi-final against South Africa. In the 88th minute he hit a free kick reminiscent of Roberto Carlos, another Brazilian wingback, to secure his side a 1–0 win and himself a more secure place in Brazil's international set-up.

So why must the world's priciest defender sit on the substitute's bench? Well, such is Brazil's strength in depth that Maicon challenges Alves for the right-back slot. The duel provides one of Brazil's most keenly debated footballing points – one that will be resolved in the summer of 2010.

OPPOSITE *Robinho (above) lifts Dani Alves in triumph. Alves had just scored the winning goal from a right-footed free kick (below) with only six minutes to go during the 2009 Confederations Cup semi-final between Brazil and South Africa.*

Kaká

Many rate Kaká as the best player on the planet. South Africa 2010 is where he must prove he belongs up there with the game's greats.

Kaká's long-time coach at Milan, Carlo Ancellotti, says: 'Brazilians assert that Kaká plays like Rai, Zico or Rivaldo. He reminds me of Platini.' He reminds Pelé of Johan Cruyff, and Zico of Socrates, and Ruud Van Nistelrooy says Kaká 'seems to play the game for fun and be a free spirit who never gives things a second thought'.

PLAYER FACT FILE

Name: Ricardo Izecson dos Santos Leite
Position: Midfielder
Caps: 75
Goals: 26
Team: Real Madrid
Date of birth: 22 April 1982
Height: 186 cm/6 ft 1 in
Weight: 83 kg/183 lb
Previous clubs: São Paulo, AC Milan
International debut: 31 January 2002 v Bolivia
Previous World Cups: 2002, 2006

STYLE GUIDE

Kaká glides past defenders, making them appear as if they have stepped aside to let him through. He looks relaxed playing anywhere in midfield, from where he strikes the ball in ways that are unimaginable until he has kicked it. Goalkeepers know the feeling especially well. Now that Kaká is in the full pomp of his skills, managers are asking him to press forward and display his astonishing yet economical and unflashy footwork in conjuring closer-range goal-scoring opportunities.

> **" Kaká is a magical footballer who creates moments of inspiration. As well as being a superb passer of the ball with excellent positioning, he can run past players, shoot and score. "**
>
> RONALDINHO

Kaká is a singular man. In recognition of his fame, ability and work for the United Nations' World Food Programme, *Time* magazine places Kaká on a list of the world's 100 most influential people. He has given a tenth of his income to the Catholic church since making what he reckons was a divinely assisted recovery from a broken vertebra in 1980. He plays every game with the words 'I belong to Jesus' and 'God is faithful' stitched into the tongues of his boots.

Kaká's speed with the ball, his intelligence and his ability to shoot on goal with both feet make him outstanding. He is the master of simple, yet clinical soccer and also a leader whom some fans argue can win games on his own. Despite this he isn't flamboyant or even always eye-catching. The consensus is, however, that he is still improving and has demonstrated the flexibility which promises that in South Africa he will play with the most appropriate possible effectiveness. That said, there is a proven consistency, efficiency and ability to rise to the big occasion with a decisive goal or assist.

Every game guarantees defence-splitting passes and he scores consistently from distance, with a one-in-three-games strike rate to underline just how attack-minded a midfielder he really is. He moved to Real Madrid for €8.5 million in 2003 and, as the focal point of attack switching between the midfield and striker roles, he helped them to Serie A and Champions League titles. He seemed set to remain in Italy, but in June 2009 Real Madrid paid a reported €65 million (£56 million) for its latest *galáctico*.

Despite the transfer brouhaha, Kaká travelled to South Africa for the 2009 Confederations Cup, where he shone and was named the player of the tournament plus man of the match in the final after helping Brazil to a 3–2 win against the United States. It could be a heavenly portent for another – more important – Kaká visitation to South Africa.

ABOVE AND OPPOSITE *There is always poise to Kaká's play. Here he is seen in action in 2009 against Italy during the Confederations Cup and in an encounter with Gareth Barry during England's friendly with Brazil.*

Robinho

Robinho will be at his playing prime in South Africa and no longer the playboy beginner with the raw skills that once reminded Pelé of his younger self. At the age of 26, Robinho must now deliver on the rich promise.

Though he looks insubstantial, Robinho is a force to be reckoned with as he drifts in from the left to occupy his favoured position in the hole behind the main strikers. Robinho is an attacker whom defensive players fear and he enters this World Cup with the impressive track record of having led Santos to their first Brazilian title since Pelé played for the club, plus two titles with Real Madrid. Internationally, he has won the Copa América and two Confederations Cups. So there's definitely a space to fill in his trophy cabinet.

Robinho's skills have matured and developed in the crucible of public attention. He served a Brazilian apprenticeship until he was 21. Despite his huge popularity with Santos fans, Robinho was too valuable to remain a Brazilian homeboy. In 2005 he was signed by

OPPOSITE *Robinho's talent – with added resolve and status after being given the captaincy in a friendly – is such that he's now a regular starter. He is pictured on the opposite page bursting free from a bunch of United States players during the 2009 Confederations Cup and (right) controlling the ball in a World Cup qualifier against Peru.*

PLAYER FACT FILE

Name: Robson de Souza
Position: Striker
Caps: 72
Goals: 19
Team: Santos (on loan from Manchester City)
Date of birth: 25 January 1984
Height: 173 cm
Weight: 60 kg
Previous clubs: Santos, Real Madrid
International debut: 13 July 2003 v Mexico
Previous World Cups: 2006

STYLE GUIDE

Robinho is an exuberant, samba-style footballer whose slight frame and ready smile encapsulate the supple happiness at the heart of the best of Brazilian football. His style is that of an entertainer, and he uses his pace, acceleration and outrageous trickery to thrill crowds and frustrate defenders. The repertoire of dribbling skills includes the *pedalada* dummy, the *bicicleta* step over and the hat, a close-range kick of the ball over a defender's head. He's not just messing about because a fierce and accurate shot brings his teams a goal nearly every three games.

European giants Real Madrid where he stayed for three troubled seasons and was never quite accepted by the Spanish hierarchy. In September 2008 he moved to Manchester City – in the shape of a transfer fee of about £32.5 million and a weekly pay packet of £160,000 – the first player bought by the club after it had been taken over by the Abu Dhabi United Group.

Robinho benefited from a more settled regime under City manager Mark Hughes, for whom he scored 15 goals in 41 appearances in his first season with the club. However, he struggled in the early part of the following season, scoring just once in 12 appearances for the team. In January 2010 he was substituted by new City boss Roberto Mancini after coming on as a replacement against Everton. Shortly afterwards he returned to his home club Santos on a six-month loan.

City fans might chant 'We've got Robinho' but their man really belongs to Brazil and he wants to improve on the last World Cup, when he was a substitute for many of the games and did not score. Since then he has captained Brazil in a friendly and played in every game of the 2009 Confederations Cup. Come summer 2010, he will take the spotlight on a world stage. His biggest test now looms.

" **Robinho is an incredible talent ... undoubtedly one of the best players in the world.** "

MARK HUGHES, FORMER
MANCHESTER CITY MANAGER

KOREA DPR

GROUP G

Heroic defending earned North Korea a place in the final eight of the 1966 World Cup. South Africa 2010 is their first World Cup finals appearance since then.

Defence remains the team's watchword and the Democratic People's Republic of Korea (recognized as Korea DPR by FIFA) had the meanest of defensive records during the qualifying stages. The goalkeeper Ri Myong-Guk provides backing for a rank of competent outfield stoppers; he is a clean-sheet specialist.

Thorough preparation will play a part too. In analysing the scoreless draw against Saudi Arabia that secured the team a ticket to South Africa, the head coach Kim Jong-Hun said: 'We focused on the defending as we had come under a lot of pressure and I think our preparation for the game was another factor. We monitored the Saudi team from the beginning of our campaign and I noticed that they have a problem in finding good strikers.'

The current Korea DPR team consists of home-grown players along with a few Zainichi Koreans who were brought up in Japan. Ahn Young-Hak, the best known of these Japan-influenced players, is a versatile midfielder who will play a key role in South Africa.

This is the first time in World Cup history that both North and South Korea are taking part in the same tournament and, if history is a guide, any footballing contest will result in stalemate and rancour. The two Koreas faced each other in a third-round Asian qualification match originally scheduled for the Kim Il Sung Stadium in the northern capital of Pyongyang. The North Korean government decided the South's national anthem should not be played and that its national flag should not be flown. After FIFA intervention, the match was played in Shanghai, China, on 26 March 2008. It ended 0–0.

BELOW LEFT *Ji Yun-Nam, Hong Yong-Jo and Pak Chol-Jin run a victory lap of honour after a 0–0 draw in Saudi that ensured North Korea a place in South Africa.*

BELOW RIGHT *Ri Myong-Guk, the North Korean goalkeeper, directs play. He did not let in a goal during the last four out of five World Cup qualifying matches.*

POSSIBLE SQUAD

Goalkeepers

Ju Kwang Min (Gigwanch), Kim Myong-Gil (Amrokgang), Ri Myong-Guk (Pyongyang City)

Defenders

An Chol-Hyok (Rimyongsu), Cha Jong-Hyok (Amrokgang), Ji Yun-Nam (April 25), Jon Kwang-Ik (Amrokgang), Nam Song-Chol (April 25), Pak Chol-Jin (Amrokgang), Pak Nam-Chol (April 25), Ri Jun-Il (Sobaeksu), Ri Kwang-Chon (April 25), Ri Kwang-Hyok (Kyonggongop), Ryang Yong-Gi (Vegalta Sendai)

Midfielders

Ahn Young-Hak (Suwon Samsung Bluewings), Jong Su Hyok (Unattached), Kim Yong-Jun (Chengdu Blades), Mun In-Guk (April 25)

Forwards

Choe Kum-Chol (Unattached), Hong Yong-Jo (C) (FC Rostov), Jong Tae-Se (Kawasaki Frontale), Kim Kum-Il (April 25), Kim Myong-Won (Amrokgang)

ROUTE TO THE FINALS

ASIA QUALIFYING FINAL GROUP 1 – FINAL TABLE

Team	P	W	D	L	F	A	Pts
Korea Republic	8	4	4	0	12	4	16
Korea DPR	8	3	3	2	7	5	12
Saudi Arabia	8	3	3	2	8	8	12
Iran	8	2	5	1	8	7	11
UAE	8	0	1	7	6	17	1

FINALS GROUP G

Korea DPR play	Date	Venue
Brazil	15 June	Johannesburg (Ellis Park)
Portugal	21 June	Cape Town
Côte d'Ivoire	25 June	Nelspruit

VITAL STATISTICS

World ranking 84th
Midfield 5/10

Keeper and defence 5/10
Attack 3/10

Strengths and weaknesses Stolid defence and solid preparation are the weapons of a team that will be difficult to break down, though more experienced sides are likely to prevail over a set of players whose club experience is confined to a pinched national stage

How far will they go? If Korea DPR move beyond the opening league matches, it will be a triumph of dullness over flair.

LEFT *Korea DPR (North Korea) v Korea Republic (South Korea), World Cup qualifying match, World Cup Stadium, Seoul, South Korea, 1 April 2009: (back row, left to right) Hong Yong-Jo, Ji Yun-Nam, Ri Myong-Guk, Pak Nam-Chol, Ri Jun-Il; (front row) Pak Chol-Jin, Cha Jong-Hyok, Mun In-Guk, Lee Kwang-Chon, Jong Tae-Se, Kim Yong-Jun.*

CÔTE D'IVOIRE

GROUP G

Côte d'Ivoire are Africa's best hope, with a cadre of players that would make it into many international squads. Any team would fear Kolo Touré at centre back, Yaya Touré and Emmanuel Eboué in midfield, and Salomon Kalou and Didier Drogba in attack.

What doesn't look so good on paper is Côte d'Ivoire's international record for, aside from qualifying for two World Cup finals in a row, the greatest achievement was winning the 1992 African Cup of Nations. However, the 2006 consensus is that they were a useful side that would have gone to the second round if they hadn't been in a tough group with Argentina and the Netherlands. They lost both games 2–1, which makes them the only team to have scored in all World Cup matches they have participated in. If they do reach the later stages, their penalty shoot-out record reveals a team resilience in winning international football's two highest-scoring penalty shoot-outs: 11–10 against Ghana in the 1992 African Cup final; and 12–11 in the 2006 African Cup quarter-final.

Côte d'Ivoire enters the World Cup finals as the highest-ranking team in Africa. Hopes are high, now that the stuttering progress in qualifiers against Burkina Faso, Guinea and Malawi is behind them. During those games, the defensive polish of Kolo Touré ensured quality interceptions and distribution. Both Yaya Touré and Emmanuel Eboué revealed their known defensive midfield skills but there was a problem making the telling pass up to Salomon Kalou and Didier Drogba.

That said, these players have had half a decade playing together and are at the core of a side with masses of big-game experience. Almost every squad member plays for a club outside his home country. They have escaped a nation where life expectancy at birth is 41 for males and where a quarter of the population live below the international poverty line of $1.25 a day. Football – in a land whose top footballers' combined transfer value would nearly equal gross national product – is the nation's big hope.

ABOVE *Brothers in arms: Yaya and Kolo Touré bring experience and skill to the Côte d'Ivoire spine. Yaya (19) will boss the midfield while Kolo (4) puts grit into defensive polish.*

ABOVE *Didier Drogba is the Côte d'Ivoire's undisputed poster boy. Hordes of fans will take the trip south to support their side knowing that if any team is going to show the world that Africans are world-beaters, their team is the one most likely to do it.*

RIGHT *Côte d'Ivoire v Turkey, International friendly, Izmir Ataturk Stadium, Izmir, Turkey, 11 February 2009: (back row, left to right) Barry, Demel, Yaya Touré, Gohouri, Romaric, Kolo Touré, Zokora; (front row) Faé, Boka, Drogba, Eboué.*

POSSIBLE SQUAD

Goalkeepers

Vincent Angban (ASEC Mimosas), Boubacar Barry (Lokeren), Ibrahim Koné (US Boulogne)

Defenders

Sol Bamba (Hibernian), Angoua Brou Benjamin (Budapest Honvéd), Arthur Boka (Stuttgart), Guy Demel (Hamburg), Emmanuel Eboué (Arsenal), Steve Gohouri (Borussia Mönchengladbach), Abdoulaye Méïté (West Bromwich Albion), Kolo Touré (Manchester City)

Midfielders

Emerse Faé (Nice), Emmanuel Koné (International), Romaric (Sevilla), Cheik Tioté (Twente), Yaya Touré (Barcelona), Didier Zokora (Sevilla)

Forwards

Didier Drogba (C) (Chelsea), Sekou Cissé (Feyenoord), Gervinho (Lille OSC), Salomon Kalou (Chelsea), Abdul-Kader Keïta (Galatasaray), Boubacar Sanogo (AS Saint-Étienne)

ROUTE TO THE FINALS

AFRICA QUALIFYING GROUP E – FINAL TABLE

Team	P	W	D	L	F	A	Pts
Côte d'Ivoire	6	5	1	0	19	4	16
Burkina Faso	6	4	0	2	10	11	12
Malawi	6	1	1	4	4	11	4
Guinea	6	1	0	5	7	14	3

FINALS GROUP G

Côte d'Ivoire play		Date	Venue
	Portugal	15 June	N. Mandela Bay/Pt Elizabeth
	Brazil	20 June	Johannesburg (Soccer City)
	Korea DPR	25 June	Nelspruit

VITAL STATISTICS

World ranking 16th
Midfield 5/10

Keeper and defence 7/10
Attack 8/10

Strengths and weaknesses There's no disputing that Côte d'Ivoire fields a star-studded side. Two questions remain: Will they gel into a team? Who is going to command the midfield?

How far will they go? They had a tough group in 2006 and have a tougher one in 2010. If they can squeeze past Portugal in the group stage, they could go on to be Africa's team of the tournament.

Even by the odd standards of international football, Didier Drogba is extraordinary. Having spent his youth yo-yoing between Africa and France, he was 21 before signing his first professional contract – with Le Mans in 1999 – and settling into the rigorous training needed to make it to the top. He is now national captain and Côte d'Ivoire's all-time leading scorer.

After his career's tortoise-like start, Drogba has hared to hero status in his own land: a street in Abidjan is named after him; one-litre bottles of Bock beer are ordered as a 'Drogba' because they're that big and strong; night clubs play 'Drogbacite' music with Magic System, a local band, backing Didier on vocals. He is also on the world stage as a United Nations goodwill ambassador.

Name: Didier Yves Drogba Tébily
Position: Striker
Caps: 65
Goals: 43
Team: Chelsea
Date of birth: 11 March 1978
Height: 189 cm/6 ft 2 in
Weight: 91 kg/201 lb
Previous clubs: Le Mans, Guingamp, Marseille
International debut: 8 September 2002 v South Africa
Previous World Cups: 2006

STYLE GUIDE
Didier Drogba's pace, strength, aerial power and two good feet provide two goals every three international games. There are plenty of assists coming in from left and right. He's a big man with the muscle to bully defenders and charisma enough to do the difficult job of both leading the line and acting as an inspiring captain.

LEFT, ABOVE AND RIGHT *Man at arms trilogy: Didier Drogba in handsome form leading the Côte d'Ivoire line in World Cup qualifying matches against Burkina Faso (left) and Malawi (above and right)*

In Britain, Drogba is always controversial, whether celebrating his goals or complaining at injustices. Managers of opposing teams have claimed Drogba has dived and elbowed his way to success – though they would say that of a player who has terrorized their defences in Premier and Champions League games. He's a Chelsea icon who has repaid the £24 million they invested in him in 2004 with a record number of goals for a foreign player. Nobody could deny Drogba's role in reestablishing Chelsea as one of the top four English clubs.

As the Côte d'Ivoire captain, Drogba talks of collective virtues. 'We must be more efficient in possession,' he says. 'Football's not an individual sport, you win and lose as a team. [At the 2006 World Cup] we had a lot of chances but did not take them. That's the difference between big teams like Argentina and small teams like us.'

An intriguing question for this World Cup is whether Drogba has it in him to make his team, and thus Africa, into a big footballing force.

> " **He needs to be lifted by the crowd, to feel the love. He's a showman, elegant, has charisma, class.** "
>
> ALAIN PASCALOU
> DROGBA'S MANAGER AT LE MANS

PORTUGAL

GROUP G

Portugal's record is formidable. The *Selecção das Quinas* eliminated England from Euro 2004 and from the last World Cup. They made it to the finals of Euro 2004, and reached their second World Cup semi-final in 2006.

> 66 **In any game of football, both teams have possibilities. Details and concentration will make the difference.** 99
>
> CARLOS QUEIROZ

Big acts are hard to follow and many big names of that era such as Fernando Couto, Maniche, Costinha, Rui Costa, Luís Figo have retired. Gone too is Big Phil Scolari, the Brazilian whose six years' managing Portugal were bracketed by leading Brazil's World Cup triumph in 2002 and getting the sack from Chelsea in 2009. Scolari's replacement Carlos Queiroz has a big problem: he can field the best player in the world but only in an average team that very nearly didn't qualify for South Africa.

Two new faces, both far from young and both little known outside Portugal, saved the day. Eduardo's goalkeeping prowess rocketed him from zero to hero in an international career trajectory that began when he was 26. From February 2009, Eduardo had a

timely streak of form letting in only two goals in 11 matches and pulling off some vital saves to enable Portugal to edge away from 2010 World Cup oblivion. At the other end of the park is Liédson, a 32-year-old striker called up for the first time in August 2009. He headed the 85th-minute equalizer in Denmark that maintained Portuguese hopes of qualification, went on to score a goal and to play in back-to-back wins against Hungary, and subsequently proved an efficient target man in the play-off games against Bosnia-Herzegovina.

Liédson and Eduardo are not the two swallows who will make a Portuguese summer. The man most likely to do that is, of course, Cristiano Ronaldo, who was unavailable for Portugal's later qualifying games due to injury. Ronaldo's raw skill was refined at Manchester United when Queiroz was Sir Alex Ferguson's assistant and the two wise old heads ensured their showboating peacock matured into the best player in the world. There's a tactical sympathy between manager and a remarkable player who, at 25, is in his prime and who is the reason many neutrals welcomed Portugal's World Cup qualification.

It doesn't take a tactical genius to realize that Ronaldo will be deployed across the park in the kind of advanced midfield role that makes Premiership fans wish he'd never left Manchester United. Beyond that, however, the prospect of watching Portugal is far from compelling. The midfield lacks a visionary player who can boss things just ahead of defence. Raul Meireles and João Moutinho have emerged since Queiroz took over in 2008 and they will probably make the

LEFT *Raul Meireles is submerged beneath a gathering of players celebrating his goal during Portugal's second leg play-off match against Bosnia in November 2009.*

ABOVE *Liédson rises above Bosnian defender Sanel Jahić. From mid-2009, the forward shot across Portugal's footballing firmament as a late, but high-scoring, managerial experiment.*

midfield cut alongside Tiago and Miguel Veloso. The spectacle of men hard at work in midfield will be more entertaining if Deco's fitness and form put him into midfield contention. Defence is less of a problem. Paulo Ferreira and Miguel are both above average right backs and in the centre the muscular José Bosingwa complements the cerebral Ricardo Carvalho. The left-back slot is a headache for Queiroz, though either Ferreira or Bosingwa could fill in.

HOW THEY'LL LINE UP

For the most part, Queiroz has retained the same 4-5-1 formation (though not the same players) he inherited from Scolari. This defence-minded line-up leaves Portugal reliant on a target man to exploit the wing play of Ronaldo and Simão or Nani. Portugal's tactical problems have been finding a player to replace the midfield prowess of Luís Figo and to find a world-class target man. Well, one name springs to mind as a combined creator and goal scorer and, luckily for Portugal, he's playing for them. But will Ronaldo's brilliance be enough for Portugal to approach the kind of progress they made at the last World Cup?

POSSIBLE SQUAD

Goalkeepers

Eduardo (Braga), Henrique Hilário (Chelsea), Rui Patrício (Sporting CP)

Defenders

Bruno Alves (Porto), José Bosingwa (Chelsea), Ricardo Carvalho (Chelsea), Ricardo Costa (Wolfsburg), Paulo Ferreira (Chelsea), Miguel (Valencia), Pepe (Real Madrid), Rolando (Porto)

Midfielders

Deco (Chelsea), Duda (Málaga), Raul Meireles (Porto), João Moutinho (Sporting CP), Tiago (Juventus), Miguel Veloso (Sporting CP)

Forwards

Hugo Almeida (Werder Bremen), Edinho (Málaga), Liédson (Sporting CP), Nani (Manchester United), Cristiano Ronaldo (C) (Real Madrid), Simão (Atlético Madrid)

BELOW *Portugal v Bosnia-Herzegovina, World Cup qualifying match, play-off first leg, Luz Stadium, Lisbon, 14 November 2009: (back row, left to right) Carvalho, Alves, Pepe, Ferreira, Nani, Eduardo; (front row) Duda, Meireles, Liédson, Deco, Simão. (Ronaldo was absent through injury.)*

ROUTE TO THE FINALS

MATCHES PLAYED

06.09.08	Malta 0	4 Portugal
10.09.08	Portugal 2	3 Denmark
11.10.08	Sweden 0	0 Portugal
15.10.08	Portugal 0	0 Albania
28.03.09	Portugal 0	0 Sweden
06.06.09	Albania 1	2 Portugal
05.09.09	Denmark 1	1 Portugal
09.09.09	Hungary 0	1 Portugal
10.10.09	Portugal 3	0 Hungary
14.10.09	Portugal 4	0 Malta

EUROPE QUALIFYING GROUP 1 – FINAL TABLE

Team	P	W	D	L	F	A	Pts
Denmark	10	6	3	1	16	5	21
Portugal	10	5	4	1	17	5	19
Sweden	10	5	3	2	13	5	18
Hungary	10	5	1	4	10	8	16
Albania	10	1	4	5	6	13	7
Malta	10	0	1	9	0	26	1

EUROPE PLAY-OFFS

14.11.09	Portugal 1	0 Bosnia-Herzegovina
18.11.09	Bosnia-Herzegovina 0	1 Portugal

FINALS GROUP G

Portugal play		Date	Venue
	Côte d'Ivoire	15 June	N. Mandela Bay/Pt Elizabeth
	Korea DPR	21 June	Cape Town
	Brazil	25 June	Durban

VITAL STATISTICS

World ranking 5th   Keeper and defence 7/10
Midfield 6/10   Attack 8/10

Strengths and weaknesses Their strength is Ronaldo, their weakness is the rest of the team who are too old or too inexperienced or both.

How far will they go? The early 21st-century form guide would have rated Portugal at evens for a quarter-final place. Another decade, another Portugal – this team will surely not do that well.

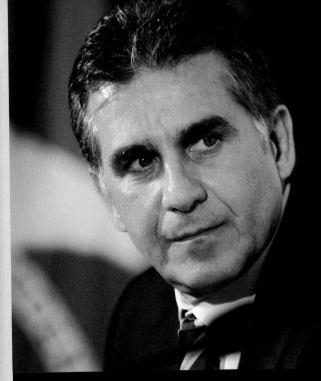

COACH **Carlos Queiroz**

Born 1 March 1953
Record: P45, W24, D14, L7

Edited highlights of Queiroz's CV would emphasise his role in developing Portugal's golden generation of players in the 1990s. Then, having nurtured talents such as Figo and Rui Costa, he did the same for Ronaldo in Manchester. He has written a book too, the *Q-Report* on football development in the United States. The raw data on his manager's jobs is equally impressive: Portugal (1991–93), NY/NJ MetroStars (1996), Nagoya Grampus Eight (1996–97), United Arab Emirates (1999), South Africa (2000–02), Manchester United (assistant 2002–03 and 2004–08), Real Madrid (2003–04) and Portugal (again) from 2008.

A fuller CV would show why he is unpopular as Portuguese manager. During his first stint in charge, Portugal failed to qualify for Euro 1992 or the 1994 World Cup. (He led South Africa through a successful 2002 World Cup qualification campaign – but was sacked before the finals.) On Queiroz's return to Portugal management after Euro 2008, his teams limped through qualification with poor showings in front of home fans treated to a loss against Denmark followed by scoreless draws with Albania and Sweden. But Portugal made it and Queiroz's fluency in front of a camera will reach a global television audience in summer 2010.

A claim that Ronaldo is the world's best footballer can't rely on statistically based evidence alone. But it's a good start. At Man U, Ronaldo scored 118 times in 291 appearances and his 84 Premier League goals helped his club to three consecutive titles from 2007. In 2008, he was the FIFA World Player of the Year, and in the summer of 2009 he moved to Real Madrid for a world record fee of £80 million.

Cristiano Ronaldo makes an impact. Few can forget the first time they saw his close control and lightning change of pace, his trademark step-overs and light-footed manoeuvres. He has a bag of tricks at his disposal. His distinctive 'twinkle toes' running style only serves to emphasize his turn of pace and ability to bemuse defenders. Equally comfortable on either foot and a good header too, he is difficult to defend against.

From the moment he joined Sporting Lisbon as a junior Ronaldo was under the spotlight. He made his debut for the senior side aged 16 and was soon spotted by Alex Ferguson, who signed the player in 2003. When he started at Manchester United, some supporters thought Ronaldo was little more than a show-boating luxury. By the time he moved to Spain, his exciting and mature performances had proved them wrong. The tricks are now deployed for a purpose: a pin-point cross, a vicious shot or a delicious through ball. Perhaps his weakness is his eye for goal, but he is a danger at corners and set pieces. The short-stepped stride has him outstripping the swiftest defender in runs that encourage more fouls than any other player. He's brave and doesn't often duck out. His acceleration is matched to an equal power of deceleration when he stops and teases defenders. His trickery bypasses whole defensive structures with flicks and back heels and lobs and passes where he looks one way and kicks the other.

PLAYER FACT FILE

Name: Cristiano Ronaldo dos Santos Aveiro
Position: Forward
Caps: 68
Goals: 22
Team: Real Madrid
Date of birth: 5 February 1985
Height: 184 cm/6 ft
Weight: 78 kg/172 lb
Previous clubs: Sporting CP, Manchester United
International debut: 16 August 2003 v Kazakhstan
Previous World Cups: 2006

STYLE GUIDE

Ronaldo's distinctive running, unique style and sublime skills will test the mettle of all opposing teams. His quick thinking is such that he can turn a game on its head in an instant.

Ronaldo says: 'I've got an ambition to always win and be the best and to win every trophy and competition I'm part of. I'll be happy when I win the Champions League, the European Championship and the World Cup.' All football fans look forward to Ronaldo's arrival in South Africa and hope he can deliver his magic from the advanced midfield role in which his manager Carlos Queiroz has deployed him. It is just possible that he will join Maradona or his namesake, the Brazilian Ronaldo, as one of those players who almost single-handedly bring World Cup victory to their nations.

ABOVE *An ankle injury prevented Ronaldo from taking part in the latter stages of Portugal's fraught route to World Cup qualification. He's pictured here in March 2009's 0–0 home qualifier battling for aerial supremacy with Sweden's Daniel Majstorović.*

❝ **There have been a few players described as the new George Best over the years, but this is the first time it's been a compliment to me.** ❞

GEORGE BEST

Ricardo Carvalho

There are few players tougher for a forward to beat than Ricardo Carvalho. The defensive maestro has spent half a lifetime thwarting top attackers. He was 20 when he won his first national title at Porto and he won four consecutive league titles in the years to 2006, two with Porto and two with Chelsea.

José Mourinho recognized Carvalho's qualities and the young manager put his young defender at the centre of the FC Porto team that dominated national and, for a short while, European football. Carvalho played in all the games that culminated in the unfancied Portuguese side becoming European champions in 2004. He then followed Mourinho to Chelsea for a fee of £19.85 million. He has remained there ever since playing his cool, unspectacular game. Injury had him losing his place to the Brazilian, Alex, when Scolari and Guus Hiddink took control of Chelsea in 2008–09, but he regained his place under Carlo Ancelotti.

PLAYER FACT FILE

Name: Ricardo Alberto Silveira Carvalho
Position: Defender
Caps: 60
Goals: 4
Team: Chelsea
Date of birth: 18 May 1978
Height: 181 cm/5 ft 11½ in
Weight: 79 kg/174 lb
Previous clubs: Porto, Leça, Vitória de Setúbal, Alverca, Porto
International debut: 11 October 2003 v Albania
Previous World Cups: 2006

STYLE GUIDE

Carvalho has the consistency common to all top defenders. He is good with both feet and commanding in the air. What makes him special is an anticipation of play that ensures he's in the right positions to make athletic interceptions. Failing that, he has the muscle to put in crunchingly well-timed tackles.

LEFT Carvalho stretches athletically for possession in a tussle with Denmark's Peter Løvenkrands during a World Cup qualifier in September 2008.

RIGHT It's 18 November 2009 and Portugal have finally qualified for South Africa. Carvalho was the old hand who took centre stage when the Portuguese celebrated their win against Bosnia.

Carvalho has been a Portuguese regular since Euro 2004. He was an unused substitute in the first match of that tournament and could only look on when Portugal lost their opening match to Greece. Big Phil Scolari rebuilt his defence on the hoof and Carvalho was brought in to replace the ageing centre back Fernando Couto. The young pretender kept his place for the rest of the tournament and delivered a run of performances that helped take Portugal to the final, also against Greece – and another unanticipated defeat. He finished 2004 being voted best defender at the European Football Awards. In 2006, Carvalho was even more influential in marshalling Portugal's defence as his team steamrollered their way to the 2006 World Cup semi-finals. It was for a stamp on Carvalho that 20-year-old Wayne Rooney was sent off in the controversial 2006 quarter-final.

Carvalho's reputation as the consummate defender will be on the line when he pulls on the red Portuguese shirt and appears for Portugal in South Africa as one of the team's elder statesmen. It will surely be the last chance he's got to prove himself a winner at the highest level of the game.

![camera] ONE TO WATCH

Liédson

Liédson da Silva Muniz, also known as *Levezinho* ('slender one'), is a nippy player who weighs in at 63 kg/139 lb and has a striker's eye for goal. When he turned 30 in 2007, Liédson can hardly have anticipated that he would be in strong contention to lead Portugal's next World Cup attack. Fair reward, though, for a player whose arrival in the Portuguese squad in late summer 2009 was the turning point in the national qualifying campaign. Like Deco and Pepe, Liédson is Brazilian born and therefore had to switch nationality to play for Portugal. He moved to Sporting Clube de Portugal (aka Sporting Lisbon) in 2003 and is a local hero with over a hundred goals in twice as many games. His strike rate is nearly as good at international level and, late in his sporting life, Liédson has nipped in to put himself in line for the title of national hero.

SPAIN

An elegant 1–0 victory over Germany in the Euro 2008 final ended Spain's reputation as the skilful nearly men of international football. That said, World Cups have so far been a step too far for *La Roja* ('the Reds'), with fourth place at Brazil 1950 being the height of Spanish achievement.

Spain has mirrored England in a consistent failure to convert club success into World Cup dominance. Both nations can look back on unlucky quarter-final defeats, terrible refereeing and lost penalty shoot-outs; both have made a habit of struggling to even qualify for their regular sessions of humiliation on the global stage. But in the run-up to South Africa 2010, both sides sailed through the qualifiers – both of them, incidentally, under managers who had led Real Madrid to championship medals in La Liga (the current England manager Fabio Capello in 2007 and the Spanish manager Vicente del Bosque in 2001 and 2003).

Spain under del Bosque dominated their qualifying group with a perfect ten victories, with double knockouts against Bosnia and Herzegovina, Armenia, Estonia, Belgium and Turkey. Del Bosque can select a squad with deep experience in the world's two top leagues – the Spanish La Liga and the English Premiership. He is popular with established players, and rather than giving lectures to the experienced, he allows them to express their talents. And there is talent in abundance.

RIGHT *When Spain won Euro 2008, their first major title since 1964, Prime Minister José Luis Rodriguez Zapatero captured the spirit of the nation: 'La Roja has always conquered our hearts. We are the champions in Europe and we have the highest expectations to be world champions.' Has their time at last come?*

In goal, Spain is spoilt for choice with Real Madrid's Iker Casillas more likely to get the spot than Liverpool's Pepe Reina. Sergio Ramos will dominate defence. The midfield is crowded with playmakers and one of the big questions of the 2010 World Cup is whether or not Cesc Fàbregas will be given the chance to play a truly creative role alongside Andrés Iniesta. Perhaps the answer has to do with del Bosque, whose time at Real Madrid had him fully exploiting the talents of Luís Figo,

"Fernando and I complement each other very well . . . We both chase down defenders, put pressure on and fight to create chances for each other."

DAVID VILLA ON HIS PARTNERSHIP
WITH FERNANDO TORRES

Zinédine Zidane and Ronaldo. And if the midfield isn't a sticky enough problem, how is del Bosque to choose the best attacking options from among David Villa, Fernando Torres, Daniel Güiza and Bojan Krkić?

The players del Bosque will have to drop would be shoo-ins to most other international teams and the selection problems of the rich are reasons enough to believe that this time Spain really could go all the way and bring the World Cup home to Spain for the first time. On Spain's World Cup journey, we can also expect to see some or all of the five young newcomers del Bosque has given games to: Bojan Krkić, Andoni Iraola, Fernando Llorente, Diego Capel and Sergio Busquets. These lesser-known names may yet receive the call if Spain's stars follow old Spanish practices of wilting at the prospect of exposure at a World Cup. But don't bet on it. The big names have shown they can stand the heat of intense competition.

BELOW LEFT *Fernando Torres has the gift of being able to concentrate at decisive moments. All Spain hopes his gifts allow him to bring home its first World Cup.*

BELOW *2002 World Cup quarter final, Spain v South Korea: Ruben Baraja gets his head to the ball to score from a free kick but the goal is disallowed.*

GREAT MATCH
2002 Spain 0–0 South Korea (South Korea won 5–4 on penalties)

World Cup, quarter-final
Gwangju World Cup Stadium, Korea

Spain's greatest ever position in a World Cup came in 1950 with a fourth place, but a penalty shoot-out victory over Ireland in the second round gave them hope of bettering that in 2002.

With Joaquin and Morientes causing problems, Spain looked like ending the joint-host nation's run at any moment. On 49 minutes Ruben Baraja headed home from a free kick, but the effort was disallowed because Morientes was ruled offside. More close shaves followed as Hierro and Morientes missed narrowly, but, eventually, Spain had a great Casillas save to thank for seeing the 90 minutes out at 0–0.

Extra time brought another remarkable decision as a Morientes strike was disallowed because Joaquin's ball had supposedly gone out of play before he crossed it. And when, in the 100th minute, Morientes turned on a long throw and crashed his shot against the left post, they might have guessed it wasn't their day. Sure enough, penalties at 4–4 brought Joaquin to the spot and the 20 year old saw his kick saved by the excellent Lee. Korean captain Hong Myung-bo converted his kick and, once again, Spain were heading home.

COACH **Vicente del Bosque González**

Born 23 December 1950
Record: P22, W21, D0, L1

Vicente del Bosque is a famously cool head in the hothouse of Spanish football. Unflappable under pressure, he has a talent to avoid confrontations with journalists, club owners or players. A reticent man and an astute tactician, his CV reveals someone able to take charge of the egotistical young multi-millionaires on whom managerial reputations must depend. In four seasons at Real Madrid, del Bosque won two Champions League titles (2000 and 2002), two La Liga titles (2001 and 2003), a Spanish Supercup (2001), a UEFA Super Cup (2002) and the Intercontinental Cup (2002).

He was approached as a possible manager of the national side in 2004, but turned the offer down; he finally decided to take the job on after Euro 2008. He quickly set about breaking international records. On 9 June 2009 in a friendly against Azerbaijan in which Spain won 6–0, he became the first manager to win his first ten games in charge of a national side, going on to chalk up 13 successive victories until a surprising 2–0 Confederations Cup semi-final defeat against the United States.

ROUTE TO THE FINALS

MATCHES PLAYED

06.09.08	Spain 1	0 Bosnia-Herzegovina
10.09.08	Spain 4	0 Armenia
11.10.08	Estonia 0	3 Spain
15.10.08	Belgium 1	2 Spain
28.03.09	Spain 1	0 Turkey
01.04.09	Turkey 1	2 Spain
05.09.09	Spain 5	0 Belgium
09.09.09	Spain 3	0 Estonia
10.10.09	Armenia 1	2 Spain
14.10.09	Bosnia-Herzegovina 2	5 Spain

EUROPE QUALIFYING GROUP 5 – FINAL TABLE

Team	P	W	D	L	F	A	Pts
Spain	10	10	0	0	28	5	30
Bosnia-Herzegovina	10	6	1	3	25	13	19
Turkey	10	4	3	3	13	10	15
Belgium	10	3	1	6	13	20	10
Estonia	10	2	2	6	9	24	8
Armenia	10	1	1	8	6	22	4

FINALS GROUP H

Spain play		Date	Venue
	Switzerland	16 June	Durban
	Honduras	21 June	Johannesburg (Ellis Park)
	Chile	25 June	Tshwane/Pretoria

VITAL STATISTICS

World ranking 1st
Midfield 8/10

Keeper and defence 9/10
Attack 8/10

Strengths and weaknesses The undoubted Spanish strength lies in an array of mature young talent with the experience of outstanding European achievement. However, their form in previous World Cups indicates that at the pinnacle of the game the Spanish are natural born quarter-finalists.

How far will they go? This time Spain have a strong chance of making it to the semis and could go all the way.

HOW THEY'LL LINE UP

Vicente del Bosque must conjure the strongest team from a squad of footballing magicians. The key cards in his hand are Iker Casillas in goal, Sergio Ramos as ball-juggling centre half, with Andrés Iniesta as midfield wizard providing David Villa and Fernando Torres with the cues to pull rabbits out of hats up front. Spain will depend on the old trick of building from the back, but in new attacking patterns that will surprise and delight a world audience. Much will revolve around Iniesta's ability to challenge strongly and then make the killer pass. The fear is that tactics and skill could vanish in a puff of stage fright.

POSSIBLE SQUAD

Goalkeepers

Iker Casillas (C) (Real Madrid), Diego López (Villarreal), Pepe Reina (Liverpool)

Defenders

Raúl Albiol (Real Madrid), Álvaro Arbeloa (Liverpool), Joan Capdevila (Villarreal), Carlos Marchena (Valencia), Gerard Piqué (Barcelona), Carles Puyol (Barcelona), Sergio Ramos (Real Madrid)

Midfielders

Xabi Alonso (Real Madrid), Sergio Busquets (Barcelona), Santi Cazorla (Villarreal), Cesc Fàbregas (Arsenal), Xavi Hernández (Barcelona), Andrés Iniesta (Barcelona), Albert Riera (Liverpool), Marcos Senna (Villarreal), David Silva (Valencia)

Forwards

Daniel Güiza (Fenerbahçe), Bojan Krkić (Barcelona), Fernando Torres (Liverpool), David Villa (Valencia)

BELOW *Euro 2008 champions, 29 June 2008: (back row, left to right) Casillas, Marchena, Ramos, Capdevila, Senna, Torres; (front row) Silva, Iniesta, Xavi, Fàbregas, Puyol.*

Cesc Fabregas is a central midfielder and playmaker whose blend of personal creativity and unflagging team spirit has lent so much to Arsenal's intricate passing game. Although always in the Spanish squad, he has not caught the eye so much in his international career.

Having signed as a schoolboy for Barcelona, Fàbregas left Spain in 2003 aged 16. Andrés Iniesta, three years his senior, had already established himself as Barcelona's creative force and Fàbregas was attracted by Arsène Wenger's approach at Arsenal. The move paid off, for Fàbregas's career has flourished at club level. At international level, however, Iniesta's consistent form has overshadowed Fàbregas and threatened to cast him in the role of midfield water carrier.

PLAYER FACT FILE

Name: Francesc Fàbregas i Soler
Position: Midfielder
Caps: 47
Goals: 5
Team: Arsenal
Date of birth: 4 May 1987
Height: 177 cm/5 ft 9½ in
Weight: 69 kg/152 lb
Previous clubs: None
International debut: 1 March 2006 v Côte d'Ivoire
Previous World Cups: 2006

STYLE GUIDE
There's a smooth economy about Fàbregas's play and he's one of those rare midfielders who seems to have more time and space than others on the pitch. He's always demanding the ball and is a natural captain with the talent to mix pinpoint passes across half the pitch with angled flicks to better-placed colleagues a couple of metres away. A cool head makes him a natural taker of corners and free kicks.

But if Fàbregas is an international journeyman, he could yet exceed the master. He was just turned 19 years old when he became the youngest Spaniard to play in a World Cup, as a substitute against Ukraine in 2006. Two years later at Euro 2008 he was assigned the number ten shirt but began as a substitute, scoring his first international goal in Spain's 4–1 win over Russia and assisting another goal. Fàbregas scored the winning penalty in the quarter-final shoot-out against Italy. He made the starting 11 in the final and put in a hard-tackling performance that earned Spain their first major title since 1964. It's amazing that he still seems something of an international newcomer.

ABOVE *The pressure was piling on Cesc Fàbregas in the penalty shoot-out to decide the Euro 2008 quarter-final against Italy. Fàbregas took the deciding shot and showed his cool to send the Italian goalie Gianluigi Buffon in the wrong direction and Spain in the semi-final direction.*

"It is very easy to play with these teammates in the Spanish side. There is a lot of competition here, which is good. "

CESC FÀBREGAS

Andrés Iniesta

Andrés Iniesta is one of the game's great all-rounders and a man whose skills are underpinned by consistency and loyalty. He's a tidy tackler and team man who is famously committed to club and country.

There is a decency and humility that endears Iniesta to football fans, who variously refer to him as '*El Ilusionista*', '*El Anti-Galáctico*' and most recently '*San Andrés*'. He dominates any midfield, whether in the *volante* holding role he played as a Barcelona apprentice or in the more advanced and creative position he now most usually occupies.

Name: Andrés Iniesta Luján
Position: Midfielder
Caps: 39
Goals: 6
Team: Barcelona
Date of birth: 11 May 1984
Height: 170 cm/5 ft 7 in
Weight: 65 kg/143 lb
Previous clubs: None
International debut: 27 May 2006 v Russia
Previous World Cups: 2006

STYLE GUIDE

Iniesta's unselfish creativity would earn him a place in any team. He's a player's player who performs in the thick of the action when the going gets tough. Wayne Rooney puts him ahead of Ronaldo, while his former Barcelona teammate Samuel Eto'o says he's 'the best player in the world and whenever he is on the pitch he creates a spectacle'.

LEFT *Iniesta shows his athleticism and determination in holding off a challenge from Samir Muratović during the World Cup qualifier with Bosnia-Herzegovina. Spain won the match 1–0.*

> ❝ **In my opinion Andrés Iniesta is the best player in the world. He's incredible.** ❞
>
> WAYNE ROONEY, 2009

In 2007 he played a couple of Champions League games as striker and scored in each game. His balance, close control and skill on the ball thrill all football aficionados but what makes crowds purr is a passing ability that Frank Rijkaard, his former manager at Barcelona, describes as 'like watching somebody hand out sweets'.

Iniesta has proved himself a big-game player who does not freeze when the spotlight is brightest. Spanish fans hope his record at Euro 2008 is some kind of a prophecy. He played in all of Spain's group stage matches and threaded an inch-perfect pass for David Villa's second goal against the Russians. Unlike most of Spain's regulars, he played in the final group game against Greece and he was the engine of the team for the quarter-final as Spain beat Italy on penalties. He was man of the match in the semi-final against Russia, when he made the cross for Xavi to open the scoring, and he was once again the dominant figure in midfield in the stylish 1–0 final victory over Germany.

He was on form during the early World Cup qualifiers but a thigh injury restricted him in the later games and he missed the Confederations Cup. At the beginning of the 2009–10 season, looking forward to summer 2010, he said: 'I am 25 years old, I like how I am at the moment and I think the best is still to come.' All Spain hopes so. Andrés Iniesta has delivered for his club in two Champions League finals (2006, 2009) and for his country at the European Championship (2008). All Spain hopes that he can do so again and that in South Africa he will once more show his tournament-winning combination of unselfishness and lack of fear on the big occasion.

 ONE TO WATCH

Bojan

Bojan Krkić Pérez was born on 28 August 1990 in Catalonia to a Spanish mother and a Serbian father, the former Red Star Belgrade player Bojan Krkić senior. He will be 19 years old during the World Cup, and his career has developed at the same lightning speed he has shown as a right winger for Barcelona and Spain.

Known to Spanish fans as Bojan, he already has a place in the record books. He broke Lionel Messi's record of being the youngest player to make the Barcelona first team. He is the youngest ever scorer for Barcelona in a La Liga match and is the first player born in the 1990s to score in the Champions League. He finished his first season at the top level with ten goals, breaking Raúl's record of most goals scored in a debut season.

A fortnight after his 18th birthday, Bojan made his national debut as a substitute in Spain's second World Cup qualifying game against Armenia. The 4–0 victory proved his country was not about to repeat former qualification struggles and ended speculation that Bojan might choose to play for the Serbian national side.

Fernando Torres

Fernando Torres is an out-and-out goal-grabbing centre forward. His name is synonymous with goals, including the single goal that secured his country the Euro 2008 final.

Unlike most of today's crop of footballers, Torres does not present himself as the selfless team player. He spends games sniffing out the spaces in which to practise his art and often seems to fade from the action until he senses a chance to pounce. He doesn't like to be used as the sole target man, preferring instead to feed off the scraps of half-chances provided by other nearby strikers. For a modern forward, his link-up play is unimpressive and he doesn't have the greatest assist rate on the planet. Nonetheless, every manager would have him in his team because he scores goals wherever he plays.

As a schoolboy, Torres was a goalkeeper before converting to striker. He scored 75 goals in 174 La Liga appearances for Real Madrid and joined Liverpool in 2007. In his debut season, he became Liverpool's first player since Robbie Fowler to score more

PLAYER FACT FILE

Name: Fernando José Torres Sanz
Position: Striker
Caps: 71
Goals: 23
Team: Liverpool
Date of birth: 20 March 1984
Height: 185 cm/6 ft 1 in
Weight: 78 kg/172 lb
Previous clubs: Atlético Madrid
International debut: 6 September 2003 v Portugal
Previous World Cups: 2006

STYLE GUIDE

Torres is an old-style goal poacher with all the physical attributes for his richly rewarded specialism. He has a remarkable speed on the turn and the rapid acceleration to take him past today's athletic defenders. He has that strange centre forward's knack of seeming to hang in the air when he goes up for a header, and his powerful neck muscles have him heading the ball harder than most could kick it. On the deck he uses the minimum of backlift to hit the ball with either foot.

LEFT AND RIGHT *Fernando Torres of Spain rises above the New Zealand greenhorns to score the final goal in a 3–0 Confederations Cup match in June 2009. He'll also stoop to conquer and is pictured right watching the ball into the net in a Euro 2008 game against Germany.*

than 20 league goals in a season. His 29 goals for the 2007–08 season took him past Michael Owen's record for goals in a season.

Torres made his debut for Spain against Portugal in 2003 and the 2010 World Cup will be his fourth major tournament and he'll be using the experiences gleaned at Euro 2004, the 2006 World Cup and Euro 2008. At 27 years of age, when he pulls on his number nine Spanish shirt in South Africa, he will be one of his country's most experienced players and a man who has outgrown his early nickname of 'El Nino' ('the Kid').

Torres is a hero in a Liverpool side where he plays number nine to Steven Gerrard's number ten. On 13 June 2009, a year before the World Cup, Torres gave an interview saying he and his good mate Gerrard had already been bantering about a Spain v England final. 'England are one of the candidates to win the World Cup in 2010, without doubt,' he said. 'Stevie and myself have often spoken about our teams. Our dream would be for England and Spain to play in the final in South Africa. But Spain would win it.' Shortly afterwards Torres scored a hat-trick to help Spain extend their unbeaten run to 33 matches after defeating New Zealand 5–0 in their Confederations Cup opener.

❝ I want to win more titles and be the most important player in Europe and the world. ❞

TORRES
AFTER SPAIN WON EURO 2008

David Villa

Villa's onfield audacity has him scoring from extravagant bicycle kicks and lobs from the halfway line. The intuitive style doesn't stop him from being a team player whose snap decisions create as many goals for others as he scores himself.

Villa's goal-scoring record is putting him up with the game's great names. *El Guaje* ('the kid' in Asturian, his north Spanish language) has hit over a hundred goals for Valencia, a club he remains loyal to despite interest from bigger sides. For Spain, he has scored an astonishing 33 goals in 52 games. He scored three goals at the 2006 World Cup and was top scorer at Euro 2008 with four. In February 2009, he scored in a record-breaking sixth successive international game in Spain's 2–0 win against England.

PLAYER FACT FILE

Name: David Villa Sánchez
Position: Striker
Caps: 54
Goals: 36
Team: Valencia
Date of birth: 3 December 1981
Height: 175 cm/5 ft 9 in
Weight: 69 kg/152 lb
Previous clubs: Sporting Gijón, Zaragoza
International debut: 9 February 2005 v San Marino
Previous World Cups: 2006

STYLE GUIDE

David Villa has the full repertoire of attacking qualities. He is genuinely two-footed and his first touch is first class. A superb personal scoring record belies the fact that he's often the man to take free kicks and corners. He's good off the ball too and has the vision to make unpredictable diagonal runs that wrench the best-drilled defences out of shape.

LEFT *David Villa beats Russia's Roman Shirokov to sidefoot the ball in a Euro 2008 match.*

ABOVE RIGHT *Another one hits the net and Villa swoops back to the centre circle having just scored against South Africa in the 2009 Confederations Cup.*

The selfishness of a natural goal scorer is well hidden, for Villa's demeanour makes him famous for avoiding the limelight off the pitch. His personality seems an ego-free zone and he prefers talking of 'we' rather than 'I', such as when describing his partnership with Fernando Torres, which might well provide the goals that earn Spain their first World Cup. 'Fernando and I complement each other very well,' Villa says. 'We get on well on the pitch and very well off it too. We're a good partnership. We both chase down defenders, put pressure on and fight to create chances for each other. We work well together.'

Talent recognizes talent. Listen to what Kaká says: 'The player with whom I would most like to play is David Villa of Valencia. He is the best Spanish footballer.'

Talent will also supersede talent. The Spanish media has long buzzed with the rivalry between Villa and Raúl Sanchez, the 32-year-old Real Madrid player who scored a record 44 goals for Spain before losing his

> ## " I'd have David Villa over Kaká and Cristiano Ronaldo. "
>
> VINCENTE DEL BOSQUE

place to Villa. Vincente del Bosque has never picked Raúl and yet Villa stands accused of taking the number seven shirt off his more flamboyant rival. 'I have not taken anything away from anybody,' Villa says, slipping easily into the first person. 'I was simply playing well for my club and the national coach gave me an opportunity. Too much has been said about the number issue. I'm not looking to cause any controversy. All I want is to be in the squad for every game, to have the Spain badge on my chest and to score as many goals as I can.'

Xavi Hernandez describes the Barcelona approach to football, saying: 'We have this active, attractive attacking method to keep possession and control the game.' For Barça read Spain.

Barcelona and Spain employ Xavi at the hub of their ultra-efficient and yet supremely attractive footballing mechanisms. Both teams use Xavi's ability to dictate the pace of play, whether in speeding things up to spring bewildering attacks from defensive seizure or, later in a game, using the dark arts to protect a lead and shut things down.

Xavi's engine-room flair was nurtured in the Barcelona academy, which he joined when he was 11, to come under the tutelage of his fellow Catalan, Pep Guardiola. The present Barcelona manager occupied Xavi's current defensive midfield role in Johan Cruyff's flowing

PLAYER FACT FILE

Name: Xavier Hernández i Creus
Position: Midfielder
Caps: 83
Goals: 8
Team: Barcelona
Date of birth: 25 January 1980
Height: 170 cm/5 ft 7 in
Weight: 68 kg/150 lb
Previous clubs: None
International debut: 15 November 2000 v Netherlands
Previous World Cups: 2002, 2006

STYLE GUIDE
Xavi operates as a hard-tackling playmaker and midfield anchor man. He's as good as any player in the world at protecting the ball with his chunky physique, and he's arguably the best at finding the precise moment for delivering a perfectly flighted pass.

side of the 1990s. An education in the creative mechanisms of Dutch and Catalan ways made Xavi a certainty for international recognition.

Xavi made his debut for Spain aged 20, having led the junior side to victory at the 1999 World Youth Championship in Nigeria and a silver medal at the 2000 Olympics. He struggled for a regular place in the Spanish squad for the 2002 World Cup, then became a regular in the Euro 2004 qualifiers only to be dropped for the finals. He was Spain's most influential player in the 2006 World Cup, and he made the running to appear in every game until Spain went out to France in the second round.

UEFA officials selected Xavi as the player of Euro 2008 in recognition of his contribution to the way Spain won the trophy. In what might come to seem a trial run for the 2010 World Cup, Xavi's partnership with Andrés Iniesta, his Barcelona teammate, brought defensive stability and a string of passes to the attackers. Xavi scored the semi-final opener against Russia and in the final against Germany his sliderule pass to Fernando Torres secured Spain the winning goal. In South Africa it could seem like déjà vu all over again.

> **When I was at Barcelona, Xavi was just emerging. Even when he was starting out he already had fantastic quality. At the time we called him the Master.**

LUÍS FIGO
FORMERLY OF BARCELONA AND PORTUGAL

BELOW *Xavi in the Russia v Spain Euro 2008 semi-final on the way to scoring the opening goal while the Russian Arshavin looks on.*

SWITZERLAND

GROUP H ✚

Switzerland will be looking to improve on their performance in the 2006 World Cup, when they created the unfortunate – and unique – record of having failed to score in the penalty shoot-out that sent them home.

The Swiss team – known variously as the *Schweizer Nati* (German), *La Nati* (French) and *Squadra Nazionale* (Italian) – might find goals hard to come by but they do, however, boast a star attraction: Ottmar Hitzfeld. He's not really Swiss, neither does he play football any more, but he's a manager of exceptional pedigree. He has won 18 trophies at club level, was elected FIFA Coach of the Year in 1997 and 2001, and is one of only two managers to have won the Champions League with two clubs, Borussia Dortmund and Bayern Munich.

'I have always dreamed of making it to the World Cup, so this is like a dream come true for me,' he says.

'Many people told me that going to Switzerland was a mistake, as it was impossible to achieve anything with the Swiss team. However, I have always been convinced that we could make it.'

Hitzfeld is known as the General and his fighting spirit has turned a lacklustre side into a coherent, hard-working and efficient unit. The captain, Alexander Frei, is Switzerland's top scorer with 40 goals and a knee problem. The troops he will muster are strongest in a defence that is marshalled by the honest endeavour of Arsenal's Philippe Senderos. Hitzfeld will hope that age and injury won't prevent Hakan Yakin and Bayer Leverkusen's Tranquillo Barnetta from patrolling midfield.

After that, it's down to teamwork, and there's no better touchline organizer than Ottmar Hitzfeld.

BELOW LEFT *Benjamin Huggel (left), Alexander Frei, Hakan Yakin and Eren Derdiyok celebrate after a 2–0 World Cup 2010 qualifier victory against Greece at the St Jakob Stadium in Basel.*

BELOW RIGHT *Ottmar Hitzfeld, the German manager of the Swiss team. In South Africa, will he continue to fashion footballing silk purses out of sows' ears? Or will his players make a pig's ear of it?*

POSSIBLE SQUAD

Goalkeepers

Diego Benaglio (Wolfsburg), **Johnny Leoni** (Zürich), **Marco Wölfli** (Young Boys)

Defenders

Heinz Barmettler (Zürich), **Stéphane Grichting** (Auxerre), **Stephan Lichtsteiner** (Lazio), **Philippe Senderos** (Arsenal), **Alain Nef** (Triestina), **Steve von Bergen** (Hertha BSC), **Ludovic Magnin** (Stuttgart)

Midfielders

Tranquillo Barnetta (Bayer Leverkusen), **Gelson Fernandes** (Saint-Étienne), **Benjamin Huggel** (Basel), **Gökhan Inler** (Udinese), **Marco Padalino** (Sampdoria), **Pirmin Schwegler** (Eintracht Frankfurt), **Johan Vonlanthen** (Zürich), **Hakan Yakin** (Luzern)

Forwards

Albert Bunjaku (FC Nürnberg) , **Eren Derdiyok** (Bayer Leverkusen), **Alexander Frei (C)** (Basel), **Blaise Nkufo** (Twente), **Marco Streller** (Basel)

ROUTE TO THE FINALS

EUROPE QUALIFYING GROUP 2 – FINAL TABLE

Team	P	W	D	L	F	A	Pts
Switzerland	10	6	3	1	18	8	21
Greece	10	6	2	2	20	10	20
Latvia	10	5	2	3	18	15	17
Israel	10	4	4	2	20	10	16
Luxembourg	10	1	2	7	4	25	5
Moldova	10	0	3	7	6	18	3

FINALS GROUP H

Switzerland play		Date	Venue
	Spain	16 June	Durban
	Chile	21 June	N. Mandela Bay/Pt Elizabeth
	Honduras	25 June	Mangaung/Bloemfontein

VITAL STATISTICS

World ranking 18th	Keeper and defence 6/10
Midfield 5/10	Attack 4/10

Strengths and weaknesses Teamwork is a Swiss strength, individual talent a weakness. Those who are into the modern cult of management will wish this team well.

How far will they go? Switzerland have already advanced further than expected and in South Africa will have only Honduras and Chile to beat to further confound expectations.

LEFT *Switzerland v Greece, World Cup qualifying match, Basle, Switzerland, 5 September 2009: (back row, left to right) Benaglio, Grichting, Nef, Nkufo, Huggel, Magnin; (front row) Padalino, Fernandes, Barnetta, von Bergen, Frei.*

HONDURAS

GROUP H

Viva Honduras! **A nation went wild with excitement when Honduras squeezed into the World Cup finals on goal difference over Costa Rica.**

The Hondurans' 1–0 win in El Salvador seemed in vain because their rivals Costa Rica were still playing and were ahead in a game that would have relegated Honduras to the play-offs. Then came an injury-time equalizer against Costa Rica and the instant creation of two heroes: Honduras's own Carlos Pavón for scoring in El Salvador and the United States' Jonathan Bornstein for equalizing in Costa Rica.

Honduras had expected to do better and have several players who could put them more firmly onto the footballing map. The best known in Europe is Internazionale's David Suazo, also known as 'the Panther', whose pace and inventiveness in front of goal were missed during the qualification struggle due to injuries. Suazo is the cousin of two Wigan players, defender Maynor Figueroa and midfielder Hendry Thomas.

Another one to watch is Wilson Palacios, whose intelligent distribution impressed Wigan fans before he moved on to Spurs. Other talents that could impress in South Africa are free-kick specialist Julio César de León and the experienced captain Amado Guevara.

Reinaldo Rueda, a Colombian disciplinarian who has managed Honduras since 2006, has prepared a side that mixes youth with age, skill with organization. Much is expected of the first national side to make it through to the World Cup finals since 1982, and Honduran football fever runs high.

Football passions reached a nightmare level when the game spilled into warfare in 1969. Riots at a World Cup qualifying match against El Salvador exacerbated political tension over El Salvadoran immigration into Honduras and triggered the four-day 'Football War', in which some 4,000 people lost their lives.

BELOW LEFT *David Suazo (11) and Carlos Pavón celebrate Honduras's winning goal against El Salvador.*

BELOW RIGHT *Honduran fans rejoice at their last-gasp qualification at the expense of Costa Rica.*

POSSIBLE SQUAD

Goalkeepers

Ricardo Canales (Motagua), Donis Escober (Olimpia), Noel Valladares (Olimpia)

Defenders

Víctor Bernárdez (Anderlecht), Maynor Figueroa (Wigan Athletic), Oscar Bonieck García (Olimpia), Emilio Izaguirre (Motagua), Erick Norales (Marathón), Carlos Palacios (Real España), Mauricio Sabillón (Marathón)

Midfielders

Edgar Álvarez (Bari), Amado Guevara (C) (Toronto FC), Julio César de León (Torino), Ramón Núñez (Cruz Azul), Wilson Palacios (Tottenham Hotspur), Hendry Thomas (Wigan Athletic), Danilo Turcios (Olimpia), Melvin Valladares (Real España)

Forwards

Carlo Costly (GKS Bełchatów), Walter Martínez (Marathón), Jerry Palacios (Marathón), Carlos Pavón (Real España), David Suazo (Internazionale)

ROUTE TO THE FINALS

CONCACAF FINAL STAGE – FINAL TABLE

Team	P	W	D	L	F	A	Pts
USA	10	6	2	2	19	13	20
Mexico	10	6	1	3	18	12	19
Honduras	10	5	1	4	17	11	16
Costa Rica	10	5	1	4	15	15	16
El Salvador	10	2	2	6	9	15	8
Trinidad & Tobago	10	1	3	6	10	22	6

FINALS GROUP H

Honduras play	Date	Venue
Chile	16 June	Nelspruit
Spain	21 June	Johannesburg (Ellis Park)
Switzerland	25 June	Mangaung/Bloemfontein

VITAL STATISTICS

World ranking 38th   Keeper and defence 5/10
Midfield 6/10   Attack 5/10

Strengths and weaknesses A few classy players and a consistent management could bring this team glory. More likely is a repeat performance of their qualification struggles.

How far will they go? This team will probably only go as far as an early bath unless they can prevail over Chile or Switzerland.

LEFT *Honduras v El Salvador, World Cup qualifying match, Cuscatian Stadium, San Salvador, 14 October 2009: (back row, left to right) Wilson Palacios, Norales, Sabillon, Jerry Palacios, Valladares, Guevara; (front row) Pavón, Álvarez, Suazo, Izaguirre, de León.*

CHILE

GROUP H

Chile has a long footballing history. It was one of the original 13 nations in the inaugural 1930 World Cup. The national side has appeared in seven World Cup tournaments and Chile hosted the 1962 World Cup, finishing in third place.

History also reveals a nation that has often played an ugly version of the beautiful game including being banned from the 1990 and 1994 World Cups following a qualifying match where Brazil was leading and Chile faced elimination. All that is now behind them for Chile's recent football has filled the country with optimism. A triumphant qualification campaign included their first-ever point playing Uruguay away; a 1–0 win over Argentina that led to the resignation of Argentine coach Alfio Basile; and away victories in Peru and Paraguay.

Marcelo Bielsa has been the driving force behind the new Chile. He found fame as manager of his native Argentina, where he was known as *'El Loco'* ('Madman'). Bielsa has stabilized a fractious squad that shortly before his appointment in 2007 had banned six senior players for 'internal indiscipline' during the Copa América. This forced a rapid adoption of youthful players, whom Bielsa has deployed in attacking formations, notably away from home. Thorough preparation and intelligent tactics secured the famous run of qualifying results.

South America has rocked to Bielsa's Chilean renaissance and unleashed a style of play that might just restore Chile's reputation The major talent to have prospered under the new regime is Mark González, a pacy left wing and the most-capped player in the squad. In that he was born in South Africa to Chilean parents, South Africa will be a kind of homecoming for him.

BELOW LEFT *Mark González, Chile's left wing and star player, heads the ball in a qualifying match against Brazil.*

BELOW RIGHT *Argentinian manager Marcelo Bielsa, the architect of Chile's transformation into a disciplined and confident team.*

POSSIBLE SQUAD

Goalkeepers

Claudio Bravo (C) (Real Sociedad), Miguel Pinto (Universidad de Chile), Nery Veloso (Huachipato)

Defenders

Osvaldo González (Universidad de Chile), Gonzalo Jara (West Bromwich Albion), Hans Martínez (Universidad Católica), Gary Medel (Boca Juniors), Waldo Ponce (Vélez Sársfield), Arturo Vidal (Bayer Leverkusen)

Midfielders

Carlos Carmona (Reggina), Matías Fernández (Sporting), Gonzalo Fierro (Flamengo), Mauricio Isla (Udinese), Manuel Iturra (Universidad de Chile), Rodrigo Millar (Colo-Colo), Pedro Morales (NK Dinamo Zagreb), Rodrigo Tello (Besiktas)

Forwards

Jean Beausejour (América), Mark González (CSKA Moscow), Fabián Orellana (Xerez), Esteban Paredes (Colo-Colo), Alexis Sánchez (Udinese), Humberto Suazo (Monterrey)

ROUTE TO THE FINALS

SOUTH AMERICA QUALIFYING GROUP – FINAL TABLE

Team	P	W	D	L	F	A	Pts
Brazil	18	9	7	2	33	11	34
Chile	18	10	3	5	32	22	33
Paraguay	18	10	3	5	24	16	33
Argentina	18	8	4	6	23	20	28
Uruguay	18	6	6	6	28	20	24
Ecuador	18	6	5	7	22	26	23
Colombia	18	6	5	7	14	18	23
Venezuela	18	6	4	8	23	29	22
Bolivia	18	4	3	11	22	36	15
Peru	18	3	4	11	11	34	13

FINALS GROUP H

Chile play		Date	Venue
	Honduras	16 June	Nelspruit
	Switzerland	21 June	N. Mandela Bay/Pt Elizabeth
	Spain	25 June	Tshwane/Pretoria

BELOW *Chile v Brazil, Pituacu Stadium, Santiago, 9 September 2009: (back row, left to right) Jara, Bravo, Millar, Vidal, Carmona, Beausejour, Ponce; (front) Medel, Suazo, Fernandez, Sánchez.*

VITAL STATISTICS

World ranking 17th
Keeper and defence 6/10
Midfield 5/10
Attack 5/10

Strengths and weaknesses The most positive thing to say about Chile is that they're not quite as negative as they used to be.

How far will they go? They are in an easy group and could go further than they have a right to expect.

Index

Acknowledgements

All images reproduced courtesy of Getty Images.
(a = above, b = below, l = left, r = right)

AFP/Getty Images, p 120b; /Eitan Abramovich, p 175; /Nelson Almeida, p 168; /Odd Andersen, p 124l; /Marcel Antonisse, pp 139b, 141; /Mladen Antonov, pp 202–03; /Juan Barreto, p 27; /Elvis Barukcic, p 194; /Gabriel Bouys, p 11a; /Rodrigo Buendia, p 54l; /Jose Cabezas, pp 220l, 221; /Fabrice Coffrini, pp 113, 218l; /Thomas Coex, p 26l; /Adrian Dennis, p 79a; /Dimitar Dilkoff, p 158; /Norberto Duarte, pp 166b, 167, 169l; /Pius Utomi Ekpei, p 58a; /Paul Ellis, p 137; /Daniel Garcia, pp 30, 44–45, 47, 51, 56r, 180a/b; /Louisa Gouliamaki, p 67; /Bertrand Guay, p 34; /Gianluigi Guercia, pp 6b, 18; /Jack Guez, p 218r; /Valery Hache, pp 35, 38b, 160; /Marcelo Hernandez, p 222l; /Patrick Hertzog, pp 138, 139a; /Andrej Isakovic, pp 39a, 120a, 121; /Alexander Joe, pp 7, 12, 163b; /Ade Johnson, p 132; /Jung Yeon-Je, pp 62a, 189; /Sia Kambou, p 192b; /Karim Jaafar, pp 117, 184b; /Atta Kenare, p 64b; /Kim Jae-Hwan, p 65; /Ian Kington, p 78; /Glyn Kirk, p 89; /Toshifumi Kitamura, p 119a; /Joe Klamar, pp 209, 213r, 216b; /Natalia Kolesnikova, p 96l; /Francisco Leong, pp 197, 198, 199, 201r; /Mauricio Lima, p 223; /Pontus Lundahl, p 142a; /Juan Mabromata, p 56l; /Simon Maina, pp 58b, 59, 60; /Pierre-Philippe Marcou, pp 90a/b, 93r, 108l, 216a; /Martin Bureau, p 37b; / Damien Meyer, p 208b; /Marcos Miras, p 177a; /Olivier Morin, pp 142b, 144b; /Peter Muhly, pp 41, 172a/b; /Sven Nackstrand,

p 145; /Alexander Nemenov, p 107; /Fayez Nureldine, p 94r; /OFF, p 31a; /Alejandro Pagni, pp 46b, 169r, 222r; /Vincenzo Pinto, pp 16, 17, 155; /Hrvoje Polan, p 96r; /Pornchai Kittiwongsakul, p 146b; / Miguel Riopa, p 200b; /Miguel Rojo, p 24l/r; /Stephane de Sakutin, p 19; /Issouf Sanogo, pp 192a, 193; /Roberto Schmidt, pp 204, 206; /Sascha Schuermann, p 208a; /Antonio Scorza, pp 174, 178b, 181b, 187r; /Abdelhak Senna, p 124r, 148b, 149; /Kambou Sia, p 190b; / Torsten Silz, p 112a/b; /Carl de Souza, p 84; /STF, p 10a; /Sergei Supinsky, pp 66l/r, 86; /John Thys, p 133; /Nigel Treblin, pp 98, 102, 106b; /Diego Tuson, p 214a; /Pedro Ugarte, p 11b; /Andrew Yates, p 136b.

Bongarts/Getty Images, Lars Baron, p 159a; /Stuart Franklin, p 6a, 104, 109b; /Alex Grimm, p 109a; /Christof Koepsel, pp 92, 93l, 176; /Joern Pollex, pp 100, 103; /Martin Rose, pp 105, 106a, 111b; / Vladimir Rys, pp 99, 108r, 110, 212b; /Patrik Stollarz, p 111a.

Epsilon/Getty Images, Dmitry Korotayev, p 57.

FA via Getty Images, Phil Cole, p 76b; /Michael Regan, p 76a, 80.

FIFA via Getty Images, Shaun Botterill, p 21b; /Mike Hewitt, p 182a; / Jeff J. Mitchell, pp 178a, 185, 215; /Michael Regan, p 21a.

Fotoarena/Latin Content/Getty Images, Caetano Barreira, p 186.

Gallo Images/Getty Images, Lefty Shivambu, pp 61, 181a/b, 184a, 190a.

Getty Images, p 154; /Giuseppe Bellini, p 97; /Shaun Botterill, pp 85l,

122, 130, 152–53, 201l, 205; /Clive Brunskill, p 75l; /Massimo Cebrelli, p 165; /Chung Sung-Jun, pp 63, 188r; /Robert Cianflone, p 115; /Chris Cole, p 129; /Phil Cole, pp 77, 88a/b, 135, 156; / Mark Dadswell, pp 116, 118a/b; /Lucas Dawson, p 147; /Julian Finney, pp 38a, 200a; /Stu Forster, pp 32, 36, 39b, 43; /Laurence Griffiths, pp 20a, 25, 125, 126, 127l; /Han Myung-Gu, p 64a; / Richard Heathcote, pp 20b, 159b, 173, 214b; /Mike Hewitt, pp 134, 136a; /Hannah Johnston, p 170r; /Jasper Juinen, pp 210a/b, 211; /Matt King, p 114; /Ross Kinnaird, p 71; /Alex Livesey, pp 72, 82b; /Jamie McDonald, pp 72–73, 79b, 82a, 83, 91, 191, 212a, 213l; /Ian McKinnell, p 3; /Clive Mason, pp 94l, 95; /Marty Melville, pp 170l, 171; /Jeff J Mitchell, pp 128, 140b; /Dino Panato, p 163a; /Andrew Paterson, p 6; /Photogamma, pp 52a, 53, 55; /Ryan Pierse, pp 68–69, 70, 75r, 87r, 140a; /Clive Rose, pp 81, 87l; /Cameron Spencer, p 119b; /Michael Steele, pp 33, 143, 144a, 148a, 150a/b, 151, 219; /Bob Thomas, pp 10b, 46a; /Mark Thompson, pp 74, 85r, 195, 196; /Touchline, p 2; / Claudio Villa, pp 157, 161a/b, 162, 164; /Koji Watanabe, pp 62b, 127r, 146a; /World Sport Group, p 188l.

Jam Media/Latin Content/Getty Images, Francisco Estrada, p 22a; / Mario Castillo, p 22b.

Latin Content/Getty Images, AlfieriPhoto, p 50; /Dante Fernandez, pp 26r, 183; /Omar Hernandez, p 220r; /Pablo Lasansky, p 52b; / Richard Rad, p 54r; /Santiago Rios, p 48a/b; /Luis Vera, p 166a.

Popperfoto/Getty Images, pp 8, 101; /Rolls Press, pp 9, 177b.